IN CASE I FORGET

Letters to my god-daughter

IN CASE I FORGET

Letters to my god-daughter

Joan Cherry

ATHENA PRESS
LONDON

IN CASE I FORGET
Letters to my god-daughter
Copyright © Joan Cherry 2007

ISBN 10-digit: 1 84401 870 9
ISBN 13-digit: 978 1 84401 870 3

First Published 2007 by
ATHENA PRESS
Queen's House, 2 Holly Road
Twickenham TW1 4EG
United Kingdom

Printed for Athena Press

Dear Ursula,

Your mother did me the honour unique in my life when she asked me to be your godmother. I love you dearly now but you were not a totally delightful child. You were the first to make me painfully aware of my antiquity when, one day, you held my hand, looked into my eyes and said: 'Auntie Joan, how old are you?' I hesitated. To a six-year-old, even twenty seems verging on decrepitude; but your mother, who was probably more interested in knowing the answer than you were, said sternly that she always told you the truth. Swallowing hard and closing my eyes, I said, 'Fifty.' Silence, then, 'Auntie Joan, are you going to die soon?'

Mind you, you redeemed yourself by bursting into tears when it was my seventieth birthday!

Time is not the same at every age; now, life, for me, is rushing by at a hitherto undreamed-of speed. Whereas I shan't know the world of your old age, you can't know the world of my childhood, the world in which I grew up. Even to me, it seems another life. We are now separated not only in time but in place. You are in a sense my posterity, so, despite Saki's opinion that the old have reminiscences of what never happened, these letters are for you.

I'll write them in batches, so that you can read it more as a story. You must try to imagine me talking to you.

I can but hope that your life and times are varied and pleasurable in their own different ways, and that they bring you happiness and peace of mind.

Love,

Joan

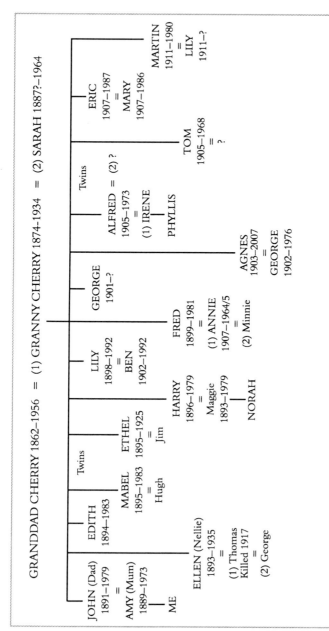

GRANDDAD CHERRY 1862–1956 = (1) GRANNY CHERRY 1874–1934 = (2) SARAH 1877?–1964

JOHN (Dad)
1891–1979
=
AMY (Mum)
1889–1973
|
ME

EDITH
1894–1983

Twins

MABEL   ETHEL
1895–1983   1895–1925
=   =
Hugh   Jim

ELLEN (Nellie)
1893–1935
=
(1) Thomas
Killed 1917
=
(2) George

HARRY
1896–1979
=
Maggie
1893–1979
|
NORAH

LILY
1898–1992
=
BEN
1902–1992

FRED
1899–1981
=
(1) ANNIE
1907–1964/5
=
(2) Minnie

GEORGE
1901–?

AGNES
1903–2007
=
GEORGE
1902–1976

Twins

ALFRED = (2) ?
1905–1973
=
(1) IRENE
|
PHYLLIS

TOM
1905–1968
=
?

ERIC
1907–1987
=
MARY
1907–1986

MARTIN
1911–1980
=
LILY
1911–?

At least nineteen cousins who had at least twenty-eight children who had at least sixteen children. I have lost touch with all except Agnes.
Those mentioned in the story are in capital letters. To avoid all confusion, all unmentioned descendents are omitted.

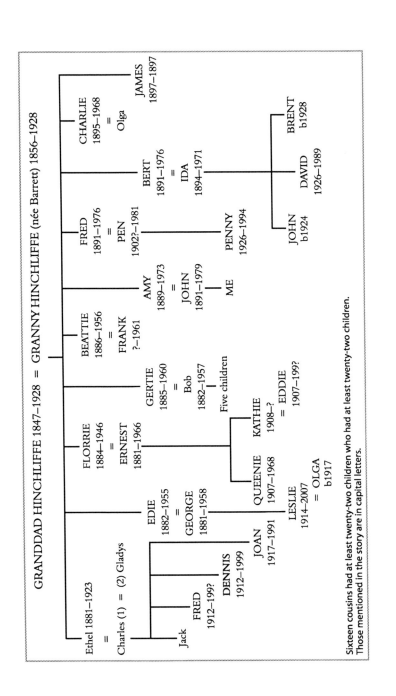

GRANDDAD HINCHLIFFE 1847–1928 = GRANNY HINCHLIFFE (née Barrett) 1856–1928

Ethel 1881–1923
=
Charles (1) = (2) Gladys

Jack

FRED 1912–19?

DENNIS 1912–1999

JOAN 1917–1991

EDIE 1882–1955
=
GEORGE 1881–1958

QUEENIE 1907–1968

LESLIE 1914–2007
= OLGA b1917

KATHIE 1908–?
= EDDIE 1907–199?

FLORRIE 1884–1946
=
ERNEST 1881–1966

GERTIE 1885–1960
=
Bob 1882–1957
Five children

BEATTIE 1886–1956
=
FRANK ?–1961

AMY 1889–1973
=
JOHN 1891–1979

ME

FRED 1891–1976
=
PEN 1902?–1981

PENNY 1926–1994

BERT 1891–1976
=
IDA 1894–1971

JOHN b1924

DAVID 1926–1989

BRENT b1928

CHARLIE 1895–1968
=
Olga

JAMES 1897–1897

Sixteen cousins had at least twenty-two children who had at least twenty-two children.
Those mentioned in the story are in capital letters.

My Excuse

This began as a letter to my god-daughter, but then my life took over.

I am told that publishers groan under the weight of manuscripts sent in by old ladies, who each feel confident that they have one book in them and who think the resulting incomparable pages of their life story ought to see the light of day. Is this, then, just one more? Well, at least it is not my only book. I am sure, of course, that not only is it worth reading, but also that it is unique, for there is no one else who has ever been, who is, me.

Early memories are like photographs in an album: fascinating to the sociologically minded, of intense interest to members of the family and close friends, giving to those who shared them either a sentimental glow or a violent desire to contradict. Life before the Second World War now has a greater attraction for it has gone for ever.

The first seventeen or eighteen years seem so much longer than any other stretch of time. The outbreak of war in 1939 is where these letters stop; my life until then belongs to another era and place. Perhaps its strangeness was already dawning on me when I began to keep a diary on my thirteenth birthday.

W. Somerset Maugham is encouraging: 'Men and women are not only themselves; they are also the region in which they were born, the city apartment or farm in which they learned to walk, the games they played as children, the old wives' tales they overheard, the foods they ate, the schools they attended, the sports they followed, the poets they read and the God they believed in.'[1] My view exactly. I cannot agree, however, with Evelyn Waugh, who felt that a person had reached the age to write about his or her past only when that person had lost all curiosity about the future; that is certainly not true for me.

Luis Buñuel in the *Observer* gave me the necessary push. 'You have to begin to lose your memory if only in bits and pieces to realise that memory is what makes our lives... Our memory is our coherence, our reason, our feelings, even our action. Without it, we are nothing.' There may be mistakes of fact in these letters; I, deliberately, haven't checked these, because it is what I remember and how I remember it that is the whole point.

Memory is fading, so I must get a move on.

---

[1] W. Somerset Maugham, *The Razor's Edge*, published by William Heinemann Ltd. Reprinted by permission of The Random House Group Ltd.

Letters

ONE

Beginnings

Settling in Liverpool

My parents, John and Amy, made a strange couple. Their 'understanding', their 'walking out together' time, their 'courting' time, then their engagement, all had been leisurely and prolonged. Even the Great War and John's call-up did not bring them finally together until his embarkation leave. Determined to 'bear his name', Amy arranged a full marriage ceremony in her home town of Shrewsbury for Saturday, 21 April 1917.

A studio photograph shows John, unrecognisable with a moustache and some hair, in the uniform of a Second Lieutenant, Amy in the characteristic seven-eighths-length white dress, low-heeled bar-strap shoes dyed white, a circlet of blossom and a veil. They spent their honeymoon of two nights and one day some fifteen miles away at the Old Post Office, Marshbrook, near Church Stretton; the listed house still adds its attraction to the lovely valley. But they spent it with Amy's sister Edith (Edie, the favourite of all, endowed with more than her fair share of charm, and prettier than any of her five sisters), her quirkily individualistic monumental stonemason husband George and their tiny 2½-year-old son Lesley. John recalled his brief stay there with pleasure; they all went for walks together. Monday morning saw him off to the Front and Amy back to her parents at 12 The Mount.

A very short spell at the Front for John was followed by a long period as a Prisoner of War. On his release in 1919, having learned much about himself and encouraged by a fellow prisoner, Rawdon Smith (who was acquainted with some of the city's important families – Melly, Holt, Rathbone), he came to Liverpool, where he and Amy spent the rest of their lives.

It is only since I grew up that I've realised what a shock Liverpool must have been to both of them, but especially to Amy, who had only once in her life travelled more than thirty miles. It was a shock to which, remaining a small-town girl, she never adapted. On John's return from Germany, she had expected to return to Shrewsbury and the hierarchical life in which she knew where she stood; she still expected to go back when he retired nearly forty years later. John was a realist who looked forward all his life and adapted to almost anywhere. Today is the tomorrow you worried about yesterday. Amy looked back unrealistically; all her life, her deep resentment at being uprooted jarred with her pride at being in a big city so that the rest of her family would be impressed by her new status.

Even now, Shrewsbury retains much that is village-like. Its friendly houses full of character still cluster together, comparatively unchanged; the shops and the market, albeit new, keep it a lively, but inward-looking place. The river Severn almost binds the town into its country setting; the Mersey, on the other hand, dictated Liverpool's power and prosperity; the city looks outward to the world.

You'll know of Liverpool because of the Beatles, yet it is still a foreign place to many English. Outsiders have even been known to hint at the need for passports. It was terrifyingly huge then; it's even bigger now as it has swallowed up villages on its periphery.

This 'pool in thick water' has a rich past, not all to its credit. John remained intrigued. The earliest settlement was probably between 2000 and 1500 BC; Scandinavians and Vikings invaded; King John hunted in what is now Toxteth. It expanded in the seventeenth century from its original seven streets – Castle, Mill, Bank, Chapel, Dale, Moor (all still there in some form) and Juggler. Lord Street, now pedestrianised, was laid out by Lord Molyneux, Duke Street was named after the victor of the battle of Culloden, the Duke of Cumberland. The eighteenth century brought the fashionable squares – Abercrombie (still patrician), Clayton, Faulkner, Williamson – and the Georgian beauties of Rodney Street. The city has more than 2,000 listed buildings.

The slave trade brought wealth but also grisly slums, appalling diseases and deaths. The iron slave rings remain on Goree Piazza, yet streets were named after the merchants who made their pile from this cruel trade as well as after those who, in the nineteenth century, benefited from the expansion of transport by sea and land to prosper in the cotton trade.

No less a personage than Queen Victoria proclaimed that the mid-nineteenth-century St George's Hall was worthy of ancient Athens. Charles Dickens gave readings in it. Millions have been spent on its restoration. Alas, the Punch and Judy show outside seems to have gone for good.

Trade caused an influx of migrants. The Potato Famine of the 1840s brought in the Irish ('feckless' as Mother never ceased to point out); 3,000-plus landed in two days in the 1840s and most stayed, mainly in the Everton and Scotland Road areas. In their wake came cholera (which is perhaps why the city pioneered the first public wash houses in Britain) and sectarian ill-feeling and passion. On the anniversary of the battle of the Boyne, people stayed indoors and shops were barricaded. There used to be – maybe there still are – no-go pubs for Proddies (Protestants). The newish Catholic Cathedral is often called, not respectfully, Paddy's Wigwam. With 'lesser breeds without the law', as the hymn phrases it, Liverpool was always a city of violence outside pubs and inside houses. In one period, my father's case, with the remains of his lunch inside, was searched before he was allowed into a cinema.

Shipbuilding, especially Cammell Laird, and shipping, particularly Cunard, attracted men from many countries. Even in the Twenties, an annual average of immigrants was estimated at 6,000. The mixture of races gave another shock to Amy, the Shropshire girl, her religion giving her one counsel, her instincts the opposite.

Lascar seamen, dockers wearing turbans or fezzes – was it they who brought the expression 'to put the kibosh on' something? It certainly sounds more exotic than putting the tin lid on it. 'Chink, Chink Chinamen' inhabited Chinatown, the oldest in Europe. Negroes (then the polite term) and Jews were Darkies and Jew Boys to Amy, nearly as much descriptive as pejorative, but the hint of fear remained.

> A B C D goldfish (Ab(i)e (Abraham), see dey goldfish?)
> M N O goldfish (Them ain't no goldfish)
> S D R goldfish (Yes, dey are goldfish)

The 1980 Toxteth riots made one wonder why this, the oldest coloured community in Britain, is still not fully integrated. Some families have been here for almost 200 years – they should be real Scousers by now. Mixed marriages brought mixed blood, a touch of the tar brush. Mind you, call a spade a spade had no overtones then, neither did Baa Baa Black Sheep.

As for the Welsh, yes, their male voice choirs sang beautifully, but

> Taffy was a Welshman, Taffy was a thief,
> Taffy came to our house and stole a piece of beef.

Feelings have never been exactly harmonious between the supporters of the two football teams, although Dixie Dean, playing for Everton, was the city's idol.

Amy came from a family which, with nine children, knew poverty, but it was a proud, often bitter, poverty, which kept itself to itself. No one should know what life was like behind closed doors. Class terminology was never used; one simply *knew* one's place and the place of others. Yet, apart from the occasional mispronunciation or grammatical error, both of which she stuck to like glue, she spoke remarkably pure and fluent English, which was amazing when her social and educational disadvantages are considered. As much of its life was lived in the streets, downtown Liverpool, with its poverty open for all to see, must have seemed another world. This wretchedness increased in the Twenties and the Thirties with the Depression and Slump.

Women were markedly the inferior sex. It was assumed that young school leavers (fourteen and upwards) would go into service with totally unregulated conditions and pay, or a factory, a shop or, better, an office such as Vernons or Little-woods. They would not have what we think of as a career. When they married, their lot became generally harsher. Amy never realised how unusually well treated she was by John. Married women went out to drudgery only if they were forced to by poverty or had been left 'without visible means of support' (although this phrase had also an unfortunate double meaning in respect of female underwear and stockings). If the former, the women were generally admired – unless it resulted in them sending out for fish and chips instead of giving their children a 'proper' meal. If they were war widows, they were pitied. Husbands who 'let' their own wives work outside the home (inside, paid or unpaid, was of course a different matter and to be expected) were shunned as failures.

The women slaved; they pawned until they could pawn no more, their main pleasure a chinwag (a lovely word for conversation or gossip) with those in similar predicaments. Feeding their children took precedence, although Amy felt they should not have been in the family way (that is, pregnant) in the first place. Compare those 'on the club' or getting sick pay, with those 'in the club' or with child. Both were frowned upon.

The workhouse was the ultimate shame. Desperation often set in when, by 1930, two and half million men in the country out of a smaller population than today were unemployed. This number rose during the decade. Amy had a never-ending, if unwarranted, fear of debt, of the dangers of clogs to clogs, or muck to muck, even riches to rags (rarely the other way round) in three generations. She was ever conscious of the need to cut your coat according to your cloth, to live within your means. Only the flighty, that is the imprudent, 'bought' things on tick, on the never-never.

Hire purchase, a later idea, was equally reprehensible. It was hammered home to me: take care of the pennies and the pounds will take care of themselves – one of the few of her admonishments which has stuck. Betting was, of course, un-Christian, whether on horses or dogs. It is true that it hurt the finances of many Liverpool families, the Grand National giving the greatest cause for concern. I still don't bet, but the main reason is probably the fear of losing. Even borrowing was considered not respectable in her house. For her, the poor used newspapers as tablecloths, lived in council houses or in one room in someone else's house, went to evening classes or the pub and bred guttersnipes.

My arrival

In due course, Amy decided that she wanted to 'bear John's child' (her phrase), which is when my life began. She had always been, and remained, very reticent about bodily functions; indeed, she never used the word pregnant: a woman was 'in an interesting condition' or 'expecting', unless, of course, she was 'no better than she ought to be' – a bewildering phrase.

Her *naïveté* was extraordinary in view of the fact that she had four younger brothers and, by this time, she was aunt to eleven small nieces and nephews, yet she did not actually realise that she might be carrying a child until she confided her symptoms to a fellow churchgoer. This woman and her husband, the Myers, became my Auntie (not 'Aunty' and not 'Aunt', for that was reserved for great-aunts) Rose and Uncle Phil – in an honorary capacity. Mr and Mrs were deemed too much for a toddler; using a Christian or baptismal name for an older person was, then, unthinkable. Times have changed, haven't they!

They, the Myers family, were much loved and appreciated as real bricks. He had a grocer's shop in Smithdown Road; fresh produce unsold by Saturday night was available for my parents, whilst their youngest daughter, Mamie (Mabel) and I had the run of their eccentrically shaped home above the shop. Christmas Day there for several years was the greatest fun.

I was 'brought into this world', not without difficulty, shortly after lunch on 7 September 1922. Was it by Dr McAusland or Dr Hope-Simpson? Fortunately, Amy was in awe of and believed implicitly in doctors. They ranked almost as highly as the best parson, and higher than many parsons.

'Thursday's child has far to go', the saying went; you, Ursula, are luckier, for 'Monday's child is fair of face'. John, my father, was thirty-one, Amy, my mother, two and a half years older. I remained an only child; she was not willing to face such an ordeal with chloroform again.

The birth was announced in the *Liverpool Daily Post* and *The Shrewsbury Chronicle*. According to custom, as it was a firstborn, Amy's maiden name was included.

CHERRY – September 7, at 34 Carrington Street, Princes Park, Liverpool, to Mr and Mrs John Cherry (Amy Hinchliffe) – a daughter.

My parents now called each other Mummy and Daddy, as though their personalities had changed. They later became Mum and Dad – to each other as well as to me. It was not until the late Sixties or early Seventies that John ever spoke of her as Amy.

Perhaps it is especially true of an only child to imagine that her real, therefore *extra*-ordinary, parents are somewhere else, and will one day turn up magically to reclaim their splendid offspring and whisk her away to some exciting land. Another characteristic, shared by only children and the mad, is to talk to themselves. Apparently, I did it frequently, even in my sleep – along with teeth-gnashing – even to the extent of carrying on a conversation ('talking the hind leg off a donkey'), although no details were ever vouchsafed.

Mother did not realise that she was starving her baby of milk. Auntie Rose and the doctor between them saved my life. I was then put on to a 'tittybottle' – surely Mother never twigged why a feeding bottle was so called. For her, masochistic on my behalf, dummies were taboo – a nasty, dirty habit, which would mean giving in to weakness. Was that why I caught any infection going and an annual dose of bronchitis?

She enjoyed spasmodic cuddling, singing:

'Go to sleep, my little piccaninny,
Daddy Fox'll to get you if you don't keep still,
Hushabye, lullaby, Mammy's little baby,
Mammy's little Alla-Balla-Coon.'

This presumably meant Alabama Negress child, although I am sure that she was unaware of this. Yet there was no knowing when she would simply push me away.

Normanby Street

Carrington Street no longer exists. I was nearly two years old when we moved to 4 Normanby Street, which was, I think, the next parallel to it. It too has gone, and rightly. University buildings and a new hospital cover the area, a welcome improvement.

I have vague memories of living in the heart of Liverpool; some may not be true memories, but rather remembrances of what I have been told, subsequently reinforced by photographs. I *believe* them to be true, which is what matters.

I was bathed in a zinc or tin bath in the yard, or, in winter, in front of the fire. After the bath, there was the performance of being dressed for bed – pyjamas with a 'gurgle [girdle] like Daddy wears', and having a tickly game played with my 'tutties' (toes).

> This little piggy went to market,
> This little piggy stayed at home,
> This little piggy ate roast beef,
> This little piggy had none,
> And this little piggy cried wee-wee-wee all the way home.

Perhaps that was how I learned the then acceptable names for the two bodily functions: Wee Wee and Big One. I was offered the choice when I demanded that 'Baby go labshie'. I later discovered that others called them Number One and Number Two, altogether less euphonious.

I do know that I felt safe in my playpen for no one could get at me or inside it; safe, that is, except when relatives were dumped on us. A doll's pram had been a pleasing possession until a cousin, sixteen months my junior, staying while his mother and father went to Paris, stamped on it. He has no recollection of the disaster, but subsequent to that and surely because of it, relations between the two families were severed. In fact, John and I met again only recently after more than seventy years, although his younger brother David made contact with my parents in the Sixties, remaining helpfully in touch until their deaths.

Another cousin, another Joan, came to stay while her mother was dying. Five years older, she was constantly badgered to be quiet so as not to wake the baby. Mother had no intuition to help her to realise that the child must have been desperately unhappy. Family relations here too were very strained.

Joan's brother Dennis remembered his visit. Aged ten or

eleven, he enjoyed his first ever car ride:

> This was in a huge limosine [sic] with Uncle John, your mother
> and other chapel friends; to me, it was another world.

Mid-morning, I apparently insisted that he have whatever I
was having – 'grapes, bananas or cake'. He played rounders
with my father and young men from the Sunday School, went
on an outing to Hoylake and walked to West Kirby, took trips
to the Dockside to see ferry boats and liners such as the *Mont
Royal*, and to see the opening of the first section of the cathedral.

> A less happy occasion was when your parents had more faith
> in my ability to look after you than was justified. One Sunday
> evening, you had been safely tucked up in bed with me left as
> your guardian, but with strict instructions on no account was I
> to go into your bedroom. You woke, no one there; a flood of
> tears from you, followed by an equal flow from me.

Family relations were then severed for at least twenty-five
years.

You know my devotion to Teddy, one year younger than
myself and given to me by my father – you've certainly added
to his family. He came everywhere with me, which is the only
reason that he has survived to a contented if battered old age.
Someone gave me a Teddy Tail brooch, but somehow it never
seemed quite right.

I had a toy gramophone. Dad bought two Nursery Rhymes
for it, but sadly, if typically, sat on one! Tears from us both,
silence from Mother. Other toys came later.

There are photos of the baby in the high pram, then in the
pramette, then riding piggyback on Dad's shoulders.

'Never run when you can walk,' commanded Mother, an
odd saying to a child who demonstrates the opposite. Have you
ever watched a youngster learning to use his or her feet?

Another incomprehensible instruction was, 'Don't point, it's rude.' But how else could you draw grown-ups' attention when and where you wanted it? I found it more satisfactory than getting things wrong.

I loved the tall, narrow, terraced house. The back step was hollowed out in the middle where people always trod and where I sat; it needed elbow grease and red carbolic soap for its scrubbing. The front door opened directly on to the pavement, unlike those in Upper Parly (Parliament) Street round the corner, which had four to six frightening steps up to the front door.

I could play with two boys in the empty street, matching their murderous Woolworths metal weapons with a wooden axe and spear (I have them still) carefully crafted by my grandfather. Mother was miffed by this mark of his interest and favour.

More easily supervised was playing in the jigger, or down the entry. After going through a gate in the wall, you came to an alleyway between these back-to-back houses. Having been warned not to tread in puddles, I remember vividly sitting in one, quite deliberately. This wasn't a matter of disobedience; I simply needed to know what it was like as it had been banned without explanation. For once, Mother did smack. The punishment didn't fit the crime. I do now avoid puddles! The wall itself was used for banging mats against or hitting them with a stick.

Some houses were 'in multiple occupancy', with cooking facilities on the curtained-off landings and shared outside privies. I wonder now what those facilities comprised. Poor wretches slept four, six or even eight to a bed.

Inside number 4 was better than the outside would suggest. The large but cold stone-floored basement, formerly used by servants, was now where clothes were washed in the copper; a 'professional' washerwoman came in to preside over the tub and do the 'rough' (that is, the scrubbing). The back kitchen, on the ground floor, had a dresser for cups, plates, etc., and a kitchen range with a high, three-sided brass fender, which had to be polished. It had a square seat at each end and, all too often, damp clothes draped over it on a wide fireguard. A black kettle sat permanently on the hob (which explains why a kettle-holder was essential) and a toasting fork hung on a hook. Have you ever used one? We received two as wedding presents even after World War II. The flat iron was heated here too. A gas mantle was in the passage and a paraffin lamp.

Above the two (or was it three?) storeys was an attic, primarily intended as maids' sleeping quarters, which served as a playroom in which there were plenty of places to hide.

The windows were in two lateral sections. When the catch in the middle was released, the bottom half could be pushed up, or the top half pulled down. They were virtually childproof because of their height.

I can now imagine the problems this house presented to my house-proud mother, although she had learned housewifery in a similarly harsh home.

Church: The bedrock of life

Both houses were convenient for my father's work in town and for them both in their spiritual home at Trinity, Grove Street, Wesleyan Methodist Church. I was duly christened Joan Hinchliffe Cherry and presented with a certificate admitting me to the chapel Cradle Roll. My mother adored her mother, so perhaps I should rightly have been called Barrett rather than Hinchliffe. It was customary – still is, to judge by birth announcements – for a wife's maiden name to become an offspring's middle name: so the name lives on, perhaps to remind the mother of earlier days. I enjoyed having an extra initial, always signing my name as Joan H. Cherry, but the name itself has been a permanent embarrassment. No one could, or can, spell it.

The general consensus is that she wanted a John, not a Joan;

it certainly seemed many times over the next twenty years that she was disappointed through the fibres of her being that I was not a boy. Her young nephew and my hero Leslie came to stay: he was her idol and remained so even when he committed the sin of marrying Olga, a Catholic girl, albeit lapsed. He came with us, when I was three or four, 'over the water' to Hoylake to dig sandcastles and make sand pies with mud, and nobly push my pram, wearing his Ludlow Grammar School cap to do so; he would have been eleven or twelve at the time. Mother took him down to the Pier Head to watch the boats. Despite this obvious partiality, he has remained my favourite cousin.

Unlike you, Ursula, I had no godparents. Why should the child have godparents, a perverse Church of England custom? In fact, it verged on the blasphemous for God is the Father of all, although my father did become a reluctant godfather to a neighbour's son, but never followed it up after the family left the area. He could take, leave or resume relationships without difficulty.

The only surviving record of church activity then – apart from my teeth marks on my father's fob watch to keep me quietly occupied on his knee during the sermon – is a sixpenny ticket for a Dickens recital on Friday, 18 December 1925 at 8 p.m. under the auspices of the Wesley Guild, of *The Soldier's Story* and *Sam Weller's Valentine* by Nathan Stephen, FSP, FPC. I can find no explanations of these letters – pharmaceutical, perhaps? I suspect that it has survived simply because Dad used the back of it to make largely illegible notes for one of his many addresses on Jesus Christ, a man's potential for good, whatever his situation, and which none of us should hinder. The more I reread his jottings, the more clearly I see this complex man. He never spoke extempore, feeling that it resulted in waffle, insincerity and lengthy self-advertisement; he never read a speech, for that led to turgid boredom – there was just much thought, prayer and notes to which he rarely referred.

One of these days, I must tell you more about him.

Friends

Whereas Mother always kept herself to herself, thus being often regarded as snooty, Dad had a host of friends; many survived from these early Trinity years, several contacting me when he died in 1979, although they had long left Liverpool.

Each church had, perhaps still has, its poor, its elderly 'church mice', those whose emotional lives derived all their sustenance and pleasure from the church, the Sunday School and the regular evening meetings during the week, and who tended to swarm round the minister, especially the young probationer on his first and nerve-racking appointment during which he was not allowed to marry. By definition, they were unmarried, indeed were known as 'maiden ladies', an incongruous adjective, for none was young; the phrase was deemed primarily descriptive and more respectful than the word 'spinster'. The sexual connection seemed unnoticed. They were occasionally accorded the courtesy title of 'Mrs'. Some had undoubtedly been affected by the slaughter of men in the Great War. Married women like Mother were condescending to those left on the shelf; this might explain, at least in part, her sudden haste to ensure her own marriage.

Bea Helms was one of these mice. Living in one room, she was a badly paid and insensitively treated companion (as were many in her position) to a pathetic, friendless but dictatorial old lady. Better off but idle women often treated a 'companion' abominably, abusing them verbally, financially, even physically.

With enough true aunts (eleven) and uncles (ten) of my own, plus nineteen more by marriage, a horrendous total of forty, with well over forty cousins, of whom only eight or so are still alive, I also collected Honorary Aunts. Bea Helms was one such. Poor as she was, Auntie Bea sent thoughtfully chosen books for birthdays and Christmases; she was one of the very few regular visitors, which, in reality, meant that in Mother's eyes, she posed no threat. There was always concern lest she outlive the old lady to whom she was the companion, for, thus deprived of money and lodging, what could she do? When I left home, I lost track of her. I don't remember what she wore; mousy brown is my general impression, certainly not pink, which was regarded uncharitably as an old maid's last hope.

Auntie Rose and Uncle Phil had four children – Hubert, Lucy, Clara and Mamie. Prone to 'crushes', I worshipped the first two from a distance, especially Lucy who was in the Sixth form when I joined the secondary school. As a lonely child who had only herself, and Teddy, to talk to, I envied the two youngest. One present from them lasted until just the other day: a two-handled cup, one-handled for many years – the loathing of, and fear of, retribution for breaking anything remains – filled with chocolates originally for Easter and subsequently filled with cold tea to put on burns. Auntie Mabel (Miss Willey), who came on holiday with us at least once, was, I think, an unmarried and direct relative of the Myers family.

Less happy is the memory of staying there twice – in May and December, 1928 – all by myself. I was abandoned by my parents, and each time they returned, a loved relation, first Granddad then Granny, had disappeared without explanation.

There were many other friends: the Corletts, whose highly respected father had his own chemist's shop (was it on the corner of Upper Parliament Street and Grove Street?), Tom, one of his two sons, inviting me during the Second World War to Magdalen College May Day celebrations; Murdoch Mackinnon – such an exciting name; Joyce Roxburgh; Miss Muriel Hawkesworth, Headmistress of, I think, a Junior School to which we went for the patriotic (but to me frightening) tableaux of Empire Day; and some of the hockey players – Georgie (Georgina) Latarche, so attractively foreign-sounding, daughter of the jeweller; and Lylie (Violet) Craig (a later visitor); and Sadie Luke.

Cory Dixon, JP, BA, a good local preacher, subsequently became Lord Mayor; he invited my father and me to an impressive Reception when I was sixteen: best dress (or frock, as it was usually called then), corduroy velvet, I guess. He showed us round the Town Hall beforehand.

Especially warmly regarded and lifelong friends were the four members of the wealthy Smith family, owners and beneficiaries of the carpet firm of J. R. Smith in Clayton Square. They lived in a big house, with a basement transformed into a light and airy games room which opened directly on to the large garden, with cellars and attic, and a sitting room with stuffed birds in it, at number 11 Sunnyside, Princes Park. Cupboards were full of curiosities, including a stereoscope, which never focussed for my odd eyes, although Mother assumed that I was just being my usual difficult self. They also owned a delightful holiday house, The Lodge, in Madeira Walk, Church Stretton, a few miles from Marshbrook; another in Aberdaron was probably rented.

The eldest, Miss Nellie Miff, was a terrifying lady, in the Queen Mary mould but thinner, who died early.

Some fifteen years older than my father, portly Mr Robert (Robert Martin, Robin to his sisters, Rob to his close friends) played a stately game of tennis in immaculate whites on their own private grass court, while guests watched from their cushioned basket chairs, wrapped in warm rugs if the weather should so dictate. We were often invited, as I grew up, to play. One special occasion of tennis plus supper ('lovely time') ended with the unheard-of luxury of a taxi home.

RMS was to be extra respected because he had visiting cards! At that time, there was a special nuance about such cards left with an edge turned down – or was it up? He wanted Dad to become a Rotarian, but Dad felt that he could not, or ought not to, afford their demands for money for charitable purposes. Both men were united in their condemnation of Masons, not really because of their secrecy or their garb, but partly because members were considered to be anti-Christ and perceived glad-handing in the sense of 'you scratch my back and I'll scratch yours'.

In Mother's autograph book some thirty years later, RMS ruled lines and wrote with care:

> Look up and not down
> Look out and not in
> And lend a hand.

This was typical of his simple philosophy.

Miss Amy wished to be known as Aunt (and her brothers as uncles), but Mother forbade it for she knew her place. They were hurt, and I was deprived; I knew nothing of this until much later. A shame, as it would have given the lady great pleasure; it is not only poverty which creates barriers.

A right-winger in politics, she hopefully passed on Kenneth de Courcy's newsletters. Accustomed to correct behaviour, she told Mother that she ought to put her daughter's nose in a clothes peg overnight to prevent it from turning up at the tip. For once, Mother was right if for the wrong reason: 'What does she know about children? She hasn't had any.'

Her autograph was also characteristic.

> God grant me the sincerity to accept things I cannot change
> The courage to change the things I should
> And the wisdom to know the difference.

Perhaps you can appreciate my mother more clearly when you know that she gave that autograph book to Leslie, not to me. Nevertheless, he felt that I should have it.

Mr Herbert, who, I now realise, was a complete hypochondriac, an old maid according to Mother, was an excellent playmate for a child. With clean sand, two tiny wheelbarrows and spades, 'working' under the names of two labourers (he was Ernie, I was Eric), we built houses together. He always gave Dad a book for Christmas. He rose further in my estimation when I saw labels in his own books – Ex Libris Herbert Smith. Do you remember the wooden-framed fire screen of tapestry in your bedroom? It was sewn by him. More impressive to a child then was his huge camel winter coat with its astrakhan collar.

Dad was on Christian name terms with them all; Mother remained Mrs Cherry.

The Smiths' maids wore formal uniforms and, as was customary with the gentry, were known by their surnames; their comfortable cook Ada, once their nurse, was an exception as was John, the firm's driver who doubled as their personal chauffeur of a cream-coloured car with a dickey seat. This, originally a seat for the servant at the back of a carriage, was then an open seat for one person. Hand signals were gradually replaced by traffic arms – neither was much use in the dark!

When I was older, we were invited time and time again to tea; in my memory, this was always outside in sunshine. We played clock golf and croquet, clubs, mallets and hoops being kept in the conservatory in special long wooden boxes. A painting session was tried – but once only! Dad played tennis on their court. After this exertion, he had a bath before dinner – such sophistication. Food, summoned by Miss Amy's foot pressing on a bell under the dining room table, came up in a lift worked by a pulley; it was served by her and then distributed by at least two maids. The gentlemen might smoke a cigarette or an Abdullah cigar after the ladies had retired to the drawing room. No alcohol was ever served.

They were never invited back to our house.

I remember the family with great affection. It was a pity that Wesleyans had no truck with godparents, as each would have filled the bill beautifully and would have so much enjoyed the more intimate connections. They had to make do with honorary nieces and nephews.

The Neighbourhood

I never heard my parents mention any neighbours from this time. In retrospect, I can see that they did not fit into the area. In our two inner city houses, they yet lived close to a 'good' district, to the houses of the rich in the Georgian terraces (of which Liverpool claimed more than your now hometown of Bath) and to Princes Park, where a handbell was rung to indicate closing time. This was surrounded by the backs of big houses whose owners had, according to Mother, 'feathered their nests'. One surprise was a disused boathouse in the style of a Swiss chalet, another the palm trees. Its larger neighbour, Sefton Park, boasted tropical trees and a palm house with statues. Also near were the genteel mansions of Rodney Street, where medical specialists lived in imagined splendour.

Gambier Terrace and Upper Parly Street, however, were already going downhill. Granby Street was the centre of riots in 1981 and apparently some years later was plagued with heroin dealers. 'Poverty has its appeal to those who have never known want': this was the 'real' Liverpool, where 'pool' was reduced in a form of self-mockery – hence Liverpudlians. Here, rough, tough boys played football in the streets, wearing shorts and jerseys conspicuous by their holes; they walked barefoot; lice often crawled in their yellowish undernourished hair. I caught the lice too; Mother harvested them with a special lice comb and cracked them with her fingernail. The Waifs and Strays Society was well named.

Little girls wore no knickers in summer and were sewn into them for winter. Sniffling, nose-picking, handkerchief-less children did cling to their mothers' skirts, for mothers wore long skirts that were clingable to, or to the strings of their sacking aprons. Women often wore a man's flat cap back to front and a shawl crossed over and tied at the back; on their feet were sometimes lace-up or buttoned boots, but more often men's shoes without laces.

Poverty was stark in the aftermath of the Great War, yet all the men, on foot or in transport, doffed their hats at the Cenotaph. It was a harrowing sight to see down-and-outs, small groups of unemployed, forgotten, workless and sometimes shell-shocked or blinded ex-soldiers, looking twice their age, many with major limb surgery helped by wooden attachments known as Dot and Carry ones because of the thump of the timber on the ground. The realistic phrase was not meant unkindly nor was it malicious, just as nigger, blackie and Chink were not truly racist. They shuffled along in the gutters, for they had to keep moving as it was illegal to stop to beg in the streets. They often carried a little placard to explain their plight, as they begged in dignified silence as often for crusts as for cash. Others patrolled with musical instruments. The Welsh sang harmoniously, holding out their caps in the hope of ½d or 1d. Perhaps 'Guide me, O Thy great Jehovah, / Pilgrim through this barren land' was appropriate to their lot. Those who could offered something in exchange: heather or matches. The organ-grinder, often an Italian, played his tunes; sometimes his clothed monkey performed tricks. The one-legged diver off New Brighton pier, a familiar but distressing sight, earned his money the hard way. They are all immortalised in the American song, 'Buddy, can you spare a dime?'

Occasionally, wounded soldiers, conspicuous in hospital blue, would be wheeled out of hospital, as late as the mid-Thirties. Others talked shamefacedly to each other on street corners.

Men wore white mercerised cotton mufflers, the ends crossed, folded over behind and tucked into their armpits; collars and ties were only for the better off. I was similarly swathed in winter – one off-white, one harsh blue – but mine was tied at the back, partly for warmth and partly so that I could not untie or lose the wretched thing. Their trouser turn-ups were scuffed. A few had old trilbies but most wore cloth caps. I used to be intrigued by the way some of them held Woodbines (when scrounged, a pride as well as a stigma), the lighted end facing backwards. They had done this originally so that the boss would not see too readily and it had become an ingrained, furtive habit. Pipe-smoking was largely an admired habit of the affluent, the toffs, the toffee-nosed.

I do remember sitting on my father's shoulders to watch the marchers in the General Strike when I was nearly four years old, another occasion for boarding up windows. He was profoundly affected – there, but for the grace of God... In the Thirties, men were driven to sifting through rubbish dumps in the desperate hope of finding something usable or sellable, or snitching coal from the slag heaps. Charity giving was not nationally organised, churches, groups such as the Soroptimists and Robin Goodfellow of the *Liverpool Daily Post* at Christmas being the main channels that I can recall.

Liverpool was such a harsh place that, for survival, a voluble and sardonic sense of humour, a sly cynicism, was needed, typified by the joke, ' "I see," said the blind man as he bumped into a lamp post', or 'A nod's as good as a wink to a blind man'. A favourite rhyme was basically cruel too; there are many variants.

> Poor old lady, she swallowed a fly.
> I wonder why she swallowed a fly.
> Poor old lady, she swallowed a cat.
> Fancy that, she swallowed a cat.
> Poor old lady, she swallowed a dog.
> She went the whole hog when she swallowed a dog.
> Poor old lady, she swallowed a horse
> [Pause for effect]
> She's dead, of course.

> Oh dear, what can the matter be?
> Three old ladies locked in the lavat'ry,
> They've been there from Monday to Saturday,
> Nobody knew they were there.

Some of these phrases might well be heard elsewhere. I know them only in Liverpool. If you wanted to get the better of someone, then 'two heads are better than one, even if one is only a cabbage' (double-edged, because who is the cabbage, you, self-deprecating, or the other person, dull-witted?). In self-assertion, 'I'm not as green as I'm cabbage-looking.' If anyone did or said something silly, then he was a 'daft ha'porth' (or halfpenny) or 'as daft as a brush' and it was 'enough to make a cat laugh'. Because cats go out at night, you 'let the cat out', that is you spill the beans, you broadcast a secret. 'A cat can look at a king' was the answer to a rebuke for staring.

A female social climber was 'all fur coat and no knickers' – more telling than simply 'common as muck'. Another, maybe 'no spring chicken', was titivated, 'all dolled up to the nines' or 'dressed up like a dog's dinner'. Older women, perhaps pushing thirty or forty, and trying to disguise their age were 'mutton dressed as lamb'.

Anyone scurrying to do this, that and the other all at once might be asked, 'Have you got ants in your pants?' – more vivid than being a 'cat on hot bricks'. For those disapproved of and who came to a sticky end, well, it was 'good riddance to bad rubbish'. An apparently derogatory remark needed the reply, 'Same to you with knobs on.' When anyone commented 'Well, well!' he would be answered with, 'Two wells make a river and your head'll make it bigger.' An unbelievable tale was 'all my eye and Betty Martin', or, more succinctly, 'tommyrot' (possibly derived from soldiers, that is Tommies, getting foot rot in the trenches) or 'rats'. Any visitors inclined to outstay their welcome would be told ambiguously, 'Here's your hat. What's your hurry?'

Are all children literal-minded? I was, so some sayings were frightening: for example, 'wiping the floor with someone', or 'don't make a face, you'll stick like it', or 'Who's she? The cat's grandmother' – it being rude to say she instead of the person's name, or 'You give me the pip' (what kind? what a funny present!) to someone who makes you fed up. 'Pip' is less ambiguous than 'willies'! 'Well, I'll go to our house,' expressed extreme surprise.

Although for years I was carefully shielded from its vulgarity, I later appreciated Liverpudlians' gruff, plain speaking, even if I didn't always understand Scouse pronunciation which is doubtless influenced by the weather and by Welsh, Irish and Lancashire accents and phrases, although Lancashire folk were generally regarded as slow, homely countrymen. The letter 't' is pronounced explosively compared with the Londoners' avoidance of it like the plague. But what of 'I'll 'it 'im on the 'ead with an 'ard 'ammer and make 'im 'owl 'orrible'? Recently the origin of Scouse was said to be *lobscouse*, the Norwegian name for a meat and vegetable stew. Well, well, indeed!

Other examples: gear, spiffing, goody goody gumdrops (great), girt big (enormous), give over (stop), gerr off, skedaddle, get out of my road, I'll do it any road (anyway), I'll do it my road (way), gotcha (you're caught); get that in yer lughole (ear, therefore, listen and absorb), shut yer gob (be quiet), watch-er whacker (hello, mate). Tarrá, or worse, tarráwell, was vulgar; tattá (but not tattá for now, immortalised by Tommy Handley) was acceptable for children, goodbye was preferable, so long for now passed muster, sling yer hook did not. 'Eh?' and 'What?', both in general use, were rude; pardon was acceptable because, dependent on the tone and circumstance, it could mean either 'How dare you say/do that?' or indicate an apology, 'I do beg your pardon.'

Some colloquialisms were possible: 'ye gods and little fishes' and 'my giddy aunt' both expressed delighted surprise; blest (as in 'well, I'm blest'), blinking, crikey (does this derive from 'Christ'?), dash, gosh, bother, golly gosh. Some, really only variations on bloody or blasted, were OK, except that OK wasn't OK and was forbidden at home. 'What a swizz!' expressed disillusion. Dash or drat was as far as Dad would go to indicate extreme annoyance; anything stronger, like damn, was a dirty and a naughty word. At school, there came the thrill of learning 'hell's bells and buckets of blood' – true emancipation! Getting your dander up, getting into a stitherum or simply being crabby were all more exciting than losing your temper or just getting worked up.

An argument which didn't hold water or was unanswerable might receive the odd remark: 'Bob's your uncle and Fanny's your aunt', a phrase having some forgotten connection with the Balfour and Salisbury families. It was a multipurpose dictum for it could also indicate 'That's that, that's the way it goes', problem dismissed, for another Liverpudlian character-istic was stoicism.

Health

Mother, although not a Scouser, took this to masochistic excess. 'You don't get owt [anything] for nowt [nothing]' led her to cut off her nose to spite her face. For example, it was morally weakening and therefore wrong to light the fire in the bedroom when anyone was ill. She spurned corn caps when her feet were killing her with corns, bunions, segs and ingrowing toenails. Shoes were not made then in the varied widths of today. If she ever admitted to feeling middling or groggy or had a bit of a lie-down, this indicated that she was proper poorly. It was mardy to complain of not feeling well, nesh to complain of, or even notice, the cold. As for a woman who was in trouble or who did complain, she was dismissed with 'she made her bed and must lie on it'.

There was a pattern of infant mortality and particularly of miscarriages for childbearing was as hazardous as life itself. There were no ante-natal or post-natal clinics. It was just assumed that all the womenfolk would rally round. All the more reason to want to go back to Shrewsbury. It was also taken for granted that a mother would never regain her figure. Mine certainly did not if her boast of a 20" waist were true; she was supported by fearsome corsetry ('stays'), which she wore throughout her life. She remained short and stubby. Older women had varicose veins which often ulcerated.

There was a saying that one came into this world as another left it; this, like hanky-panky, caused bewilderment. I wasn't even given the conventional explanation that a baby came out of its mother's tummy. No, 'never you mind'; storks brought many, others were found under gooseberry bushes. My knowledge of such matters was of the order of:

> Where did you come from, baby dear?
> Out of the nowhere into here.

Hymns did not help much:

> Away in a manger, no crib for a bed,
> The little Lord Jesus laid down his sweet head.

'Offspring of a virgin's womb' might as well have been in Greek. Only slightly easier to understand was a later reply: 'from Nantycumpuffyn, where the ducks fly backwards', I've never seen the place written, so my spelling is approximate. I don't remember ever noticing the bulge of a baby, maybe because pregnant women then wore loose garments and remained in semi-purdah. So why the concern and the complications? And what did they mean by a girl who was no better than she ought to be? Certainly, she was thus if she wore garters which were flashy, instead of normal suspenders. The smaller point of garters pinching the legs and being bad for the circulation didn't come into the matter.

More adults were misshapen, more children had harelips, club foot or were in leg irons with rickets. You've probably never seen a child with rickets; their bones developed badly as a result of poor diet and environment, so that they looked sadly deformed with, for example, bowed or bandy legs, knock knees and spinal distortion. For spinal curvature, which afflicted my cousin Fred, the only treatment was to lie down for twelve months in/on a spinal carriage. I've never seen albinos (people with white hair and pink eyes) except in Liverpool. Some unlucky folk had St Vitus' Dance, their involuntary movements striking us youngsters as hilarious. One or two local lads had no roofs to their mouths; we mimicked their speech. Children were markedly cruel; perhaps fear of the unknown and the unexplained comes into it, but cruelty, albeit non-violent, is not a modern phenomenon.

Although everyone knew what was meant by Rainhill, the local asylum, the word lunatic was not mentioned. There were many euphemisms, however: loony, dippy, dotty, potty, doolally, dimwit, dumb-dumb, not all there, were perhaps the kinder ones. More picturesque were 'thick as five short planks' (Liverpudlians always had to go two or three better), 'having a screw loose', and, my own favourite, being 'tuppence short of a shilling'.

Maladies which are hardly heard of or easily treated now were rampant, although others have taken their place. You were 'taken' by an illness; if you were 'took', you were carried out feet first, the illness having completely taken you. With TB, no respecter of class or status, the victim was packed off to a sanatorium, impossibly situated in the countryside for visiting, or, if rich enough, to Switzerland, as was the son of a church friend. Liverpool's weather, raining cats and dogs, did not help such patients. Whereas we thought of East England as colder and windier, we hadn't heard of the poor air quality associated with the dampness of the North-west. Galloping consumption carried off so many that my paternal Cherry and maternal Hinchliffe stock must be fairly sound.

Meningitis and pneumonia with its feared 'crisis' after six to eight days, after which it was hoped that the patient had turned the corner, were all too often fatal. Other common afflictions were rheumatic fever, mastoid, anaemia (Iron Jelloids) and goitres which produced bulbous eyes. Faces were pasty and spotty; I was lucky in this regard, as spots, boils or acne, of which I had none, were considered to indicate bad blood and/or poor upbringing. Nails were brittle and often badly bitten. Gumboils were normal. It is probably hard for you to imagine a time without antibiotics.

'No Spitting' was an essential notice. For congestion of the lungs, one sniffed the tar as men made or replaced the roads. It was exciting to talk to these men as they sat round their brazier, drinking their strong tea from enamel-lidded and enamel-handled tea cans. Bronchitis, poor tonsils and bad adenoids added their contribution to the unique Scouse accent. The doctor put a spoon down your throat; you wanted to be sick. There were two schools of thought: painting tonsils distressingly or removing them altogether. My parents refused surgery which then involved having a chloroform pad put over the nose, leading to nausea. November illness when we went through handkerchiefs (made out of old sheets) at a rate of knots was an accepted fact of life.

So we suffered chilblains, sometimes on the hands (dannies) but usually on the toes; always hot and itchy and all too often agonisingly broken, they were probably not helped by a hot-water bottle, a large, dark beige stone tube with a stone screw knob in the centre of the top surface, nor by freezing bedrooms, and they were certainly made worse by warming the extremities by the fire. Mother claimed that she did not feel the cold, yet she had chilblains and her fingers went numb as mine do today. Perhaps poor circulation is a Hinchliffe trait. For chapped hands – no rubber or plastic gloves, no creams – there was no cure.

With infectious diseases such as scarlet fever, which meant up to six weeks' isolation and a medical certificate, all toys were baked or even burned. I was successfully inoculated against it and still bear the scar. The dreaded diphtheria (dip) and chickenpox were often lethal. In the epidemic of 1932, a curtain was hung over the front door to indicate an infection in the house. Bedrooms were fumigated, unless the sufferer had been incarcerated in an 'isolation hospital', which caused a stigma.

Avoiding all these, instead I caught measles – not once, not even twice, but three times! Was this, as was suggested, the cause of my eye problems? Four days of blindness followed by double vision (I can still hear myself saying plaintively: 'No, I don't want two pieces of bread') were inadequately and unsympathetically dealt with, after endless waiting, during the frequent visits to the terrifyingly morgue-like St Paul's Eye Hospital. Spectacles were bought privately, which gave my parents a choice of frames – I had no say in the matter, but then I was only three or four years old. For those on 'the panel', or list of those who were too poor to pay, frames were all the same. They were tortoiseshell, but a metal bar over the nose made the top of that organ very sore, whilst a so-called flexible wire hurt behind the ears. For a while, glasses were not always worn in case they got worn out! From then, it was Plain Jane and no nonsense – hardly a morale-booster. I couldn't even rise to rosy cheeks like you, still less a dimple. For adults, there were then no contact lenses, no bifocals, none on a string; pince-nez looked alarming, but there was always the hopeful fear that they would fall off.

The tendency, medically, was to use home remedies until a critical point was reached, for unless you were poor and on the panel, visits to and treatment by doctor, dentist and optician were expensive. These specialists were usually paid in guineas. Have you ever heard of them? A guinea was a pound plus the same number of shillings, so that three guineas equalled £3 3s 0d. It seemed so professional – and subtly added to the cost: twenty guineas meant £21. We would have hated to regard ourselves as poor. Relations remained formal: 'Yes, doctor; no, doctor.' 'Do this, Mrs Cherry' – not, as now, 'Hi, Joan, how's life?'

Most families had a stock of their own tried and trusted procedures and remedies. Mother's began with the dictum:

Early to bed, early to rise,
Makes a man healthy, wealthy and wise.

Regular bowels were essential; a recent writer to *The Times* obviously suffered the same *régime*. 'Regularity was almost a religion.' Prunes 'are good for you' – a poor gambit psychologically.

For digestive disorders, coyly referred to as 'pains in one's Mary' or 'in Mary Jane', arrowroot and milk, rhubarb and senna, the milder milk of magnesia, even Eno's fruit salts or castor oil, which acted as a personal Jeyes' Fluid, were all possible means to a 'good clear-out'. Syrup of figs and sulphur tablets, which caused rude smells and equally rude noises, are still a distressing memory. Dad favoured Andrew's Liver Salts internally and Sloan's Liniment externally. Calves' foot jelly was reserved for the well-off. Gyppy tummy (whence 'it gives me gyp') – was that Egyptian in origin, perhaps from wars in the Sudan?

After graduation from the potty (no connection with driving people potty or up the wall), my morning wee-wee and big-one were supervised in the sense that I was not allowed to pull the chain or 'jiler' even when I could reach it as I was not trusted to tell the truth, as that might involve any of the horrors I've just mentioned. For years, there was no toilet paper, but on a hook neat squares of newspaper with which to wipe my rumpy (or rumpie – I have never seen the word written down). I had no idea that it was twee or diminutive for that part of my backside. Was it a family word, in common parlance or in folklore? Such matters were not discussed – but it came as a shock later to discover a more technical word. It wasn't considered nice to have the lavatory in the same room as the washbasin or bath.

Public lavatories cost money; they weren't posh either like those at mainline London stations nowadays. You inserted a penny in the slot on the door – hence the euphemism to spend a penny, just as you did for chocolate, hence the euphemism 'has the penny dropped?' for 'have you understood?' You then turned the door handle. There were no washing facilities. Another apparatus, usually on station platforms, which also cost one penny, was the public weighing machine. When the coin was fed into the slot, the whirring began and a card came out, giving as well as your weight a motto or warning of the most banal kind.

Special night vests, that is, day vests not pensioned off but past their prime, were impregnated with camphorated oil. We sang:

Camphoramphoramphorated,
camphoramphoramphorated,
camphoramphoramphorated,
so we rubbed her with camphorated oil

to the tune of 'Glory, Glory, Alleluia'. These oily garments were articles of faith worn in bed in the winter in a vain attempt to ward off or counteract coughs and colds. For winter too, we took spoonfuls of cod liver oil and malt, or the superior halibut; cod, believe it or not, was the cheapest fish then; this was for 'growing troubles, weaknesses, anaemia'. In the spring, to clear out the winter's microbial deposits, when blood was out of order, there was brimstone and treacle (which caused a tremendous pong), replaced later by the more socially acceptable, and more pricey, Sanatogen tonic.

For coughs and colds, we inhaled Friar's balsam in a basin of hot water, a towel over our heads, sucked tablets of linseed, liquorice and chlorodine, sipped butter, sugar and lemon juice for especially tickly coughs, or, best of all, drank home-made blackcurrant tea. Was there any native of Liverpool who did not have nasal or chest problems, trouble in their 'bronicals'? Feed a cold and starve a fever.

For eye troubles, styes being more common then, Golden Eye ointment was favoured; for swellings, bread poultices, as iodine hurt on open wounds. Cuts were covered with Germoline (Germy), then sold in a tin; I don't recall any tubes. 'What you need is a little bit of bandage' or 'Let Mummy kiss it better' – both with a low success rate. Perhaps, who knows, this encouraged an early disillusion with adults. Aspro or aspirin was judged the soundest product for a severe headache. Hands were dipped in egg water to 'cure' warts – or was it the other way round? Was it that if water in which eggs had been boiled were spilled onto a hand, then warts would develop?

Advertisements for cures were ubiquitous. Virol was extolled on every railway station and on countless hoardings. I found recently an old envelope on which Mother had listed purchases of four bottles (3/9 each) in six weeks, a bottle of emulsion (1/-) each month and Glaxo (eight tins in six weeks) at 2/6 each – what an expense over three winter months that must have been! Scott's or Anger's Emulsion would surely build us up.

Publicity turned her against not only Sal Volatile (a four-syllabled word) – no Hinchliffe should be so feeble as to feel faint – but also against Dr Williams' Pink Pills for Pale People, Dr Carter's Little Liver Pills, Phyllosan (said to fortify the over-forties), Beecham's Pills ('worth a guinea a box'), Veno's Lightning Cough cure, and certainly against Dr J. Collis Browne's Chlorodine, Honey and Glycerine – 'safe and reliable family remedy for Influenza, Colds, Coughs, Catarrh, Asthma, Bronchitis. At all chemists, 1/3, 3/5. It would be difficult to name a more complete and reliable medicine to keep at hand under all climatic conditions.'

Granny and Granddad

Despite weighing a good nine pounds at birth, I was allegedly delicate, born with a weak chest which had to be covered in flannel. I was, if you can believe this, very tiny. I remember still the terrifying 'whoops' of a bad case of whooping cough.

As I was too ill for the train, we were taken by the Smith's chauffeur John in the car to Shrewsbury. Cars were generally boneshakers, or baby Austins, but this was the height of luxury. Horns when pressed generally gave forth a frightening sound, but not this one; it was fun squeezing the bulb to make the genteel noise. There was a screen between John ('the salt of the earth') and the passengers, who could give him instructions through a speaking tube. The journey, during which I was very sick over Runcorn Transporter Bridge, was the beginning of the highlight of my pre-school life.

We stayed just over the Welsh Bridge across the River Severn, at 12 The Mount (the numbering has since been changed and the large and original number 12 now looks less than pristine), Frankwell, with my maternal grandparents. You were luckier than I was in that you knew your maternal grandparents throughout your childhood and youth. This was my only acquaintance with mine. They were kinder to their grandchildren than they had been to their own offspring – six girls, followed by four boys, the youngest, James, surviving only three weeks. This fact was for long a matter of strange pride: 'I once had an uncle three weeks old,' for death simply fixes a person at whatever age it occurs.

In the back garden (there was no front one, the steps going straight down to the pavement), hens, fed by Granny by hand, pecked, which was alarming as was the noise they made. I don't suppose that I had ever seen a hen before – I was only about three and a half or four. At the bottom was a dark, exciting but frightening little house – the wooden-seated lavvy – so potties were used indoors. Whenever anyone said, 'I'm just going out the back,' everyone knew why. Beyond that was Granddad's top garden – it was never called an allotment – full of vegetables, including taties or tatties, for everyone ate great dollops of spuds, and fruit that I'd seen only in shops. I didn't know that a gooseberry grew on a bush, which made the explanation of where a baby came from even less acceptable.

To a town child used to a backyard, this was indeed bliss. Inexperience led me to mistake a pile of soot for a pile of earth. The mess was cleaned up in a stormy scene in a hip bath in front of the roaring fire, the water being heated in a bucket hung over the fire on a hook. A harsh wielder of a big stick with his own family, Granddad encouraged the splashing and the blowing of soap bubbles. As well as Woodbines, he smoked an old clay pipe; a small one was found for me to resemble the Pear's Soap adverts. It was removed as soon as we got home, as blowing bubbles was not considered 'nice'; blowing through straws, a later novelty, was similarly frowned upon.

For the old man, nothing was too much trouble for the one he called Skipper Sardine when I wore my sou'wester (a deep face-encircling rain hat) and wellies (not gollies; galoshes, despised then, might well be welcomed now). When the rain teemed down, it was 'nice weather for ducks'. It is odd how one's childish language returns in old age: for example, it's 'pournin' nainin' ('it's pouring with rain'). I loved to snuggle up on his knee and run my fingers through his long white beard; my father was virtually bald and I'd never seen anyone in Liverpool with a beard. I thought that they must be reserved for granddads. He also owned a heavy iron last, which had served him in his trade as a carpenter, and which he then used for mending shoes or knocking in nails. We found it in our shed after my father died.

Granny was more forbidding, although she was considerably younger then than I am now. Her face was deeply lined, she always wore black, including a black goitre band which hid, at least partially, a sagging neckline, and occasionally a white lace cap. In other words, she assumed that she was old. As well as a cameo brooch on her neckband, she wore 'gold' sleeper earrings which were reputed to be a help for weak sight. None of her daughters followed this example, Mother thinking them vulgar. She was, nevertheless, emotionally attached to her mother, criticising her father (not, of course, to his face) for causing so many children, another concept bewildering to a child with a sheltered upbringing. At home, but not to outsiders, she praised her mother's courage for taking in the washing of the well-to-do, especially in such primitive conditions. Granny wore a man's flat cap when hanging the clothes outside; Granddad wore his inside the house as well.

Mother's admiration was given to few people, and then not always for any logical reason: Mr Johnnie Williams, a well-off Shrewsbury Wesleyan, who sent his shirts to Granny for washing; the Rev. F. Paul Bacon, the minister who officiated at her wedding; her brother Fred, although she condemned his charming wife Pen as pretentious because she lisped and did watercolours.

Indeed, family relations were strained. I didn't realise for many years just how strained. I sensed that I was different, kept apart, partly by geography, but mainly by my mother's pride – she, through my father, had risen socially, and they were going to give me a better educational chance – and her shame. Not only poor, both grandparents had had a less than complete belief in Divine Guidance, to say nothing of insufficient sexual restraint. Much, much later, Mother's relatives let bygones be bygones in most charitable fashion.

Of the tall house on The Mount, I remember little. There was no electricity, no gas, no running water – fun for a few days. The oven was to the side of the kitchen fireplace; food was not merely cooked in it, but kept delightfully hot. Pots hung over the fire for water or vegetables. I do recall with a shudder a glass dome on a landing; it contained stuffed fish and birds' eggs.

Staying there was not considered a proper holiday. A fortnight (not a shaming week) in the summer at the seaside, in a boarding house advertised in Dad's Civil Service handbook, was *de rigueur* for Mother. As a baby, I first accompanied them, I'm told, on a church outing in 1923 to the Wirral; this was doubtless a dummy run for the first orthodox holiday, bed and breakfast and the rest self-catering, stay in Llanfairfechan and in 1924 Penmaenmawr, then Llandudno twice and Rhyl in 1927. For Penmaenmawr, the address was Moel View, Brynmor Terrace. I can't have remembered it, as I was only two, but it has somehow stuck.

1926 was the year of the great Church Stretton camp, for which Dad wore his ex-army clothes. One photo shows sixteen boys, an elder sister of one, cousin Leslie, Mother and me. I am told that I refused, howling desperately, to set foot in a tent. That refusal has, so far, been maintained!

All change!

Problems were arising at home in Liverpool, although I knew nothing of this at the time. Doctors advised moving out of the city for my health.

More seriously, my father had been attacked; notes threatening his wife and baby had come through the letterbox from an ex-Service man crazed by the 1914–1918 War. This happened because Dad worked first for the Liverpool Welfare and Pensions Committee, then for the Ministry of Pensions. He was, I discovered subsequently, given police protection. He was notified many years later of the man's death in Broadmoor.

Dad enjoyed this good, well-paid and senior post, but had no security of tenure, for it was thought that such war-caused problems would not be long-lasting. The 1926 General Strike tipped the balance and he took a much lowlier post in Inland Revenue in India Buildings. He was much looked up to, not only as having a safe job – or rather, post – but an almost governmental one which allowed him to use his considerable arithmetical skills (no calculators then) and to be usefully informative to others.

Dumped one day on Auntie Rose, I found myself in the evening transported, without warning or explanation, from the centre of my universe. Yes, I was only four, but I'd have liked to have been told. I couldn't have put my feelings into words then, but I recognise now that my parents had betrayed a trust. A newspaper article recently urged that children should always be involved in moving because of their need to feel secure. The writer expressed incredulity that the first time some children see the new house is on the day they move in. Maybe this is why, as I grew up, I felt that I was living in my parents' house, their home, and so never suffered homesickness for either of their next two abodes.

How did you feel about your moves when you were a child? In my next letter, I must tell you about Hunts Cross.

TWO
Hunts Cross

Outside 24 Roskell Road

Strange to find a village road named after an eighteenth-century watchmaker who exported 30,000 timepieces to South America alone. At least, that is the only origin I can find. But it was our road, *our* pronounced with pride. Now postcoded L25, Hunts Cross was then a village outside the city boundary. At the bottom of our road, on the other side of the country road leading to Woolton, where you might see a car on a busy day, was the golf course with its background of woods. The other direction took you to Speke, incorporated in the city as long ago as 1932.

At the top end was Mackets Lane, where, in September, Dad and I filled bowls with blackberries, fruit for pounds of jam and jelly, causing multiple scratches on legs, arms and hands and the comment: 'You look as if you've been dragged through a hedge backwards.' Mother often spoiled the berries for me by stewing them with apples. I loved to trample in my wellies through the fallen leaves in autumn before we collected them in sacks for the midden (compost heap).

Beyond were fields of buttercups and daisies ('Oh, the pretty flowers!'), and big dog daisies. 'You mustn't pick wild flowers', not for reasons of conservation, but because 'you don't know what's been on them'. Buttercups were the flowers by which you knew if your sweetheart loved you – he loves me, he loves me not, he loves me, as you picked off each petal; on the other hand, if you picked a dandelion, then you would 'wee the bed', a strange belief not confined to small Liverpool children; consider the French word for the flower, *pissenlit*.

I stood open-mouthed here nine years ago. Mackets Lane retains the name but is now a main road and seems to have displaced in importance the old Speke Road. Now, there are houses on each side as far as one can see and more houses behind them, so that the fields and the flowers have gone. No more leaf-gathering, no more blackberrying.

It really was a village, with its own conundrum: What made Hunts Cross? Because Halewood Speke – Speke with its alleged 9'-high giant and its first tiny aerodrome, with the attraction of joyrides or flips at 5/- a time, dependent on the wind. Not very long ago, I saw in an article on the apostrophe, Hunt's Cross, as though a cross belonged to a man called Hunt. Whatever its derivation, an apostrophe would not have been tolerated in the Twenties and Thirties.

Hunts Cross was an idyllic spot.

We'd never sunk to an Alley or Court, but now we lived in a Road not a Street. Parallel with our road was, then, Pinfold Road; there are now three more. True, there was Stuart Avenue behind us; it had older and bigger houses; later there was Kingsmead Drive, but a Road was an especial delight to Mother after two Streets. She was mutely envious when, in the Fifties, we bought not only a detached house but in Curthwaite Gardens. From (comparative) rags to (comparative) riches in three generations.

The house was much, much smaller than 4 Normanby Street. It was one of about sixty, with the odd numbers on the other side of the road, and it had a name on the wooden front gate, thus breaking the ignominy of having just a number, though it was a name difficult to spell and difficult to pronounce – Trelystan (Trelústan). You've seen the board now adorning our garage. This strange choice was the name of the isolated village where Mother as a child spent a frightening, lonely and hated time with her fearsome grandmother. Was it another manifestation of masochism? Even now, it is a lonely, unspoiled, unchanged, secretive place; the only noticeable difference probably is that now and again an odd car comes up or down the hill past the llama farm between Welshpool and Montgomery.

I think that number 24 cost £250, but it was neither council-owned nor rented. A mortgage was the only purchase allowed on the never-never, for a mortgage was different.

It wasn't long before major repairs had to be put in train in this owner-occupied, semi-detached home with pebble-dash walls, because of dry rot; the excavation and replacement of floorboards of the sitting room led to trauma, although mercifully we didn't know the word then. The nearly five-year-old me loved the upheaval and made great friends with the workmen. Men were always brought in to redecorate or to mend things. Neither parent really believed in what is now universally called DIY; Dad was too nervous and anyway worked hard and it was simply not a woman's job. So, in order 'not to spoil the ship for a ha'porth of tar', they both rationalised the matter as giving employment to those who needed it.

Each house had its own obligatory privet hedge, golden privet being definitely superior if you had it, a trifle flashy if you hadn't. Many had a notice by the side of the number on the gate: 'No Hawkers; No Circulars; No Canvassers'. More upsetting was 'Trespassers will be Prosecuted' – clearly a grown-up misspelling of 'Persecuted'. Did that mean that they could be killed or even eaten alive, as in the Bible? I wondered. But we are supposed to forgive them that trespass against us – it was all too bewildering.

I was now to be brought up in a lower middle-class world. Contemporaries would say that there was nothing remarkable in that, although it was to my parents and my mother's family, who hadn't two ha'pennies to rub together – another puzzling statement, for why would you want to? To your generation, it's probably meaningless as social distinctions and classes are blurred. Money has taken their place; there are still the obscenely rich, the fat cats, the 'haves' and those on or below the poverty line, the 'have-nots'. Most people then wanted the chance to better themselves. This brought the beginning of the growth of too-often maligned suburbia, its buildings and its pattern of life. Hunts Cross was spared the unplanned spread which disfigured then as now so many rural outskirts of towns. Other districts not in the centre also had lovely names: Old Swan, Gateacre (pronounced Gatt-ica), Wavertree and, made famous by Ken Dodd, Knotty Ash. Fazakerly was always good for a laugh.

There was room at the side of the house for a garage; when we last saw it, one had been built with a room on top, so that, contrary to usual experience, it looked bigger than I remembered it. In the Twenties and early Thirties, there was only one car owner in the road. Most inhabitants had a garden shed built at the back, on the far side of the tall wooden side gate.

The front doorstep here had also to be kept clean with hot water and a stone, preferably when no one else was about, yet Mother would go out into the road to collect horse manure, almost as it dropped, for the garden without embarrassment. This was, presumably, because it was common procedure in the country, being economical and sound practice. For both of these tasks, she wore a hat, not her Sunday best, but a proper hat nevertheless. The front door, with a top pane of glass in it, had a door knocker, but no light, no bell.

We didn't have an entry (back alley) any more; we didn't just have one garden, we had two. Gardens, especially front ones, bore an importance out of proportion to their size. This is my nine-year-old's verse:

> The rockery was small and sweet,
> To see it was a perfect treat.
> The little rose-flowers were in bloom,
> They took away all thoughts of gloom.

The primroses – and pansies too –
In pretty colours yellow and blue.

Knowledge and inspiration clearly ran out at this point, for the
poem concludes suddenly:

And hosts of other pretty things
Brought me that joy a garden brings.

I was undoubtedly influenced by the too-often repeated hymn:

All things bright and beautiful,
All creatures great and small,
All things wise and wonderful,
The Lord God made them all.

The nineteenth-century hymn writer went on to mention:

Each little flower that opens,
Each little bird that sings,
…The purple-headed mountain,
The river running by,

[after praising the seasons, he concludes that]

The ripe fruits in the garden,
He made them, every one.

You opened – and closed – the front gate, and on the left,
leading to our front door, was our front garden. The square of
grass was kept immaculate, first by hand shears, then by a
hand-worked mower; it was surrounded by old-fashioned,
cottage-garden flowers, according to season: wallflowers (gilly
flowers), bulbs, Michaelmas daisies (from Granddad's top
garden), antirrhinums, lilies of the valley, forget-me-nots,
lobelia, London pride, Canterbury bells, pansies – that sort. As
for rhododendrons, hydrangeas and lilies, they belonged

rightly, to the larger plots of Stuart Avenue.

The back garden was long. Rambler roses and sweet peas grew along the adjoining fences. The cinder path divided the land unequally. To the right was our wooden shed, full of heavy metal garden and washing equipment, and beyond it a long narrow patch of well-tilled earth. To the left was first another rough path along the back of the house, a tiny obligatory rockery, flower borders, a small rectangle of grass and then the garden proper for vegetables and fruit: potatoes, sprouts, beetroot (to be pickled in vinegar, which I adored), peas (with cotton twisted over them to deter birds), gooseberries (goozzgogs), raspberries (Mother's favourite, although the seeds got under her plate, that is, her dentures), blackcurrants (my choice), rhubarb and runner beans. Fruit was bottled in Kilner jars (nine of which are still in use for our marmalade) or made into jam (waste not, want not); beans were salted down. You made a silent wish when you ate the first and the last of seasonal goodies. Although you could get a penny back on any jars, all were saved for jams, marmalade, lemon cheese (never lemon 'curd') and mincemeat. Smaller ones were ideal for home-made potted meat, a sort of 1930s *pâté* – a word we had never heard of. This was used for sandwiches and was very popular with brawn, meaning mixed cold meats, at church functions. Occasionally, a small pot of tasteless bloater paste was a 'treat'; generally, shop-bought remained a term of the greatest scorn.

Contempt for those few whose gardens were less than extremely tidy and usefully productive was total. Mother dealt mainly with the weeds. Dad did the heavy stuff, dressed for many years in his ageing khaki army jacket and puttees ('long bandages round legs'). Clothes were tough in those days; that jacket did for holidays first, then gardening, for at least twenty years. I had my own tiny patch; enthusiasm never ran high and interest was always short-lived. By the station, some few minutes' walk away, were a few allotments for those men who wanted, or needed, to grow more vegetables.

The bonfire on 5 November, a small affair compared with that of the grown-up boys in Stuart Avenue, was made of what we now regard as compostable material, for only leaves were used on the midden. A woman (was her name Miss Leece?) came round Dad's office with a case of stuff; he brought home sparklers and a few other treats. Mother disapproved of the expenditure, refusing even to watch. I don't know which of us – Dad or myself – was the more frightened as we were both cack-handed. I was, wisely, never allowed even to touch a match. Cheekier lads knocked at doors asking for 'a Penny for the Guy', which accompanied them in a wheelbarrow.

Inside

The tiny hall had its inevitable hatstand, a wooden structure with a mirror in the middle, glove drawer, hooks for clothes, a shoe rack (for galoshes) and an umbrella stand.

Immediately to the left as you came in, after wiping your feet carefully on the outside brown doormat, was the doleful front room (as most Liverpudlians called it) or sitting room – not that anyone sat there, although it had the obligatory three-piece suite – settee and two chairs – upholstered in off-grey material. Except for regular piano lessons and rarer practices, the room was opened up once in a blue moon, and then only for church folk, such as an unmarried or visiting parson who came for Sunday tea, although most of them were accommodated in the dining room, which should have been more accurately called the living room.

A Jacobean gateleg table, an object of pride, stood in the window; it was the devil to polish, to open or close, as, like Arkwright's till, it nipped fingers. On it and on the window ledge behind were pots for maidenhair fern and an aspidistra (bad enough, but not Gracie Fields' 'biggest aspidistra in the world'). The top windows had leaded lights – very swanky. No windows were ever opened. There was never a fire in the small grate and it had only the morning sun, so the room was permanently cold. Long sausages of material at doors made an unavailing stab at preventing draughts.

Mother was conventional in most ways, but not on the matter of curtains. She refused to have both lace and lined curtains, because they were secretive and they reduced the light; she had nothing to hide. Curtains of heavier material were changed at spring-cleaning time for lighter ones.

The well-tended room was worthy of the looks of nosy parkers. Especially did she wish everyone to see the Rushworth and Draper piano, preserved and kept tuned for over thirty years in case I should ever master the instrument, and the piano stool. We brought both when we moved down here, paid regularly to have the piano tuned, never used it and sold it for a pittance.

The only time curtains were closed on their rods was for funerals, as 'a mark of respect', even if we did peep between the joins. The door knocker would be swathed in black. In some households, pictures would be similarly treated. In the poorer districts, 2d per week insurance was paid towards a cortège and an appropriate burial, when someone 'popped his clogs'; this was sometimes followed by violence between Papists and Proddies. The phrase 'bury so-and-so with ham' began as a sensible idea, as folk might have travelled some distance and be in need of sustenance before returning home; it became a posh affair, keeping up with, then surpassing, the Joneses.

Men wore black suits, or at the very least, a black crepe armband, as on 11 November. When Dad's office black jacket and pinstripe trousers had 'gone home', dark clothes were acceptable, especially after all four grandparents had died. A black tie was always kept handy. Women wore black, borrowed or rented; mauve (half-mourning) was just about tolerated for the young, and was permissible for the most closely bereaved after three to six weeks. A strict widow might remain permanently in mourning, as Victorian women had done. It all meant a bonanza for dyers. Mother kept her set of black clothes in reserve at the back of a cupboard for many years; in her seventies, she decided that mourning garb was stupid.

I often wondered, why black? Maybe travelling or fear of catching your death (of cold) in a draughty country cemetery was involved. If you believed in Heaven, surely white or even brightly coloured clothes might be more appropriate. For Wesleyans, one didn't die; one passed on, over or away. This was not a euphemism, although my father grew less and less sure as he grew older. Both parents were surprisingly modern, especially when compared with their family circle; they refused to contribute to wreaths as a waste of money and wished to be cremated, with donations for good causes. I think that you know that I've gone a stage further in leaving my body for medical use or for research.

The dining room was at the back. In winter, a heavy chenille curtain hung on a rod to minimise draughts. The table was permanently covered by a heavy brown chenille cloth with fringes and bobbles; a runner, usually hand-embroidered, had to be placed exactly (not 'skew-whiff') diagonally across it, for a bowl of 'daffies' (a horrible abbreviation), tulips or whatever was in season in the garden to be placed absolutely in the middle.

For knife-and-fork meals ('Tuck in, you're at your granny's' was the vivid Scouse phrase) the runner would be replaced by a white cloth with coloured edges, often bought cheaply as surplus to shipping requirements. For 'afternoon tea' (as distinct from ordinary teatime meals) and especially on Sundays, a checked cloth with cross-stitch border or, later, an elaborately embroidered square (there were half a dozen of these, new and untouched when Mother died) would be placed carefully. Dad had a white serviette (not napkin), not quite the double damask dinner napkins of the rhyme, but ship's surplus; his silver serviette ring was monogrammed JC, whilst I had a painted wooden one. No one came unannounced or uninvited; the few visitors allowed had small white squares folded to a triangle. Mother never had a serviette: in the daytime, a crossover pinafore covering what was known as a washing frock; in the afternoon and evening, an apron over a better or afternoon dress. The apron remained on until she went to bed. A cousin has confessed to putting on an apron when she knew Auntie Amy was coming; it would be one that she had received as a present, for no such present could be thrown away. Dad deplored this apron-wearing habit – in vain.

Willow pattern plates were in use for tea, the remains of Granny's plain white china for other meals. Their wedding present tea service set was untouched except for two cake plates; all were intact when I inherited them, for any breakage was regarded as a major catastrophe. The teapot was camouflaged in a knitted crinoline-lady tea cosy.

A leaf or leaves could be removed from under the table and inserted to provide a ping-pong table for Dad and me and, again, the occasional unmarried parson. It was enjoyable, albeit somewhat cramped and dangerous. Mother sat in silent resentment.

One afternoon stands out. Left rarely alone in the house, I was terrified by a knock on the front door and hid under this table, but was soon startled to see the caller looking at me through the back window.

The coal fire was almost surrounded by a polished fender with seats at each end and a fireguard. Lovely pictures were visible in the flames and in the shadows thrown on the walls. The fire heated the water as well as causing scorch marks on my legs. Rarely, bread was toasted on a wire toasting fork.

There were, of course, no power points for electric fires, no central heating. Coal men with sacks over their heads as protection sold just one sack if requested; they humped it round through the side gate and emptied it in a shower of dust into the large coal shed between the garden shed and the bin. The Corpy

(Corporation) bin men lugged the bins out and back each Monday. The grate was black-leaded, the fire lit by a match – Bryant and May had a factory near by; there were also Pilot matches and Swan Vestas for smokers. It set fire to a newspaper spill which ignited the newspaper firelighters (one of the few manual skills which, during the War, I mastered) and chopped wood under the coals. Nutty slack was cheaper but less reliable. A newspaper was frequently – and dangerously – held over the whole opening to encourage the fire to 'draw'.

Smoke billowed up the chimney. A long-handled flue brush was used weekly, but it needed its annual clean-out by the soot-begrimed chimney sweep. It was exciting to watch his broom coming out of the chimney pot, although an unpleasant amount came down the chimney. He left the soot for the garden. It was considered lucky if a sweep were the first person to cross the threshold to wish the household a Happy New Year. In some families, the oldest male dressed up as one and knocked – just to be on the safe side.

There were four sit-up-and-beg chairs, a special one with arms for Dad. The old rocking chair from Granny's, which provided a gentle pleasure, was returned as it was regarded as suitable only for pregnant and nursing mothers; there was no way that Mother was going to need it again. Instead, there were now two easy chairs, each with its cushion in a hand-embroidered hessian cover and each adorned with the obligatory antimacassar, lace, embroidered or fringed. This gave rise to a silly question: Who was Auntie Macassar and why were such horrid things named after her? The true explanation of being a protection against gentlemen's hair-oil was too prosaic.

Mother was obsessive: cushions had to be rearranged as soon as anyone stood up. The daily paper was hidden from view under a cushion. Mother's easy chair faced Dad's. His was ladder-backed, so could be moved to different positions. I had to make do with a pouffe or stool, or I could sprawl happily on the carpet.

On Dad's side of the fireplace was his bureau, which Mother considered an unnecessary encumbrance. Nevertheless, it was regarded by all of us as private. It supported two top fitments, one belonging to a very solid cupboard which she had, astonishingly and courageously, bought for £5 at auction in the early Thirties, the lower handmade to fit his handmade bureau.

On the other side was a book cabinet, with two leaded-glass fronted doors, on top of a cupboard – allegedly ex-Eton college furniture – the whole standing about 7' high. Along the side wall a sideboard almost blocked the doorway. No food kept in its two cupboards nor, apart from an occasional bowl of fruit, displayed on it; there was no cutlery in its drawers. This veneered furniture was considered 'better' than Granddad's solid home-made variety.

On the heavy mahogany mantelpiece, a wooden framed clock took pride of place. Solemnly each night, Dad wound it, together with his watch on its chain. He alleged that a wrist-watch didn't function accurately, but wore one for the last fifteen years of his life. On each side of the mantelpiece were, in the spring, hyacinths in glass bowls or bell-like special jars, which had been put under the stairs then brought out at the right time into the light. The roots looked quite nasty.

Neither parent, mercifully, was keen on silver-framed photographs. The pictures which I remember – I'm sure that there were more – were a large portrait photograph in an enormous dark wood frame of a much younger Dad, an embroidered 'Stokesay Castle', 'The Light of the World', 'The Gleaners', and a simple but beautiful 'Hands joined in Prayer'. Each hanging on strings from a movable hook on the picture rail was described as 'picture-skew' (was it because picturesque sounded la-di-da? extravagant? boastful? – or merely a heavy joke?).

A rectangle of carpet was in each room, a smaller strip in the hall and on the landing. A fitted carpet was too expensive, and was, therefore, effete. I never remember them being cleaned. Newspapers provided the underlay. The surrounds were stained with Darkaline. I recently found a strange large postcard-size advertisement for 'Flooryline Varnish Stain for Floors. Beauty and Economy. Quick Drying, Sanitary, Decorative. Supplied in many shades. Each tin contains FULL IMPERIAL MEASURE. A FREE BRUSH of best quality is supplied with each tin'. This wonder cover was obtainable from Cooper and Co.'s Store, Ltd. The other side of the card is a pink blotter. Floors were polished regularly with Mansion Polish.

No one smoked. Dad had tried it to pass the time in his POW camp, but it had made him sick. An ashtray was ostentatiously provided for the odd male addict, for, of course, no *lady* would smoke.

Christmas

I'm now going off at a tangent.

In December, the Christmas tree stood in the window. Despite grumbles about its shedding of needles, it was, although small, an essential part of the season. Holly or tinsel was draped round the cord of each picture, and mistletoe hung at the front door – theoretically to enable kisses to be exchanged. Decorations were kept from year to year. A few crackers – they frightened me – yielded paper hats and the odd incomprehensible riddle.

Dad signed all the cards: most were from Mr and Mrs Cherry; some from John and Amy; and, for a few, very few, from John. The postage was less – ½d as for postcards with five words only – if the envelope was left unsealed and no letter was enclosed. I wonder how the household finances were made to stretch to cover the manifold extra seasonal expenses.

Carefully graded Christmas 'boxes' had to be prepared for all regular callers: 1/- to 10/- for milkman, greengrocer, dustman, window cleaner, postman. This last came every day except Sunday. Because of hospitality on the way, he was always slewed/sozzled/plastered by the time he reached our house on Christmas Day, laden with cards. This was the only time that I can remember my parents laughing at drink, even when he was once found fast asleep on the doormat. I wish that I could recall how they handled that situation.

Each of us ritually stirred the pudding mixture, together with their obligatory hidden silver three-penny (pronounced 'thruppny') bits (or joeys, to distinguish them from tanners or 6d), which had been saved all the year round; each then made a wish before all was divided between four basins, one for Christmas, one for New Year, one for my parents' wedding anniversary on 21 April and one for Dad's birthday on 4 June. With a cloth tied over the top, all were cooked for hours in the large marmalade- and jam-making pan of boiling water. On Christmas Day, it was served with a sparkler on top and custard.

The main meal was sometimes capon but normally a goose. Mother turned up her nose at turkey. Was it less tasty? Too expensive? Or simply too big?

Christmas pudding, and, for tea, Christmas cake tasted scrumptious, although I would have preferred two layers of icing sugar (pleasingly soft and yummy) with its crystallised fruits, purple violets and hundreds and thousands on top instead of one layer on top of Mother's favourite almond paste (displeasingly solid). Mincemeat for individual pies and plate-size tarts, with caster sugar scattered over the top, also took time to prepare as each currant, for example, had to be washed and picked over.

Christmas service included the well-known hymns: 'O Come All Ye Faithful'; 'Christians Awake, Salute the Happy Morn'; 'See, Amid the Winter's Snow' (which I recently discovered originated with Martin Luther); 'It came upon the midnight clear / That glorious song of old'; 'The First Noel'; 'As With Gladness Men of Old'; and the one with the most attractive tune, 'Silent Night, Holy Night'.

A shiny new coin, chocolate coins wrapped in gold or silver paper and in a 'gold' string bag, a pink sugar mouse, a farthing (a quarter of a penny) and a tangerine were always, a Christmas annual sometimes, in the stocking – actually a pillowcase – at the end of my bed. One year, one of Dad's sisters stayed with us; relations between her, an intelligent but acerbic spinster who doted on her brother, and Mother were always strained and did not improve when Auntie Edith and Dad were found giggling outside my bedroom as they filled the pillowcase.

This delightful custom of pillowcase-filling survived my rumbling of Father Christmas (never Santa Claus) who received letters of request and thanks, a glass of milk and some chocolates. This seemed strange when he was supposed to be bringing presents for us, but, after all, he was a grown-up too, and we all know how unpredictable grown-ups can be. On a visit to the old gentleman in a shop grotto, 3d or 6d entrance fee governed the present received after the obligatory and unpleasant kiss – on the cheek if you could manage to steer it that way.

J. B. Priestley once wrote, 'We always had snow for Christmas when I was a boy'; for me, it meant special food and presents and, usually, a happy day.

Boxing Day was spent, as was the day after my birthday, in dropping a line, that is writing thank-you letters. Dad made chewing movements, of which he was quite unaware, when he wrote. Therefore, so did I. The prestige of a good hand was great in both families, as more than one aunt and uncle had difficulties in reading, let alone writing. Sometimes, one put SWA(L)K on the back of the envelope – sealed with a (loving) kiss.

Letters not over 2 oz, or about 52 g, bore a 1d, later 1½d, stamp. They did arrive within twenty-four hours, even overnight, or, locally, even during the same day, for there were always two, sometimes three, deliveries. Sticky stamp-edging was saved for multifarious repairs. Postage ate into pocket money if neither parent was writing at the same time to the same recipient. It became an especial burden when one was locked into a chain letter; what might be the fearful consequences of not copying the rubbish and sending it on to five more people! Fortunately, one 'con' was enough when I received no replies.

A telegram of nine words could be sent in 1935 for 6d, twelve words for 1/-, as could parcels of up to 2 lb. For birthdays and special occasions, there was the beautifully ornate Golden Greetings version.

New Year's Day was not as important as the following day, 2 January, Mother's birthday. I used to sleep heavily; when I was fourteen, I forgot to wish her a happy birthday the moment she woke me – result, a pursed mouth for a week.

Back inside again

Let's go back to look at the rest of the house. The scullery was now called a kitchenette and was used for washing clothes and for cooking. Food was kept on a cold slab in a door-less cupboard known as the pantry, hardly on the scale of a typical butler's pantry. The great summer Saturday when a dog stole the cooling joint because the window had been left open was remembered ruefully. Henceforth, it rested under a dome of wire mesh, before being put on the top shelf of the meat safe, with its mesh-covered door. Some houses had one of these safes on the outside wall. The kitchen itself, minute compared with that at Normanby Street, had whitewashed walls; all other rooms in the house had dark patterned paper so as not to show the dirt; woodwork was stained dark brown.

Two brown Windsor chairs (one still in active use in our garden room, but now painted white) were tucked under the wooden kitchen table scrubbed with soap, white or brown Windsor; packet products (Vim, Rinso) came later.

Cooking equipment – iron pans, a cast-iron mincer, iron scales, stone storage jars, a stone pastry bowl (still useful) and a wooden rolling pin – was heavy. The old-fashioned oven was a gas one; electric was too modern and self-evidently too expensive: that 'stands to sense', as one loses money as it heats up. There was, of course, no fridge; freezers and microwaves were probably just a glint in a scientist's eye.

A washing-up bowl remained permanently in the sink, which had a single wooden draining board to one side on which there was always a 12" square dishcloth knitted on large wooden, later steel, needles, in dishcloth cotton. Making one of these was how I learned to knit. This was a step up from French knitting, where wool was wound round pins in the top of a used cotton reel and sometimes something came out of the hole – it didn't work for me. I didn't understand it then; I'm still in the dark. My first effort was not uniformly successful: Teddy's scarf grew a hole in it – for his head.

Hands were wiped on a roller towel which was pulled over its wooden roller as required. Near the ceiling there was a wooden slatted clothes airer, worked on a pulley by a cord; one was advertised recently as a decorative feature! Under the stairs in the hall, the narrow, low-ceilinged cubbyhole housed wellingtons, brooms, cobweb brush and other cleaning equipment, all in unlit Stygian gloom. I've grown up with the tradition that its other name, that of 'glory hole', was because Catholic priests hid in the tiny space in times of persecution. This may or may not be true.

You went through the kitchen to reach the back door. Coming in, you cleaned your shoes on the iron shoe-scraper. The stairs led up almost from the front door; you certainly had to squeeze past the hallstand. The strip of carpet on each tread was secured by a stair rod fitted into metal slots, and the uncovered sides were stained with Darkaline.

After ten or twelve steps, there was a sharp right-angled turn to the left, with three more steps to the landing. Going

upstairs was always intriguing. I learned to memorise much of
A. A. Milne:

> Halfway up the stairs
> Is a stair where I sit,
> There isn't any
> Other stair
> Quite like
> It.
> It isn't at the bottom,
> It isn't at the top.

And, as with Christopher Robin:

> All sorts of funny thoughts
> Run round my head.
> It isn't really anywhere!
> It's somewhere else
> Instead.

I used to think of the distance I'd travelled after climbing six or
seven stairs. I'd left the world of the kitchen, breakfast porridge
and dinner rice puddings and hadn't yet reached the bedroom,
the place of dreams. Imagination ran riot. What would I do
when I grew to be a big girl – write books, be in plays as a
clown or a villain, be school tennis captain – I didn't mind
which. I could give free rein to my thoughts, on the stairs. My
Teddy Bear was Winnie the Pooh; we used to go upstairs
together and sleep together for many years. He was – still is – a
person in his own right, not like soppy Bo-Peep or the over-
energetic Tom, the son of the piper, or an upstart heffalump
(elephant).

One's attitude to stairs changes with the years. To watch a
baby with its short stubby legs climbing step by step with its
mother reminds one of how great a performance it is. And
what about the glee and pride of a child who reaches the top

step all alone for the first time? Sadly, for me, this is becoming a bit of a struggle again!

To the right was the bathroom, with a claw-footed bath and a medicine cabinet in which Dad kept his bottle of Milton. In the winter, it was freezing cold, all too often literally so. Although cramped, the room was a real treat after the tapless tubs of Liverpool 8. Baths for Dad and me (although frequently averring that cleanliness was next to godliness, did Mother ever have more than a 'wash down'?) were on Saturday nights, so as to be clean for Sundays. The temperature of the water was tested by an elbow. For years, Dad bathed me and we splashed each other noisily; it was great fun and I don't know which of us enjoyed it the more. Mother was not amused but dared not interfere. Because of the need for a fire to heat the water, we had even fewer baths in the summer.

There was great pride, as if it were a personal achievement rather than a geological phenomenon, in having soft water; pipes were considered exempt from furring up. It was a boon when soap was rationed during the War. Less pleasant to drink than hard water, it is certainly kinder to the skin and economical on soap which was the same in the bathroom as in the kitchen. Not for us 'Pear's Soap. Prepare to be a beautiful lady'. Palmolive did come later.

I normally tried to get away with a catlick, a lick and a promise, but Mother had an unerring eye for a tidemark, checking neck and wrists carefully. 'Soap and water never did any harm!' 'Have you washed behind your ears?' Why was it so necessary to specify this small area, especially when someone *naïve* in the ways of the world was described as wet behind the ears?

Mother cut my nails; unlike many children, I never felt the need to bite mine. She was proud of what she called her 'filbert' nails, marred occasionally by white spots ('filbert' was probably one of her own unsupported adjectives; it seems a strange thing to be proud of, but she was like that). Dad clipped his carefully with clippers. Few girls grew up without receiving at least one manicure set as a present.

Hair was washed over the kitchen sink and with kitchen soap, not shampoo. Friday night, according to the advert, was Marmi night – undoubtedly our mis-rendering of Amami, a new shampoo product – but for me it was Saturday, again the need to be clean for Sunday. Hair was always tangled, although a slide, like a flat clothes peg, clipped together to fasten some bits down. Later, a 'bandeau' or circular tortoiseshell band was both a fashion statement and a practical controller of errant hair. The ends were sometimes singed to prevent them splitting. I envied frizzy hair – then. Mother kept a lock of her auburn hair after it was cut off; she boasted that she could sit on it when she was younger. Literal-minded from a tender age, I asked why she would want to sit on it. I was told not to be cheeky. My pleas for long hair, which admittedly was not much in fashion, were refused on the grounds that her own slight deafness, which she used to her advantage and which increased her suspicion of people, had resulted from going to bed with still-wet hair. It was also tiresome to wash and dry: no hairdryers then.

Dad stropped a leather to sharpen his cut-throat razor, one of his few manual skills. The only time he experimented with a safety razor, he cut himself! Not merely unable to use any model which did not fall apart in his hands, he nicked my ear when he tried to cut my hair. Like father, like daughter. I still recall our mutual embarrassment when he attempted to shave my armpits.

Teeth were always a problem. There were then fewer fillings; I remember no crowns, not even the term. There was much less awareness of dental care and the effects of diet; people did not go regularly to a dentist. I was quite surprised that people even brushed their teeth, let alone regularly. Despite nocturnal teeth-grinding, I had no false teeth until I was eighty. I began to use Colgate toothpaste simply because a sample came through the letterbox one day, which suggests that advertising pays, at least sometimes.

It was a terrible shock when my first teeth (toosy pegs) began to fall out (I kept one under the pillow for luck), as I had no assurance that others would take their place. The poor had to go to the Dental Hospital. There was no anaesthetic, no injection, except for major operations as when, in the Thirties, both parents had all their remaining teeth extracted at one go, with gas, because of pyorrhoea. I have just looked up that condition in the encyclopaedia: 'inflammation of the gums causing a discharge of pus' – I won't go into further grisly details. They spent a week on 'pobbies', namely bread and milk, and suffered agonies from ill-fitting false teeth at the end of it. Their dentures were left overnight in a glass of water – an ugly fascination. Dr Mercer took a tooth out for me when I was fourteen; it never hurt while he was doing it, but after, ugh. Filling, too, was distinctly unpleasant. Be thankful that dentistry has made great strides.

The lavatory was separate; they are separate in our house now as it was built in the Thirties. Bliss it was to have no longer a chilly outside affair, but a proper lavatory, with a polished mahogany seat; the top was covered in a crochet cover as were many in similar households; we had a chain to pull. Even after fifty years of pressing a lever to flush, I still mentally use the old phrase of pulling the chain. We called ours the lavvy; toilet was regarded as begging the issue, loo hadn't been invented. Whilst newspapers were still cut into neat squares, a roll of paper was kept for the odd visitor. I don't remember washing my hands after 'going', or even being told to, although Dad always did.

The two main bedrooms had the minutest of straight and narrow grates; they were not only useless, indeed dangerous, for fires, but also excellent conductors of draughts. The airing cupboard was in the back bedroom; its door was not to be opened, but it was, and the heat was comforting. Despite this, pipes froze every winter, twice with consequent disastrous flooding. A bedside mat, either rag type or handmade on canvas or hessian with a hook and Turkey rug wool cut on a grooved wooden strip and meant as a prayer mat, increased the warmth, for only a square of old carpet graced part of the floor by the window. Fluff collected under the bed, so it was wasteful to have a carpet there. Mats were still taken downstairs, still shaken outside then beaten against the house walls. As Mother grew more skilled, rugs appeared everywhere and were given as long-lasting presents. Just one still exists here. Lino (linoleum), which had to be scrubbed, was penetratingly cold to the feet; 'beddyslips', warmed by the fire, were essential.

Furniture? In a small wardrobe with shelves, the clothes bar was inconveniently at a right angle to the door. The coat hangers were covered with material, except the broad elegant ones for Dad's suits. Occasionally, Pullars of Perth would be allowed to clean a winter coat. Each drawer in a small chest of drawers contained a handmade lavender bag and a couple of balls of camphor to guard against moths. The washstand had two cupboards underneath for pos, or potties, off-green in colour, and for my personal possessions, such as my few beloved books. The never-used jug and ewer on the tiled top had once stood on a washstand at Granny's. In season, apples were laid out for future use. When I got matric, a blue Lloyd Loom chair was somehow squeezed in, despite there being no room to swing a cat. In some houses, hair-tidies hung on a doorknob, on the end of a bed or on the dressing table.

Above the tiny mantelpiece hung a Margaret Tarrant picture, 'All Things Bright and Beautiful' – Jesus in a sort of modern garden.

The bed was large, with slats at the head and a floppy feather mattress, at that time highly regarded. Bed linen came from white sales, which were auctions from decommissioned ships;

when holes or threadbare patches appeared in sheets, they were turned sides to middles to prolong life. Beds were turned down at night. To me, Samaria meant the pattern on my white coverlet before it signified a Biblical area. These counterpanes were replaced after World War II by folkweave. Sheets were cotton in summer, that is, April to August, and flannelette in winter, September to March, regardless of the temperature at the time. At the changeover, they were rough dried and rolled, un-ironed, into a ball. I've only just wondered where they were stored. The eiderdown (eidy) went on top. Clothes suffered the same fate, so that for fluke days in September or April, no one had suitable outfits. 'Winter draw(er)s on' – by no means an idle saying. 'Cast ne'er a clout till May be out' was an arguable proposition: did it mean the blossom or the month? Mother made her own unbreakable rules.

I always wore pyjamas, cotton in summer but warmer win-ceyette (whatever was wincey?) in winter. Pyjamas and handkerchiefs had their own home-made cotton containers or cases. Mother wore voluminous nightdresses and a hairnet; only her face was visible. She didn't even own a dressing gown, whilst a bedjacket would have indicated either gross self-indulgence or ideas above her station. During the day, she was never less than fully clothed.

Snug as a bug in a rug, I had hot milk in bed, enjoyable unless there was a nasty thick skin on top. The beverage improved first with the arrival of cocoa and was finally made with the new-fangled chocolate – not Ovaltine, however, with that nasty publicity jingle: 'We are the Ovaltinies, little [or was it happy?] girls and boys.' No night-light, no torch, but in those days, I didn't have to get up in the night! Much, much later came the thrill of a watch and an alarm clock with two bells and a luminous dial.

The window looked out on to the back garden and, if you craned your neck, on to fields.

This was my winter establishment, moved into in the back

end of the year, that is, September. 'Last back end' meant September of the previous year.

The minute third bedroom, really a box or lumber room, at the front end of the landing, with its tiny bed and wardrobe, was for my summer occupation. It boasted a window seat with a tiny drawer in it. Sitting on this gave me a marvellous view of the comings and goings in the road when I was supposed to be in bed, be it in the evening or during the compulsory and boring after-lunch lie-down before I went to school. Teddy, infuriatingly, was allowed to sit there and look out any time.

> I've had my supper,
> And *had* my supper,
> And HAD my supper and all…
> I've cleaned my teeth,
> And I've said my prayers
> And I've cleaned and said them right
> And they've all of them been, and kissed me lots,
> They've all of them said 'Good night'…

…and I was left alone in the dark.

The light had to be switched off promptly, a habit which has stuck. There was to be no reading in bed; in summer, when it was still light and I wasn't sleepy, I was reduced to reading the data on the Germoline tin.

> Bless this House, O Lord we Pray,
> Make it safe by night and day.

The original 'House' was surely meant to be the church, but the song or hymn was sacred to Mother, who had a sampler of the words framed on the wall of the front bedroom. I recall but little therein. I was allowed in on extremely rare occasions, usually if I was too poorly to be left alone. Once, I had been naughty, not an abnormally infrequent occurrence in the struggle to learn what behaviour was acceptable and what was not. I had, stupidly, run to this room to escape – howling. The usual retort from Mother, 'I'll give you something to howl for' (I never stopped howling then for I'd have regarded that as a sign of weakness), was followed by her usual energetic steps to carry out her word. We dodged each other round the bed for long enough, until I was so frightened that I had to give in. Even if I chunnered (muttered under my breath) an unfelt 'Sorry', I got nowhere and 'I'll tell you for why': the reply would have been, 'Fine words butter no parsnips' or, illogically, 'I want no more of your lip.' It wasn't only children who lived in a world of their own! I felt like Mr Nobody.

> I know a funny little man,
> As quiet as a mouse,
> Who does the mischief that is done
> In everybody's house.

All the sins committed were listed: plates cracked, books torn or left around, buttons lost, pins scattered, carpets soiled by mud, papers mislaid, ink spilt, doors left ajar, unoiled (so that they squeaked) or spoiled by finger marks – all Mr Nobody's fault.

I learned the wisdom of a naughty story or fib of the 'I wasn't running. I was just walking fast' variety; even though it didn't always work, it was sometimes worth a try.

Parents automatically had the front bedroom, although it was colder and had an uninteresting view of other houses. There was a dressing table in the window, with three mirrors and a ring-stand. Dressing-table mats, called a Duchess set, complemented the downstairs lace mats and table doilies.

Any lady visitor kept her hat on unless she was staying for a meal, for which few were deemed suitable or worthy; she would then be conducted upstairs to leave hat, coat and gloves and therefore to comb her hair. A man would hang his belongings on one of the hooks which protruded each side of the mirror in the hallstand. Mother kept a comb, brush and mirror, all three with long tortoiseshell handles in a lacquered box – now reduced to holding Denys' screwdrivers. A broken mirror, of course, meant seven years' bad luck. The household linen in regular use was doubtless kept in a chest of drawers.

Everyone kept holiday trunks in the attic. There was no way to reach them other than by standing on a chair and leaping up into the unfloored darkness. There was no light. More than fifty years later, the pipes were still lagged with the newspapers of 1928.

THREE

Routines

Mother's Week

And now, dear Ursula, what happened inside this house?

Mother's Week never varied; everything had to be done in a fixed routine, otherwise she was moithered or anxiously disconcerted. She had the Protestant work ethic, proclaiming smugly, for she hoped to be corrected, that there was no rest for the wicked. Its converse was that Satan finds mischief still for idle hands to do, which meant scorn for those who 'pig it'. Not for her a house wreathed in dust. Not for her was W. H. Davies' question:

> What is this life if, full of care,
> We have no time to stand and stare?

She had two guiding principles. If a thing's worth doing, it's worth doing well. In my philosophy of housekeeping, I changed the last word to badly. Never put off until tomorrow what you can do today, although the rigidity of her programme meant that she could not always follow this in reality, yet she always thought that she did. If interrupted, she would reply 'just now', which meant when she was ready.

Monday was Wash Day, so a cold or minced meat dinner, two veg and rice pudding. There were no gloves, no washing machines, so that her hands became badly chapped. Washing was a major activity, performed in her 'washing frock', usually a striped shirtwaister.

Whites were separated from coloureds, as they needed Recketts or a blue bag (also used to put on stings) and, sometimes, Robin's starch for cuffs and detachable collars. She made difficulties for herself by refusing to have coloured towels as they 'hid the dirt'. A large bar of Sunlight soap was put ready; Lux came much later. The fire had heated the water overnight. Neither parent can have seen the advertisement for the Liverpool Corporation Electricity Showrooms: 'When a job requires lots of really HOT WATER the best way is the electric way. Hire an Electric Water Heater 3/- a quarter. Free wiring up to 50 ft. Free maintenance. No fixing charges.'

First then, garments and household goods were put in a dolly tub, brought in from the shed and worked with a long-handled stick to activate the suds. There was a three-legged stool, but, after so many years, I'm not sure whether the tub or Mother sat on it!

Then came work on a grooved scrubbing board; materials were tough then. The metal copper was used for boiling clothes; steam poured out of it. After that, clothes were folded and put through the heavy wooden rollers of the mangle by turning a heavy iron handle. The water flowed into a zinc bath placed strategically underneath. The size of the 'machine' diminished as newer models gave greater ease of use. All were put into a large wicker clothes basket, then fixed to the line by wooden, springless pegs bought, a penny a dozen, from itinerant gypsies and kept in a peg bag on a nail inside the shed. The cord line was reached by the cinder path; it was secured to two stout wooden posts. When full, it was heaved up by a long pole.

The weather was watched eagerly: would the old adage hold good?

Red sky in the morning,
Shepherd's (or sailor's) warning.
Red sky at night,
Shepherd's delight.

Best pray:

> Rain, rain, go away,
> Come again another day.

In any case, the clothes had to be in by lunchtime, for it was not done to show work in the afternoons. If rain were tippling down, they would be put on the rack in the kitchen.

Stuff to be ironed was folded or rolled in readiness. However thorough the washing learned from her expert mother, white clothes lost their lustre because of all the smoke and pollution in the atmosphere. Mother could get things clean and they lasted; some huckaback towels, dated in marking ink 'Nov. 11, 1919', still functioned as glass cloths by the same date seventy years later.

If anyone dirtied anything after Monday morning, that was just too bad. It had to wait a week; she was not going to 'rub through' anything or wash in penny numbers.

Tuesday was Ironing Day – no ironing boards (in fact, she had her first for her eightieth birthday, having consistently refused the offer until then), so the ironing was done on a plank covered with old sheeting, placed on the kitchen table, first with a flat iron (literally made of iron). She soon replaced this heavy appliance heated on burners, for, at Hunts Cross, there was an electric point in the kitchen, so she could have an electric iron. This had no heat settings, so that it was touched with a finger or brought near to the face or simply smelled. She provided herself with a small saucer of water to sprinkle on anything which had got too dry overnight. Things sizzled when the iron touched them. She ironed beautifully, again having been well trained, and had had much practice in her youth. In the evening, clothes could dry off or air on a clothes horse (or maiden) in front of the embers and/or in the airing cupboard.

Even when she was 'all behind like a cow's tail' (overbusy), she would never let me near, then grumbled that Joan never did a hand's turn, 'born idle, reared lazy and never got rested'. Any offer of help was usually spurned: 'Here, let me do it. You'll only make a mess of it', which, obviously, I did on the rare occasions when an offer was accepted. I have since learned from cousins with whom she felt obliged, strictly for their own good, to discuss private matters from corsetry to childbearing and rearing, how bored and heartily sick they became of hearing her say with a mixture of pride and fury that, of course, Joan didn't help in the house for she always had her head in a book – the very activity for which I was blamed at home. Basically, for her, time was lost which should have been spent on practical matters; all ought to improve the shining hour with deeds. Relatives all had the firm impression of Joan, and I quote, as a 'toffee-nosed little swot', 'all la-di-da', 'a snooty bighead', 'a clever clogs'.

It was not done to say nice things to a child's face, it was tantamount to spoiling, so I always felt second-rate. Her suspicion of a brainy female was shared by many of her type and generation. She was a great underminer of confidence; it is now obvious to me that she had but little herself and was jealous of anyone who had or seemed to have. If ever someone was inclined to boast of any achievement, or even to talk excitedly about it, the response was 'Did you ever', or 'Well I never!', mocking a child who has spectacular news to impart. It took me years to realise that I was in a no-win situation, that I was on a hiding to nothing. She was also an expert Job's comforter – making an ambiguous remark which meant apparent sympathy but, when analysed, could mean the opposite.

Wednesday was Upstairs, entailing a 'pound of elbow grease' and 'working her fingers to the bone'. This was no mere flicking of a duster which, incidentally, was never bought. Shirts which had 'done many turns', which had 'gone home' and thus were totally beyond the pale even for gardening, were used as dusters, floor cloths or winter handkerchiefs, appropriately called nose-dusters. When they had gone beyond any of these uses, they would be kept for the rag-and-bone man who weighed them before making an offer.

The wood surround had to be polished; the phrase 'use your gumption' (more vulgarly in Scouse, 'use your loaf' or 'your nouse'), meaning your brains – did it come from the floor polish or was it simply coincidental? For years, she used a Eubank carpet sweeper; I still tend to call every model a Eubank, just as the electric kind is a Hoover. She moaned if she did not keep up with her own punishing schedule.

The evening was devoted to darning – 'a stitch in time...' She was particularly skilled with socks, and that without the aid of a toadstool or mushroom. If a spud (hole) appeared subsequently, the garment had to wait until the following Wednesday. Just very occasionally, if the tear were an awkward one or in an inconspicuous place, she might mutter, 'I don't think it'll notice', but generally she did not agree that what the eye does not see, the heart does not grieve over. In any case, her own eye was all-seeing. She put embarrassing tucks in the sleeves of Dad's shirts – no armbands; even though he was a tall six-footer, sleeves were always too long. Fortunately, he was rarely jacket-less. Pinning was the lazy woman's way; she had to tack. She kept a store of press studs and hooks and eyes, and a large tin of old or spare buttons, all of which I inherited.

Thursday was Downstairs, a similar performance but lengthier because of kitchen and steps. A mop being considered lazy, the kitchen steps would be scoured; on her hands and knees, she washed the tiled floor with a cloth wrung out in a pail. Furniture received Mansion Polish.

Friday: in the morning, silver and cutlery, pre-stainless and kept in a drawer, were, together with ornaments, polished with Brasso or Silvo, knives with bath brick. Even the never-used silver-plated teapot and sugar tongs had to suffer, for she believed in spit and polish. Everything had to be shining, as clean as a new pin. If ever I tried to help, I got black stuff everywhere.

Cooking – puddings, cakes, sponges, buns, pastry, tarts, meat, fruit, vegetables – filled Friday afternoon and Saturday morning, so that Mother was always especially awkward by Saturday midday.

Meals

This seems a good time to tell you about our meals as you earn your living by cooking. I don't think that you would have been impressed.

The table was set, not laid, and meals served on the dot in the dining room. There were house rules, of which the first was Grace.

> Thank You for the World so sweet,
> Thank You for the Food we eat,
> Thank You for the Birds that sing,
> Thank You, God, for Everything.

I copied it into my father's autograph album when, as he noted, I was eight and a half. I had to say this Grace, regardless of who was present, and long after I had grown out of it. 'Say Grace before it gets cold', for plates were not heated. Still, it was an improvement on the two by Norman Gale in my *Treasury for Children* (selections made by Albert Broadbent, published 1919).

> When baby Tom, who's very small,
> Says grace for me, and Nurse, and Paul,
> He asks the Lord to make us all
> 'Ter-looly fankful'.

Socially distasteful as well as… I'll spare you the two more verses in the same vein. As for the other:

When Baby settles in his place,
With folded hands he says his grace,
Thank God!

Four more verses this time. Dad always said, 'Bless this food to our use and us to Thy service'; he wiped his eye and said it silently when eating outside home.

The second rule was: don't put your elbows on the table; the third: hold your knife and fork properly; and finally: it's rude to leave anything on a plate when you are out and, worse, it's ungrateful when you are at home.

Breakfast: it was considered almost immoral to stay in bed once awake – as for having a meal there…! When I was there because I was poorly, I was, by definition, too ill to eat – just Wincarnis or Phospherine Tonic Water, perhaps, to give one strength, or home-made beef tea.

The meal began with porridge or porrage, topped with treacle or honey and made with Quick Quaker Oats in a special pan which I now use as a steamer. The main dish was always cooked: usually fried, cured bacon (a troubling idea, that, to a child: cured of what? were 'they' absolutely sure it was better?), egg (1d each, thirteen for 1/-) and a piece of wet, that is, fried, bread (white, of course). Brown eggs were more expensive and so a special treat. If my egg was boiled, I tapped the top away, and my bread was cut into soldiers to be dipped in the runny yolk. Poached egg was reserved for invalids. Eggs were preserved, pointed end down, in isinglass. I've just looked up the word to check its spelling. It sounds horrible – 'a variety of gelatine, obtained from the dried swimming-bladders of different fishes. It is used principally for culinary purposes and for clarifying beer and wine, and also for making cement and plaster'. I'm relieved that I didn't know that at the time. Sausages, scrambled egg or haddock brought very occasional variety. In summer, Shredded Wheat was substituted for porridge.

The meal ended with home-made Seville orange marmalade – no time to light the fire and wait for it to glow sufficiently to make toast, no grill. Butter was socially superior to 'maggyan' (margarine, or marge, both pronounced with a soft *g*); there was no question of nutritional values. Later came the question, 'Can you tell Stork from butter?' Occasionally, to make you 'go', prunes, soaked, cooked, then de-stoned, were unappreciated, both then or as a 'sweet' with custard.

All this was because a man could not be expected to go to work on an empty stomach.

Mid-morning might produce milk or Oxo (1d a cube); Bovril, more expensive, claimed to prevent that sinking feeling. A biscuit to 'put you on' might be, at worst, plain Marie or the misnamed 'Rich Tea'; at best, fig biscuit or gingerbread. You cracked it under your elbow; if it split into three pieces, that foretold good luck. Coffee was a new, pretentious and pricey fad, raffish or fast. Fortunately, Camp was so dire that I didn't feel that I was missing much. In fact, I had no coffee until I was grown-up, when it was a blissful revelation.

Lunch, not a usual term at home, being saved for when it was eaten out in a café, and dinner were often confused, depending on who was in at midday, or rather at 1 p.m. Mother felt that the main meal should be at that time as late dinners were not good for the digestion and meant that she would be on the go longer. On her own, she enjoyed bread and dripping or bread and cheddar cheese. Before I took sandwiches to school, she and I would have our hot meal at midday. I enjoyed Heinz Baked Beans and, a rare treat, scrambled eggs. To heat the beans or spaghetti (for you never knew where they had been), a hole was pierced in the lid of the tin (never a can) which was then placed in boiling water; the contents, therefore, took longer to heat and were extracted from the hot container only with difficulty.

Dad's portion would be put between two soup plates and

kept warm over a pan of hot water, which meant that he had to catch the 5.20 train. If he missed that, the 5.40 brought him home several minutes late, which meant a reproving silence implying that he had done it on purpose.

After I started grammar school, we were all together for this 6 p.m.-sharp meal. Two courses were served: never soups and the word starters hadn't been invented, and no cheeses. If you had soup, that meant that there wasn't enough to follow; if you had cheese, that meant you hadn't had enough. The only proper time for cheese was midday, or, unfortunately, in a filling sandwich.

We all enjoyed a roast on Saturdays, usually of beef or lamb (with mint sauce); it must never be the same joint, nor indeed the same animal, two weeks running. The meat was rationed by money and not, as in the War, by weight. Occasionally, there was a chicken, always boiled. The hot joint had roast potatoes, the cold had boiled or mashed. Mother had done all the cooking, so the least my poor father could do was to carve. He attacked it with nervous stabbing motions and never quite got the hang of it. Sometimes, there would be rabbit, steak and kidney pie, Irish stew, Lancashire hotpot, or more rarely, delicious black puddings. Dumplings helped to eke out and fill up. It was unacceptable to eat food off the knife – for reasons of good manners, not of safety. Unlike many Liverpudlians, none of us liked tripe.

With Monday's cold meat and Tuesday's mince, there might be HP Tomato Sauce, Maconachie's PanYan or mustard from a Colman's tin.

Fish was rare and always boiled, so much boiled that it was never easy to decide which it was – haddy (which I then never connected with haddock), cod (the cheapest), plaice or halibut (Mother's favourite). It was served with egg sauce and new potatoes on Good Friday.

Potatoes, if new, were boiled with a sprig of mint from the garden (and, like the fish, boiled until they were exhausted), roasted if older (and delicious) and mashed if they were to be reheated. Peas were very popular: 3 lb for 3d. I shelled those from the garden as a treat. I was put off cabbage, cauliflower and sprouts, as were so many of my vintage, until I learned to cook greens with very little water for a very short while. Mushrooms were avoided as being sure to be poisonous. As you know, we now love them. That a watched pot never boils did not prevent Mother from standing over it, willing it to do just that. I wasn't too keen on carrots even though they were supposed to make you see in the dark. Boiled whole onions, allegedly able to increase brainpower, were revolting. I adored beetroot from the garden, boiled with care then pickled in vinegar.

Vegetables came to the table in vegetable dishes. I was never allowed to serve myself (too clumsy), or to say how much or how little I wanted. I was served – 'get that across your chest'. This, incidentally, was quite different from getting something *off* your chest, meaning out with it, don't hold back what you are thinking. Salt was provided in a tiny glass basin with a small spoon. If you spilled any during the delicate transfer, you must throw a pinch over your left shoulder, a strange superstition to find in this religious household, for it was thrown to appease the devil. There was no pepper in the house.

For the inevitable 'sweet', there might be jam roly-poly, spotted dick (Dad's favourite), suet or bread-and-butter pudding, turnovers, pies or tarts with garden fruits. In retrospect, stewed fruit seems to have turned up regularly – especially rhubarb; rice pudding recurred too frequently. All were eaten with just a spoon; on the rare appearance of a church visitor, a fork would be provided, but not for family. The 'upmarket' members of the family (Auntie Pen, Uncle Bert and Auntie Ida) were never invited anyway. Nothing, not even water, was drunk with any meal.

I had to ask if I wanted to get down from the table. Permission was rarely given. This was irksome, as Dad ate purgatorily slowly.

As I had a healthy appetite, Mother averred that she would rather keep me for a week than a fortnight. The trouble is that a child has little or no appreciation of when a straight-faced older person is making a joke. For example, 'You want jam on it?' 'Yes, please' – but it meant the equivalent of gilding the lily – that is, you are making extravagant demands.

After the meal, the stove was cleaned.

I don't remember anyone being invited for a cooked meal, unless, like Dad's youngest brother Martin, almost twenty years his junior and only eleven years older than I was, his fiery brother Harry or his unmarried sister Edith, they were staying with us as, to Mother, unwelcome guests. For her, each one turned up like a bad penny, whereas I loved having them.

Tea was really the dominant meal, especially at weekends. It was the only one for which anyone was asked. I felt left out, as I could not, cannot, keep the liquid down. Despite the evidence, Mother never accepted this finicky behaviour, but fortunately thought that milk was more appropriate for a growing girl. Tea (Co-op, because of the 'divi' or dividend, the equivalent of today's supermarket reward card, which came in so handy when extra goods were needed) was kept in a tin caddy with a special caddy spoon. A special tray, with yet another embroidered cloth, was kept for the teapot, the 'cream' jug, sugar basin and tongs (cube sugar for visitors only), hot water jug, slop basin (a horrid phrase) and strainer. Locals let it 'mash', that is, draw or brew before serving. Milk-less tea with a lemon slice was regarded as an affectation.

In some circles, it was deemed polite (for women) – it seemed daft as well as unappreciative – to leave a little on the plate to show that you had a ladylike appetite. It was occasionally a useful ploy if you didn't much like what was on offer. At least no one crooked her little finger as she drank from her teacup.

Doilies were used whenever conceivably possible. High tea was quite an elaborate affair on Sundays, high days and holidays. Because we had to hurry to Sunday School, lunch was a scratch (minimal) meal of scrambled egg or sausages. Tea was at 4.30 p.m. to allow time to get to church for the 6.30 service. Often it was ham and salad (namely home-grown lettuce and tomato), plus 'my' beetroot. You poured directly onto your plate from a bought bottle of yellowish salad dressing. Most things in tins were highly suspect for fear of metal poisoning. Among a few exceptions were salmon and ham (Princes, bought from Cooper's, of course), and silds (herrings).

Platefuls of white bread (Hovis was another affectation, although brown was, eventually and grudgingly, admitted to be a cut above white tin), well-cut and buttered (not doorsteps, but with the crust left on – waste not, want not) and home-made jam or Golden Syrup or honey were followed by a mixed fruit salad, not of fresh fruit (which was bizarrely regarded as laziness), but out of an approved tin. This was served on special occasions with conyony (Carnation condensed milk), or jelly and blancmange (pronounced bla-monge) and ever-present custard (Bird's). The only bought fruit that I remember were oranges and, post-war, grapefruit for breakfast. Trifle, with a solid sponge base and a layer of jelly, was a birthday treat.

Why did grown-ups solemnly pronounce at odd times that you cannot have your cake and eat it? Surely that was obvious. Scones (pronounced scownes), mince pies in season, little jam tartlets, rock cakes, maids of honour, shortbread (once in a blue moon) or cake: a Victoria (why?) sponge sandwich with a thin layer of jam in the middle and a dusting of caster sugar on top, parkin (a cake of oatmeal and treacle) or a good solid fruit cake, one slice only or I'd end up like Greedy Gretta, who came to some untimely but now forgotten end in a story. The only bought delights were piping hot Easter hot cross buns or Eccles cakes. Eccles, near Manchester, was relatively close, so it was felt that they didn't have far to travel. It would have been nice once in a while to have enjoyed a bought 'fancy'.

Mother was a good, plain cook, apart from vegetables; her cakes were tasty, her pastry light (it was vital to have a light hand), but monotonous. I never knew her to try a new recipe or even to modify an old one. She was neither adventurous nor innovative.

Miscellaneous excitements

Saturday was pocket money day; from each parent ½d, then 1d, rising by stages over a number of years to a total of 1/-. I had to ask for it, otherwise it was assumed that I neither needed it nor wanted it. Neither of them was aware of the embarrassment this requesting caused in view of the general atmosphere of economy. When I mentioned it to my father half a century later, he was astonished that I'd been upset. I was given an extra penny for church collection.

Aged fourteen, I had to manage my own finances a little more. Having collected my 6d from each parent, I supplemented it with an unexplained 3d from Dad plus 1d for an A in English, a total for January 1937 of 4s 10d. Out of that came 8½d for stamps, 3d for something called 'Milk for Primary', missionary money 4d, Sunday collections 7d, church class money 1d and Mother's birthday present 11d, so 3/- spent. I guess that 1/- would go on National Savings stamps and the 1d would either go into the NS account for an emergency or a bigger bill or be kept in a tin for expected expenditure another month or to help out when I 'forgot' to ask.

Savings were encouraged. Twelve stamps of 1d each filled a sheet which was then exchanged at the Post Office for a 1/- stamp and so on until 15/- worth had accumulated to buy a NS certificate. This, as you can work out, took a prodigious time. I kept any threepenny bits (joeys) which were given to me as presents or found in the Christmas pudding. One day, I had two in a pale blue bag on a strap, which I left on the tram. Tears. Slaps. Oft-repeated remarks such as, 'Joan would lose her head if it was loose.' Finally, the bag – and the coins – were recovered, at the cost of 6d, from the Lost Property Office.

Perhaps it was just as well that eating in the street was forbidden, for pocket money hardly allowed a splurge, although an exception was made at half-terms by way of a visit to Billy Sims' shop, past the tiny St Hilda's Chapel of Ease, built in 1898 (I've never seen it open) and beyond the station. He stocked everything, from a ha'porth (½d) of sweets to the day's newspapers, and all kinds of cigarettes – Woodbines (Wild and Mild), Park Drive and Black Cut (smoked at least in part for its coupons by one of my Irish uncles), Kensitas (which somehow had a feminine aura), Player's Navy Cut, de Reske Minors, Senior Service, Craven A, Wills' Passing Clouds – and tobacco – Gold Flake and Capstan Navy Cut.

It was almost excitement enough just to stare at the huge glass jars of boiled sweets which Billy picked out with his fingers and weighed before putting them into a cornet of paper. He had Liquorice All-Sorts and sticks of liquorice (which made your tongue black), barley sugar, dolly mixtures, pear drops, Victory V gums, aniseed balls, toffee (our home-made efforts always refused to set), acid drops, gobstoppers which changed colours as you sucked so that you had to keep taking them out of your mouth to have a look, humbugs, jubejubes, wine gums, jelly babies, bull's-eyes and sherbet dabs – these last so very special that I cannot now recall what they looked like. I was never attracted to chewing gum: I didn't like the taste and people chewing it looked, and still look, so awful.

And his drinks! Bottles with marbles in the neck so when you pushed them down, the fizz came up: Tizer, Dandelion and Burdock, Ginger Beer – they couldn't compete with Sarsaparella. We sat on the stairs in my friend Mary's house and enjoyed the fizz which came back down our noses, even more exciting than the later thrill of drinking through a straw. All were a great improvement on Robinson's Barley Water and home-made lemonade concocted with the help of a ½d packet of powder. As for ice creams – 1d a cornet, 2d a wafer (that is, a sandwich) – a van came round with its logo of 'Stop Me and Buy One'.

Alas, Billy Sims' shop is no more. On his corner, there are now traffic lights. There must have been four roads meeting at that corner then, but there wasn't any traffic. No one had to tell us to look both ways before crossing. There is now a little parade of shops by the station: not the same at all.

After lunch on Saturdays in the summer, Dad changed into white flannels (never shorts, although he did wear knee-length ones on holidays), a white shirt and scarf, white socks and shoes, took his racket out of its press, put six tennis balls into a net (an early string bag) and went, just past the station, to Hunts Cross Tennis Club and its two grass courts.

The club had many athletic young male members from the older (and richer, therefore more snobbish) and the newer communities of the village. It offered a Visitors' Day and an annual American Tournament. Ladder matches were great fun when you managed to beat enough opponents to reach the top. Away matches against such as a team from Bryant and May's factory were especially good. Getting a new racket (Dunlop, of course, but not of the top brand) was a thrill out of this world. Bigger and posher clubs had red shale courts, hard on feet and on white clothes.

Self-taught with no backhand or volley to speak of, Dad yet played for the club and won the men's singles more than once, because of a strong, accurate service and a wily sense of court craft. His wife never watched him once, even when he was in the finals, nor later, when I'd graduated from the juniors and played victoriously with him in the mixed doubles. She had to see him play on holidays as to have absented herself would have aroused comment. He never played on Sundays as everyone else at the club did. She had been so jealous when he had joined a whist club that he had given that up, but tennis, no. She had no cause for alarm, although he loved talking to vivacious young women.

Mother's guiding rules

Cleanliness was her first priority, so she would have no truck with animals. Airedales were popular pets in the road; most dogs seem to have been called, or ought to have been called, Rover, the smaller ones Bonzo. But they did their 'business' everywhere. No notices then about clearing up after them. Her objection probably originated with her father's dog, which enjoyed the garden and the fields down by the Severn – those fields still exist.

Cats too were, by definition, dirty. Don't touch! As a result, animals always approached me, doubtless scenting my fear. It took years before I could enjoy their affection. Strangely, in Liverpool, a cat was a moggy; in Shrewsbury, a moggy was a cow or calf. Even the goldfish, cared for during a neighbour's holiday, died just as their owner returned – or rather, just after their return – as I had misguidedly asked if we could keep them just a little longer.

Mother's strictures were bewildering and endless, especially when no reason was forthcoming. 'Don't make rude noises': how could you prevent or stop these involuntary and unintentional horrors? – it's not my fault. 'Take your hands out of your pocket.' 'Don't put your finger in your mouth', after reading anything, especially a newspaper. 'Don't lick your finger to turn over a page.' Yet, on the other hand, 'A peck of dirt never hurt anyone.' 'Ask no questions and you'll be told no lies.' I eventually worked that out to mean that she could not find a suitable answer. If she could not, or would not, answer the question, 'Who…' then it was sure to be 'Aunt Jane's sister's young man's aunt'.

'Don't speak until you are spoken to' – quite impossible, and on occasion, downright rude. 'Never say "What", say "Pardon".' Why? 'Never walk under ladders', although I had to find out for myself the hard way that this a sensible precaution rather than a foolish grown-up taboo. 'Look where you're going' – fine in principle, but maddening when there was so much to see all around. 'Use your head to save your legs' – apparently, I didn't. 'Pick your feet up' – now, that was odd.

She used many age-old generalisations: proverbial sayings were her stock-in-trade. They saved thought and added picturesqueness to the conversation, although she would not have recognised this. They sprang unbidden at major and minor crises of life; they covered every eventuality and now often rush back. Although criticising her blunt Yorkshire father, she kept at least three of his utterances. One justified physical or harsh punishment: 'That'll learn [learn meaning teach] you.' Another chimed with her view of economics: 'If ever tha' does out for nowt then do it for thissen.' Another was demonstrably untrue in his own life: 'Where there's muck, there's brass (money).'

Granny's wisdom, homespun through experience, was the source of most of the wise words. 'Better safe than sorry', 'God helps those who help themselves' – liable to misinterpretation, don't you think? Here it meant not 'nicking' but 'pulling yourself up by your bootstraps'. At least, it didn't quite match the cronyism of 'scratch my back and I'll scratch yours'. 'Little girls should be seen and not heard': they had to be seen because they could not be trusted if they were out of sight. 'Spare the rod and spoil the child', 'There's none so blind/deaf as those who won't see/hear', when she considered that her daughter was being contrary. 'You can't make a silk purse out of a sow's ear' – who would want to? 'Pigs might fly' or 'When pigs have wings' – very confusing because the sentence was never finished; it would have been something like 'before you can have/see/do/eat whatever you wanted', so – never. 'What the eye doesn't see, the heart doesn't grieve over' meant little; her eye was all-seeing.

How often was any show of happiness dampened by 'there'll be tears before bedtime', for 'he who laughs last laughs longest', and 'the sooner you go to bed, the sooner tomorrow will come' – alas, this becomes less and less true as one gets older. Perhaps all this explains my contribution to her autograph album, written in script on ruled lines and dated 15 April 1932, aged nine:

> If you can't have what you like,
> try to like what you have.

A lesson not yet learned.

Is it fanciful to suggest a change in outlook from my contribution some eighteen months earlier? Had I grown up just a little?

> I would be a merry sunbeam,
> Shining all the day,
> Clouds and darkness I would scatter
> With my brightest ray.

Oh dear!

When crankily she didn't feel like playing Diabolo or spinning a top or skipping, she used her father's phrase of being 'weet in the leds' (weak in the legs), or, more often, she had a bone in her leg. It was years too late before I could think that it would be stranger if she had not. She would surely have countered with, 'Don't answer back.'

If I was unwilling to get on, then 'well begun is half done', so untrue to my nature. If I sulked – 'Who got out of bed the wrong side this morning?' – I was compared with a bear with a sore head, and told, 'Don't care was made to care', or warned to 'stop pulling a face or you'll stick like it'. If worried, then 'do your best and leave the rest', but what she considered best was 101%, not simply 100%. If I stood in the window, instead of explaining why she wished me to move, it was 'your father wasn't a glazier'.

If I consorted with a non-approved friend or a known non-Wesleyan Methodist, 'you can't touch pitch without being defiled'. It was common to say Mam, snobbish to say Mamma, unfeeling to say Mother. My little playmates at Hunts Cross did not appreciate being told by me that they must be common. Mother advocated the principle 'Speak as you find', but followed it only in private.

The truth was considered vital, yet usually bore such dire consequences – slap, isolation, silence – that I was tempted to avoid or sidestep the issue and tell a white lie. It was no use thinking 'touch wood and hope to die'; she had a sixth sense; the resulting inquisition was often worse than the original punishment would have been – and I had that as well. A confession of wrongdoing was expected when 'a little bird told me' was followed by an expectant silence. With Dad, it was his clear quest for perfection that led me to try to toe the line rather than let him down. It was often difficult to work out why she was cross. For example, when I repeated something a grown-up had said such as John for Daddy, I was slapped hard for being rude. I can now recognise that the harmony between the two of them was, over me, at times fragile.

He rightly resented her threats: 'I'll tell your Daddy... Wait until Daddy gets home' – for he left the daytime upbringing entirely to her. He slapped my shin with the flat of his hand, more, I think, to support her decision or to rebuke my awkwardness with her than to punish the original offence. He was overanxious to inculcate high standards not merely of behaviour but of moral outlook. A slap was emotionally and physically hurtful, for he found it hard to be aware of a small child's physical frailty, but I knew where I stood. From her, a crisp verbal lashing or a slap was rare. When she did hit, she always chanted, 'This hurts me more than it hurts you', which dented her credibility. What was usual was total silence; this, on one dire occasion, the reason for which has totally vanished, lasted one whole week.

My dreadful *Treasury for Children* did suggest, in its saccharine and trivialising way, that my problems were not unique:

Dear mother, if you just could be
A tiny little girl like me,
And I your mother, you would see
How nice I'd be to you.
I'd always let you have your way;
I'd never frown at you and say:
'You are behaving ill today;
Such conduct will not do.'

This is the first of six verses; it might have worked for the mother of the writer, one Sydney Davre.

Jemima

There was a little girl, who had a little curl
Right in the middle of her forehead [always pronounced 'forrid'],
When she was good, she was very, very good,
But when she was bad, she was horrid.

She stood on her bed, on her little truckle-bed,
With nobody by for to hinder;
She screamed and she squalled, she yelled and she bawled,
And drummed her little heels against the winder.

Her mother heard the noise, and thought it was the boys,
Playing in the empty attic,
She rushed upstairs and caught her unawares,
And spanked her, most emphatic!

The author's name is not recorded.

In default of anything else, matters in our house always ended with the unacceptable but unarguable MOTHER KNOWS BEST.

FOUR

Roskell Road

The Neighbours

R. M. Delderfield wrote, rightly, of suburbia that the people are 'almost always decent, hard-working folk, concerned with minding their own business, improving their standard of living, paying their taxes'.

Despite the boringly uneventful lives of the women, there was, in Roskell Road, very little gossiping over the garden fences, and virtually no casual dropping in, which seemed a pity when our house was so clean! It was considered adequate just to pass the time of day.

This didn't prevent Mother from talking at home about everyone. When she didn't quite have the face to get rid of any caller who outstayed her brief welcome, she muttered to herself in the kitchen. After being a visitor herself, it was 'home, James, and don't spare the horses'. Anyone pretentious was cut down to size either by 'she hasn't a penny to bless herself with' or 'handsome is as handsome does' or 'all togged up and nowhere to go'. Others were usually in the wrong (unless it was six of one and half a dozen of the other), for 'give an inch (or an ell) and they'll take a yard'. As for herself, 'sticks and stones may break my bones, but names will never hurt me' – they did, however. She thought that she was little and good, which made Dad big and good for nothing; he and I settled for big and better.

First, the grown-ups. Eda' and Cha', who lived in the other half of our semi – Mother mocked their use, especially in public, of pet names, for she would never dream of referring to her husband in any way other than Mr Cherry (this to make everyone keep their distance) or, to the few members of the family with whom she kept in touch, Daddy or Uncle John. At least she never used the word hubby. It's only fair to say that he behaved similarly. Occasionally, she called him John after I'd grown up and left home. The nearest I ever saw them touching was when they were walking formally and she took his arm. I never saw them kiss or even hug. To many of their ilk, touching meant the degeneration of society. I guess that is why I have a longing to touch and hold – whilst remaining choosy as to whom.

But back to Eda' and Cha'. Although not halls adjoining, the walls of these houses were remarkably soundproof. The couple were deemed snobs with four major disadvantages – in Mother's eyes, for I never heard Dad comment on anyone: they had, 'selfishly', no children, did not go to church, played golf in dashing plus fours and a cap and drank at the club house. She particularly, therefore, was no better than she ought to be. I wish now that I'd known them a little. Did I ever know their surname? I doubt it.

With their back door facing our back door (both doors at the side, incidentally, and separated by a fence) were the Tushies, the Tushinghams, excellent and helpful neighbours. Long after they moved, I discovered that he was Harold (Hal) and that she was Connie. He brought home the odd delectable goodie from Cooper's where he worked in some managerial capacity. This, *the* grocery emporium in town, advertised in theatre programmes. Its 'Superb Tea was awarded the Grand Prix and Gold Medal at the International Exhibitions of Antwerp, Brussels and Paris. THREE SHILLINGS PER POUND. Try a sample quarter pound and test its outstanding fragrance... Only a few paces separate (the busy housewife) from the Grocer, the Butcher, the Fishmonger and the Fruiterer.' Hal once took Dad and me to a 'lovely tea' at a Mr Meiner's: was he a Cooper's man?

Connie had naturally curly hair and could wear frilly clothes, two reasons for admiration, although only the first for envy. She once took me to town to the cinema and, even more appreciated, to tea in Owen Owens. Kind Mr Barkla (I'll tell you more about him another time) agreed to drive her to hospital on the strict condition that her baby was not born in his car. Now a ten-year-old, I became less enthusiastic when this new son meant less time for me. In fact, however, Edmund became known as my boy; even though I once gave him a pinny (pinafore), we spent many hours together. I washed him, took him to have his hair cut, 'had to wait ages… got proper fed up, and so did he'.

Mother once took him, me and our sandwiches to Egremont in the Wirral, where we had a 'fine time'.

Their second son was Alan; coping with two was beyond me. He was Dad's godson. They moved to Newcastle when I was fifteen, but came back to see us several times.

I took to talking to Jacky Grace, a bearded veteran who seemed as old as Father Christmas, who reminded me of my Granddad and lived opposite. Mother tried to discourage the friendship, convinced that he wasn't quite nice. He probably didn't wash as often as was advisable, but he was patient, pleasant and friendly; it's just struck me that he lived on his own and was probably lonely.

Kathleen Penlington lived on the other side of the road; it was her father who had the unique car in the unique garage. An asthmatic and about seven years older, she invited me to stay with the family in Ormskirk – I think that it was on a farm. Did they have two houses? Surely not; one must have belonged to relatives or was rented for a holiday.

Living further up were two connected with church. Lorna Sharp taught in Sunday School; I later cycled over from our next home for her twenty-first birthday party, twenty-one being the age of grown-upness then. Almost opposite to her was the immensely tall Mr W. O. (Wilfred Oliver) Little, whose short, stubby wife gave birth to a daughter years after such an event was deemed seemly. I'll come back to him later as well.

At the bottom end lived the Jones family – a brother and two spinster sisters. The elder woman was 'in business' in town; the younger, Miss P. E. Jones, LLCM (Licentiate of the London College of Music), always wore black and was unable to control a dewdrop. I was 'apprenticed' to her later for Saturday morning lessons which lasted an interminable hour of practising mind-destroying scales. I had to have her as she was cheaper; she charged first 10/-, then 15/-, rising per term not because of inflation (a word known only in connection with balloons) but as I 'progressed'. Mr Barkla's gifted but lazy son charged £1. He added to his standing by having four pieces of 'pianoforte music' published; in ability, he was head and shoulders above Miss Jones, but the relationship might have been considered embarrassing.

It was felt that playing ('tickling the ivories') would be both a useful personal accomplishment and handy for Sunday School and guest house holidays. One must have at least one party piece, whether recitation, which came much more easily to me, or musical performance. Despite receiving a much-coveted black music case, rather like a long sausage-shaped handbag which folded over, I hated the lessons. Miss Jones didn't always turn up, so perhaps she hated them too. I was marginally more successful with a comb and tissue paper! The only pleasure was showing off by playing cross hands. 'Why can't you play the piano? You're bright', or worse, 'You're supposed to be bright', only increased my sense of failure.

I must show you sometime the two certificates which I did achieve: First Class Primary, December 1932, and First Class Intermediate, July 1934, of the London College of Music. At least I was the only one from Hunts Cross in the long lists of successes and passes. Characteristically of the period, over 92% had been taught by women, most of whom had no formal qualifications. Of these, six were married and six were self-styled Madame, which preceded the incongruous surnames of Hughes, Ingham, Lloyd and Still. Out of 78 students, only 17 were boys.

To encourage me, my Auntie Florrie sent for Christmas 1933 a tome published by the *News Chronicle*, *Music for the Home*, edited by Sir Landon Ronald, price 2/6.

When I finally admitted to myself that I'd progress no further and sold the instrument, I was amused to find sheet music still in the piano stool: Geoffrey Shaw, *Worship*, 4d; *Warsaw Concerto*, 2/6; Rubinstein, Melody in F; Intermezzo from *Escape to Happiness*; Billy Mayerl, *Four Aces*, 2/6; Beethoven, *Sonata Pathétique*; Gershwin, *Rhapsody in Blue*, 100 French francs; *Celebrated Waltzes*, 1/6; *Piano Selection from Showboat* and from *Snow White*, 2/6. What a jumble!

Catherine lived two doors (never houses) away, but she was Welsh. From her, I learned *Cae dy geg, muchyr bidi* (not knowing that it was somewhat rude) and *nos da, carriad bach* (more suitable for polite society). Mother, being part Welsh, did not trust these 'foreigners'. In fact, the Roberts trio was one of two 'foreign' groups. The girl was congenitally incapable of distinguishing truth from falsehood, what was right from what was a naughty story. My parents were old; I know that parents always seem old, but mine gave the impression of never having been my age. But Catherine's parents seemed to belong to my grandparents' generation, to donkey's years ago. Black-haired with a sallow complexion and narrow pointed teeth, Mrs Roberts was thought to have been a layer-out of the dead.

Next to them lived Doreen, a little older, and Clarice, a little younger, the Jarretts. We had little in common, Clarice and I, but we called ourselves the Unstuckabubbles, to indicate undying friendship. We told each other 'secrets' between you, me and the gatepost and warned each other:

Tell-tale tit,
Your tongue shall be slit,
And all the doggies in the town
Shall have a little bit.

One's best friend at that age is more often than not a matter of convenience, or availability.

One of the two developed St Vitus' Dance. Our Dóreen – 'our' was often put in front of the name of a sister or brother, 'our kid' if it were the youngest (thus 'good on you, kid'); it was part of the family spirit against intruders (Mother thought it common) – well, she went to a Central School in Arúndel Avenue, where there were standards not forms, and talked frequently and respectfully of Sister Vida (Vee-da).

Their Welsh father was a hunchbacked ex-miner, suffering from the miners' disease of pneumoconiosis; their Welsh mother seemed slightly flighty. One morning, at breakfast, there was a knock on our front door. As I got up to see who it was, I called back, slowly and calmly, 'Mr Jarrett's dead.' To this day, I don't know how I knew who the caller was, let alone her news. I went on with my breakfast while Mother consoled the widow and then held a conclave in our rarely used sitting room, so I concluded that death must be a serious business. His old miner's hands were blue-veined with coal dust; his death was attributed to silicosis, an occupational lung disease. His relict suffered immediate sorrow and eventual relief.

There was a macabre Liverpudlian expression of amazement: 'Well, I'll put my head in the gas oven!' Well, almost opposite our home, a middle-aged spinster, one of two spinster sisters, did just that in an unsuccessful bid to commit suicide. No one seemed to question why she was driven to such an extremity; it was generally felt that it betokened a severe lack of moral fibre. I never discovered any more about her.

The local simpleton lived up the road, a harmless, gormless lad of about twenty who was an excellent playmate when I was six or seven. We investigated new houses, skipped, played ball. But I grew older. There was an unearthly fascination in watching this great lout clapping his hands with delight at activities which now seemed childish to me. I was frightened but enthralled. Mimicry finally decided my parents to try to find new and more desirable acquaintances.

Ernie the builder and Eddie the carpenter lived – at least worked – at the top end of Roskell Road towards Mackets Lane, in the rich, dark orange soil. They consumed gallons of tea daily from metal billycans or enamel jugs heated on a fire of sticks and smoked their Woodbines. Always willing to talk, they treated a child so gently and thoughtfully.

The milk came in churns, on a float pulled by a horse with his nosebag on, from Mr Lunt's farm; it was then poured into a two-pint china jug. At that time it cost 7d a quart. In the house, the jug was fitted with a muslin cover, with beads at suitable intervals round the edges to weight the cover down and keep the milk free of bluebottles. He also brought new-laid eggs – all free-range then. During the Thirties, the horse gave way to engine power, bringing the worry that the mechanical joltings would 'addle' the milk. Mother was saddened at the loss of manure for the garden. I was pleased; although I loved the horse, I was by then embarrassed by my mother's sorties. Mr Lunt's daughter, Alice, preceded me to High School.

Everything was of course delivered, with the occasional exception of meat. Nothing was left on the front doorstep; if no one answered the front door, the delivering man would open the side gate and come 'round the back' to what was still referred to as the tradesmen's entrance. Mother was usually in, for delivery times, believe it or not, were adhered to, and she didn't like leaving the side gate unlocked. Her purse was always on the edge of the dining room sideboard. It had sections for the coalman, the baker, the grocer and the milkman.

Earnings (daily, weekly) or salary (monthly) were never discussed publicly, certainly not before the child. I don't think that Mother ever knew her husband's financial situation, whether salary, savings or slight flutters in stocks and shares. She never owned a cheque book; actually, cheques were still a bit suspect, in the way that credit cards also were at first. Each cheque cost 2d; those for cash were left uncrossed. Postal orders were a more usual means of exchange, especially for sending money by post.

I can't tell you the glamour of holding a gold sovereign, a £1 coin. Any which turned up were carefully hoarded until they could be sold, first for 30/- each and later for three guineas to 'a man at the door'. The vast £5 note, which never appeared in our household, had to be signed.

Mother was given household money and a tiny dress allowance, the latter for clothes for herself and for me. During holidays, the former was withheld, for it had to help with the family expenses. Her own spending money then – cards, stamps, personal presents – had to be the result of her economies. For family presents for birthdays and Christmas, she usually did the shopping and kept the accounts scrupulously. A general reckoning was then made, so that each paid exactly half. She remained terrified of Dad's generosity, which she considered impetuous and thoughtless, petrified at the very notion of penury, of the pawnshop, or, worst of all, of the workhouse.

Thrift was a religion; one must always save for a rainy day, one must always pay on the nail; debt was a social horror. I still have the odd twinge of guilt when we take a taxi or when I spend money on myself which is not strictly necessary. In all honesty, spending has become easier and more pleasurable since I passed my allotted span!

Mr Ashe, a venerable and trilby-hatted gent who was always given the title of 'Mister', called at the front door for the weekly grocery order written down in a fat notebook. The contents of the cardboard box (no plastic bags), delivered the next day at the back door, had to be checked meticulously with him. He must have overlapped to an extent with the Co-op man, membership number 4156; the receipt tickets had to be saved, counted and taken quarterly to Garston for a divi – of, I think, one penny in the pound. The bread man and the meat man also came once a week – but to the back door. The laundryman called at the front door of other houses; Mother never trusted the Lune, the 'laundry for perfect laundry'.

There was a tendency to regard anyone who knocked on the door carrying goods as gypsies, much feared as they took away babies and small children. There were at one time real gypsies off Mackets Lane, who peddled baskets of laces, buttons, bows, allegedly home-made articles, clothes pegs and hairpins. The women tried to stimulate custom by having an infant in their arms. Tramps had tea-cans and occasionally asked for hot water.

Any caller was suspect, none more than the door-to-door Hoover salesman: 'it beats as it cleans as it sweeps'. It was difficult to distinguish between the false sellers and the genuine ones, often resulting from the 1914–1918 War, who were trying to salvage a little pride in their wrecked lives. Later came the Kleeneze man (to be avoided), selling brushes and difficult to dislodge; others peddled insurance ('the man from the Pru'); another sold, or failed to sell, Brushes for the Blind – obviously not to be trusted. Breton onion-sellers called seasonally; their strings were appreciated. The knife-grinder worked a foot-propelled contraption which set a noisy wheel spinning; he also sharpened razors and scissors and mended pots. The rag-and-bone man, with his cart, horse and bell, gave 2d for a bag full of rubbish.

The front and side gates were always left open on Monday mornings for the bin men. On their heads, like the coal men, they wore sacks split up the side to form a cloak and hood, and leather epaulettes, and hoisted the lidless dustbin (never abbreviated) over their shoulders from outside the kitchen door, humped it down the path and tossed the contents onto a lorry. When this was full, they went off to some mysterious depot, emptied the lot and then returned.

Playtime

.We were told to go out to play; maternal eyes could keep watch. Anyway, we might have messed up the garden and were in the way in the house. How different from today! In this respect at least, we were luckier. Everyone played together in the traffic-free road; here, there was no suggestion of 'class'. I don't think they did in Stuart Avenue or in the newer Kingsmead Drive; actually, I don't remember any young children there.

An important superstition when you were outside was never to tread on the cracks between the pavement slabs – this meant bad luck.

Each season had its own favourite game, for the weather was the determining factor.

We had to know all the names and numbers of the houses and their inhabitants for treasure hunts, which probably caused my first dislike of the intractable surname of Jones. Unfortunately, a prize had to be provided, even if it were only a sweet; sometimes, it was a convenient way of disposing of an unwanted present. The carefully thought out clues, heavily dependent on laboured childish puns, would be in notes folded over and hidden in the splits of fences or garden gates. Some names rush back, although I can't now recall where Peter Bastin or Ada Blamire (a difficult name for any stutterer) lived.

One lucky boy had a scooter, others went roller-skating. I was mortified to be forbidden; probably, with my track record, the prohibition was a wise one. Graduating from a 'tryke' (three-wheeler) to a 'fairy cycle' (small two-wheeler), I taught myself to ride by going up and down the pavement clutching the fences with one hand and getting umpteen painful splinters in the fingers. Still later, as a reward for passing the Junior City Scholarship examination (eleven-plus by another name), I wanted a proper bicycle for school travel. Mary had a three-speed Raleigh; mine was a cheaper job from the Co-op, with chain-guard for dresses. Had the financial aspect been carefully explained, I might have understood. One dreadful day, it fell apart with four spokes and one wheel buckled. This was tragic as by then I was cycling daily to and from school. Mother had ridden a penny-farthing but was terrified of the modern ones.

She claimed that she had skated as a child on the frozen Severn. Where would the money for skates have come from? I suspect that she meant sliding, although she now never risked even that. Dad and I slid happily on any frozen pond. Those nearby strips of water have now doubtless disappeared. One blissful time, the pair of us went tobogganing.

There was an obligation to make a snowman, with pebbles for eyes, nose and mouth, as well as to clear the way from the front gate to the front door; otherwise, how could the postman get in? I suffered badly from the cold and was 'fair clemmed', although some sources say that adjective means hungry – I was that too, of course! Mother regarded me as over-susceptible, or 'nesh'.

Skipping, with and without singing and chanting, was the usual pursuit. You might have a proper bought individual rope with handles at each end, or a group would make do with an old clothes line. One at each end would turn the rope and everyone else would skip, or one end would be wound round a tree or lamp post so that only one person had to be 'out'. The more proficient could skip a double turn, or speed would increase as we chanted 'One, two, three, Allera', or 'Salt, Mustard, Vinegar, Pepper', until we ran out of puff.

The variants for chanting games were many. One player counted, others forming a circle; the last one left was the counter next time or had to be chased or chased all the others. Rules varied according to the dominant participant. Sometimes we just jigged round and chorused:

> One, two, three, four, five, six, seven,
> All good children go to Heaven.
> Penny on the water,
> Tuppence on the sea,
> Threepence on the railway,
> And out goes she.

Or:

> X is no good,
> Chop him up for firewood.

Or:

> One for sorrow,
> Two for joy,
> Three for a girl/kiss,
> Four for a boy,
> Five for silver,
> Six for gold,
> Seven for a secret never to be told.

Or:

> Eenie, meenie, mina, mo,
> Catch a nigger by his toe,
> If he hollers, let him go,
> Eenie, meenie, mina, mo.

I don't recall ever identifying this 'nigger' with a black man. What other word of two syllables would fit?

Ring a ring a roses,
A pocket full of poses [sic]
Atishoo, atishoo,
We all fall down.

Ups-a-daisy.
More boisterous were:

I'm the king of the castle,
Get down you dirty rascal.

And:

London Bridge is falling down, falling down,
London Bridge is falling down, my fair lady.

Mother knew several choruses from her early days; some references remain obscure, but that did not matter – then:

Five for the symbols at your door,
Four for the Gospel Makers,
Three, three, the Rivals,
Two, two, the Lily White Boys,
Clothéd all in green-o.
One is one and ever more shall be so.

And:

Ti la shibá, ti la shibasha,
Corabella, corabella, ching-ching-a-chinga,
For (s)he shall be a Cora, a Cora, a Cora!

The spelling is mine, for I have never seen it in print.

Belonging to all generations are 'Tinker, tailor, soldier, sailor, rich man, poor man, beggar man, thief', and 'Here we go round the mulberry bush, all on a Sunday morning'.

Sunday reminds me of the strangely mischievous Bible-based rhymes such as, 'I saw Esau / Sitting on a seesaw' and 'Adam, Eve and Pinch-me-tight' who did something totally unmemorable.

What other relatively unskilled games were there? Leapfrog, when you leapt first over one person's back, then over two until you failed. This remained very popular at high school where landings were less uncomfortable on grass. Tick (not tig, as often in books), when you were chased; if touched, you became the chaser. Staring, or making faces, at someone until (s)he cracked and laughed. Trying to get up to someone with his/her back to you (who would be counting silently up to an agreed number (speed at discretion), without that person turning round sharply and catching you moving; if caught, places were changed. Two held joined hands over a space, the others ducked to pass under quickly for if they pulled down and caught you, you were out. 'Pinch, squeeze and pass it on' defeats me now.

Others demanded more skill and involved a struggle, positively, for mastery or, negatively, not to be outdone. Taunts were involved: 'cowardy cowardy custard', usually against me. I asked first, 'Bags I do,' usually from me. A swing and battledore and shuttlecock were both a bit posh, because a big garden and special equipment were needed; none of us rose to either.

I never grasped the principle of hitting conkers on a string, but Yo-Yo, price 3d or 6d, yes. A Yo-Yo is apparently one of the oldest toys in the world; it may have been used in ancient Greece. It was introduced in 1930 in the USA; sales soon reached millions. My Yo-Yo Club certificate from Lewis' store in town, admitting me as a member, states that Miss Joan Cherry has passed the preliminary three tests. The first must have been normal down and up, the second throwing the contraption forward, and the third? Up and over? Mother had played Diabolo, a sort of string with wooden ends and a ball to balance on it. With tops, whipping and spinning, she was more skilled than I was, so I affected not to like them much. The poor in town had iron hoops; mine was wooden and you bowled it along with a stick; again, her technique was superior to mine. Marbles could be played in the gutter – if you owned marbles. French (why?) cricket involved any old bat with which you defended your feet as the others threw a soft ball at them. You were not allowed to move your feet, so backward defence was not easy. You were out if the ball touched them.

Sometimes, we played Silly Ollies, once a game with little white balls, which came to mean doing nothing, messing about – doubtless 'the Devil finding mischief still / for idle hands to do'.

Several of us had little notebooks in which we jotted down car numbers; for any success, we had to go to the bottom of our road and wait patiently for a car to come. It was a trifle unprofitable, but it was cheating to swap numbers or to accept one as a 'present'. This unproductive sport soon palled.

On 1 April you had to play a trick on someone – before noon, otherwise 'You're the Noddy [noodle, simpleton] and I'm not'.

When we had to go indoors for our respective meals, we chanted, 'See you later, alligator' and responded with, 'In a while, crocodile.'

Of course, when we first arrived in Hunts Cross, I was too tiny and too timid to join in these pursuits and had to play in the house. Mother got rid of all my toys as I grew older and particularly during the War; I was never asked if any were important to me.

I never went overboard on dolls; continual warnings against breaking them meant that I rarely played with them and so never did break them! My beloved Teddy was both cuddlesome and unbreakable. Miss Amy gave me a brown doll; she wore beautiful white knitted clothes and was far too beautiful to touch and thus get dirty. An overweight china doll closed her eyes if you tilted her head back. I wonder why she was known as Dorothy Green? Giving them tea in the garden in the summer from a tiny blue tea service, undressing them, putting them to bed or wheeling them in a doll's pram, accepted as the norm, afforded little excitement.

I was fond for a while of Wilfred (so named after Pip, Squeak and Wilfred), a violently purple rabbit with long, wiggly ears, of Sunny Jim who came with enough packets of a breakfast cereal, and of a golliwog. Again, I never dreamt of any connection with negroes; in fact, mine was given to me by one. Nigger Minstrels were, after all, painted white men, whilst negro spirituals were poignant. The toy was considered not quite 'nice', not, or not simply, because of racial prejudice (a phrase I never heard before the War), but because black was not quite 'nice' for a child. I did once dress up as one for a Co-op fancy dress competition – I didn't win. Black never seemed strange to me, although it often seemed beautiful. I was not alone in my *naïveté*: there is the story of the Liverpool child who said to the great Learie Constantine: 'Oh, Uncle Learie, why didn't you tell me you were black?'

The *pièce de résistance* was my dolls' house, made by Uncle George, Leslie's father. The front was open, so that two floors were visible with matching minute furniture. You remember the Smith family? As well as treating one seriously, Mr Robert had a sense of humour which delighted a child. I still have the letter, typed on the firm's headed notepaper.

J & R Smith (R M Smith & H Smith)
19, Williamson Square,
Liverpool.
Carpet and Linoleum Dealers and Importers of Oriental Carpets
Telegrams: Carpets, Liverpool
Telephone: Royal 300

To Miss Joan Cherry
'Trelystan'
Roskell Road
Hunts Cross

25th January, 1928

Dear Madame,

We beg to thank you for your order received this morning. The sizes of your rooms are somewhat unusual, but we hope you will find something in the range of patterns we send herewith.

Yours faithfully,

(Signed) Robert Martin Smith

(J & R Smith)

It came in the firm's envelope, at printed paper rate, namely 1½d, the address written by RMS himself. I remember my delight – in the formality of the letter and the adult tone adopted by a revered grown-up, not to mention the perfectly fitting cuts of lino. What also strikes me now is the supreme confidence of the telegraphic address.

To digress for a moment. He wrote a charming letter, still on lined paper, when we were getting married.

> Herbert and I would like to have the pleasure of sending you a wedding present and wonder if you would like us to give you a carpet for one of the rooms. [We could hardly tell him that, at that time, we had only two box rooms.] Please let me have full particulars if you would like a carpet. I almost think a square carpet would be best in your case as it might come in more handy in the case of your moving at any time.

> We should like a rough sketch of the room with fireplace shown and position of the windows also what decorations, tiles etc and whether you would like a plain, tone on tone (diaper) or well-covered pattern.
>
> We haven't one at present, but we get a few every now and again and have hundreds of folk waiting.
>
> This cold weather [the notorious 1947 winter] has closed most of our factories for 3 weeks and has made things more difficult than before.

After signing, he added a postscript:

> We hope you will both be supremely happy and that you may have a long life together, of joyous service.

My train set was not an elaborate affair like that of my cousin Leslie; his, with its countless additions and library, still fills his attic. Mine had a circular steel track, the three or four components of which did not always remain locked together, so that, when wound up with a key, the poor little yellow-brown engine, its coal tender and two or three carriages rarely finished their journey. I played with it on rare occasions: 'You'll break it, you know.' Mother regarded me, correctly, as awkward, but such remarks did not help to build confidence.

Plasticine soon palled; it just would not do what was required of it. Flour and water paste, for sticking pictures into albums, was possible on rainy Saturday mornings – wet inside as well as out! Similarly with transfers which involved a complicated system of wetting and pressing down; I never mastered which side was which.

The farmyard was more manageable, being a collection of animals and implements. You simply had to use your imagination as none of them had actually to do anything. Building bricks, on the other hand, were troublesome as, despite efforts to follow the given patterns, they consistently fell down. I was never allowed toy soldiers; was it because I was a girl or, more likely, because of Dad's understandably pacifist leanings? I didn't mind. Meccano, thank goodness, was strictly for boys.

The only game that Mother enjoyed was Peggoty – if that was how it was spelt – which involved, again if I recall rightly, putting pegs in holes in order to get a certain number in a straight line, which it was the opponent's purpose to prevent. I did graduate to dominos but never to chess, which for Dad was too slow; he enjoyed draughts. Other board games were Ludo and Sorry – I wonder now what we did. Noughts and crosses or rubbing paper across a coin to replicate the pattern provided short-lived pleasure. Bridge was too *élitist* and often money was at stake.

As I grew older, I collected things, sometimes putting them in bought scrapbooks, sometimes in boxes or tins: tram tickets, farthings and cigarette cards (in thoughtfully provided books) were much prized. My cousin Eddie and others donated Player's cards on trains, butterflies, birds, flowers, Kings and Queens, stars of sport – what they represented hardly mattered, it was the acquisition, the one-upmanship (an unknown word then) which counted. It satisfied the need to have things which were your very own, partly because adults didn't want them! Alas, they too disappeared during the War; they would have been quite valuable by now.

The other mania was stamps. Numbers increased steadily. My parents gave me my first album for Christmas when I was nine. As each one was stuck in with stamp hinges, so the total was adjusted. Duplicates too were collected profitably; for 100 of Edward VIII's short reign, one received 1d, for 500, 6d. It was a matter of honour not to buy any for the collection. I passed my two albums on to Leslie's granddaughter only a year or so ago; his own collection was a less haphazard, more professional affair.

When I began Science some years later, a chemistry set was bought; it was simple, but quite beyond me, although I did enjoy the mess I made for about a month. I do recall school instruction on the difference between hydrochloric and

sulphuric acids, and that Pb stood for plumbum or lead.
Anyone whose initials were P. B. was in for a bad time.

Books have always been a delight. I learned to read sitting
on my father's lap. As he read to me each night, he traced the
word with his finger and often I read some words with him. I
never had to cope with 'modern' methods, phonemes and the
like. Did you?

No fashion changes more than children's books. With due
account made for family background, it is almost possible to
work out someone's age, or at least decade, by what he or she
read as a child.

The Christopher Robin books gave great satisfaction,
although I gather that modern youngsters find them sissy or
soppy. I can now sympathise with A. A. Milne's son, who must
have suffered from his own contemporaries.

> Hush! Hush! whisper who dares,
> Christopher Robin has fallen downstairs.

Or, more accurately:

> Christopher Robin is saying his prayers.

I remember Jemima Puddleduck and the Dr Doolittle stories
which began the year before I was born. In 1988, they were
revamped to excise the racist element, of which we simpletons
had been blissfully unaware.

What else? There was a rhyme to the tune of 'Frère Jacques':

> William Shakespeare, William Shakespeare,
> Shelley as well, Shelley as well,
> Ella Wheeler Wilcox, Ella Wheeler Wilcox,
> Ethel M. Dell, Ethel M. Dell.

The *Everyman Encyclopaedia* comments that the American Ella
(born 1856) wrote verses 'mainly noticeable for their plati-

tudes' and that the stories of Miss Dell, who died only in 1939, 'appealed to readers who unite a love of romance with pious orthodoxy'. These ladies were popular with my mother's generation; they were clearly above my head at this stage and not to my taste subsequently.

At Christmas 1926, 'wishing her a very happy time, the girls Daddy blows the whistle for', namely Trinity Church hockey team, presented *The Chummy Book*, written in moderately large print 'for all boys and girls who are good chums'; its 288-thick pages contain no fewer than 64 items – stories, verses, pictures, drawings. I might have been able to read such as *Green Feathers* about Tony Twinkles ('a little boy who lived with his mother in a tiny house by the Willow-Willow Green') and Tony Tall (an unpleasant dunce) or *The Puff-Puff Jingle* in which:

> A stands for Ar-ri-val,
> The station is here…

and continues through Buff-er, Coal ('What a stock'), Dri-ver ('with face rather black'), En-gine, Flag, Guard, Hand-cart, In-cline, Junc-tion, Key, Lugg-age (two trunks), Queue, Ro-cket, Sig-nal, Tun-nel ('which no one need fear'), Un-der-ground, Van, Whist-le, X-mas,

> And now we are coming
> To Y and to Z,
> Time to put pictures
> And puff-puffs to bed.

Later came a clever-stick rhyme:

> 2YYs U R
> 2YYs U B
> I C U R
> 2 YYs 4 Me.

I could copy drawings, join up dots to make a picture, 175 for a man, 31 for a fish; you must see the results on your next visit. Or I could learn how youngsters made a jazz band out of household utensils, how Jack loved his naughty monkey Jacko, sympathise with *The Fairy Muffin Man*, feel envious of the girl's Wendy House, her nurse and cook and be frightened with the Wee Wanderer who lived on Pixie Common and met the Green Ogre. All this, but I was dependent on my father; I could not have lifted the book then; it's heavy enough now. A much-loved present.

Another tome, a present for my fifth birthday from Miss Amy Smith, was *The Old Fairy Tales*, with black and white drawings and four coloured pictures, written simply, but neither archly nor patronisingly – 'Jack and the Beanstalk', 'Red Riding Hood', 'Cinderella', 'The Three Little Pigs', 'Puss in Boots', 'Beauty and the Beast', 'Hop o' my Thumb', 'Jack the Giant Killer', and, my favourite, 'The Three Bears', with its simple repetition which made it easy to learn – 'Who's been sitting in my chair?' I was less keen on 'Goldilocks', as my own hair was short, straight and less than golden, although my father kept all his life an envelope marked 'April 19, 1924, Baby's HAIR, First Cutting'. I was amazed to find it after his death, for he was a most unsentimental man in respect of possessions.

A simplified version of *Alice in Wonderland*, with hyphens between the syllables, was bought for 1/- because it was thought that I ought to read it, but it has always failed to attract. Occasionally, *Tiny Tots* or *Tiger Tim* came as a Christmas annual, never a weekly expenditure. Comics and dailies were banned; the former had to be begged or borrowed. The only regular broadsheet for me was *The Children's Newspaper*.

As I got somewhat older, the Katy books appealed. What could life offer more blissful than lying on the carpet on one's tummy and reading *What Katy Did*, *What Katy Did Next* and *What Katy Did at School*, then *Little Women* and later Richmal

Compton's William series – a fantasy world with both brothers and sisters. Mother had a tear-jerker, a prize for her Sunday School attendance, *Jessica's First Prayer*; she had 'inherited' a book by Silas Hocking (a Methodist favourite) and *Self-Help* by Samuel Smiles and talked of an unlikely-named Mrs George de Horne Vaisey, but all that she read was *The Shrewsbury Chronicle* or *The Wellington Journal and Shrewsbury News*. Another weepy was *A Peep Behind the Scenes*. I wonder what I'd think of *Daddy Long Legs* now. I wonder too if you have even heard of these books of my childhood.

In the bookcase were *Black Beauty*, a handsomely bound *Swiss Family Robinson* (of which I never managed more than the first few pages) and Gene Stratton Porter's *Girl of the Limberlost*. There was a set (ten or twelve blue-bound volumes) of *Harmsworth's Encyclopaedia* – or were they Arthur Mee's *Children Encyclopaedia* or did Dad's searching mind need two sets?

Mother was not far out when she complained that I always had my head in a book. The fascination with words began early; the written word has always seemed the most worth-while and satisfying art.

FIVE
Woolton

A comparatively short letter now to introduce Woolton, which became the centre of our lives.

The Village was one-and-a-half to two miles away along Speke Road, a winding country road with a highish stone wall on the left which followed the golf course then the rook-laden trees of Woolton Woods. Nothing here has changed.

A bus did run, but infrequently, and was expensive (1d) at a time when money was tight. To a small child, the road was long and hilly. I held my father's hand; he became embarrassed at this before I did. My older self found a short cut by climbing a stile and cutting across the links. This came in handy once when a flasher urged me (I was aged twelve or thirteen) to hold what seemed to be the protruding end of a coat hanger, but which felt warm and slimy. Although totally ignorant of what was on offer, I somehow sensed that if I said anything about the incident at home, even the few freedoms which I still enjoyed would be curtailed. In fact, I told my father some forty years later; his sole comment then was, 'Tut tut.' Although the gate to its right is now open, the stile is still there; the wooden steps on each side are now bolted to a stone slab. Generally there was no danger in the streets, none even along this unlit road at night.

As Speke Road curves at the top of the hill, on the left is School Lane where the tiny seventeenth-century school is situated, taken over by an Anglican body for the Education of the Poor in 1819. Behind it are the Woods and what was once the Manorial Hall of which, strangely, I have no recollection and yet it is an important building believed to be by the architect Robert Adam. A few sandstone cottages are sandwiched together along the road.

On the right, where there is now a new suburb, were Manor Road and, when we first knew the Village, only Watergate Lane. Evocative names; the latter simply petered out at the bottom of its incline where cattle grazed in a great meadow in the fourteenth century. There was once a Catholic Priory, which proved too small for the influx of Irish immigrants. Argument still exists as to whether the tunnels which were discovered came from Woolton Hall cellars or were escape routes for Catholic priests.

Past the 5W tram terminus (the line of the tracks in the middle of the road still noticeable under the grass) is the Village itself with its Cross. Absorbed into the City just before the Great War, it has yielded slender evidence of an Iron Age encampment. What is more certain is that it was Uluentune in the Domesday Book, then became Wulfa's Town, then Wolueton Magna and Parva; these remain as Much Woolton and Little Woolton.

Two other certainties are that, together with Speke and Allerton, the Village sent troops to Flodden Field and that, from 1180, the Knights of Jerusalem were Lords of the Manor for nearly 360 years. It was Crown property for fifty years, later Lords being members of the Salisbury and Derby families. The name of the then portly Lord Derby was, in my childhood, always spoken reverently, with what might be called a tug of the forelock in the voice. I even thought it worth noting in my diary at the age of fifteen that I had seen him.

Several of Mother's sisters kept their hair long, which they did up in a bun or coiled as earphones, later regarded as suitable only for old maids. When Mother came to the big city, she had her long hair cut off, first into a bob, then a shingle, then a Marcel wave with curling tongs heated over a flame. Now she went to the hairdresser every fortnight and bent her head over the basin. It was not a salon as we understand it: the two Tomlinson sisters, with initiative but no formal training, worked hard in the back room of their home, on a machine from outer space. There were usually out-of-date weeklies to pass the time under the dryer – *Home Chat*, *Women's Own* (both 3d) and, occasionally, *Titbits*, the popular editions of which were collected and bound into an annual volume.

A whole head perm, £3, was a fearsome affair: hair, screwed up with curlers, was threaded into plugs dangling from electric wires attached to a sort of chandelier. Cotton wool in the ears was a necessity. Between perms came the regular set.

Mother's style henceforth remained constant: side parting, curls all round (no blow-dry, no layering then), which necessitated a hairnet for sleeping or for windy beaches – only, of course, when it was too windy for a hat. Her hair turned grey late in life and never became silver or white. She had a wart or mole on her chin with a protruding tuft of hair. She never thought, or at least never mentioned or gave the impression of thinking, that she could or should do anything about it.

I inherited to a mild degree the Hinchliffe tendency to auburn; not the copper knob of Mother when young or of several cousins, just enough to make my delicate skin prone to sunburn between countless freckles and just enough to support the automatic assumption that I must be short-tempered. I wasn't actually, since I was too timid then. For years, the cut (3d) was straight: not an Eton crop, more of a pudding basin, just straight, with a straight fringe, a centre parting which never kept straight, and hair just long and fine enough for a slide to slip out of it. Kirby grips saved one's self-esteem. It was more thrilling to have it cut in a big store in town, where a child could enjoy sitting on a stuffed animal. Sadly that privilege cost 6d, twice as much as a normal cut. A wet cut was an unthought-of skill. Anyway, you couldn't go out with wet hair – you might catch your death (of cold).

Hair could be grabbed as an aid to discipline, so perhaps

short was a good thing! Even though I enjoyed combing my own hair and that of anyone willing to be a victim, hair still tangled.

When I was older – judging by photographs, thirteen or fourteen or so – I was allowed to have just the ends permed (30/-) to provide a pageboy bob, first with the ends turned under, later with them curled outwards. Pipe cleaners served as DIY curlers. Not alas for me a kiss curl on the forehead, the Veronica Lake peek-a-boo look, with a bandeau or even ties of ribbon (shoelaces were 'in' later) or plaits (too much trouble for all concerned).

Dad had his few strands 'trained' by a barber in town, for there was not the slightest thought of a unisex salon. The word probably did not exist. For men, Bryl Cream was 'The Perfect Hair Dressing'. His pair of brushes, still in use, have lasted over eighty years.

We also had to go to Woolton to see the doctor, unless one was almost dying, so, however poorly, we made the one-and-a-half-mile trek there and the one-and-a-half-mile trek back. Appointments could not be made as no one had a phone; so the wait for any panel (that is, non-paying) patient could last hours. I hated the embarrassment of being, unjustly, ushered in before someone I knew. I think that a consultation cost 5/-, which was a lot of money; home visits were more expensive. Doctors dispensed their own medicines for private patients.

I still remember some of the little shops and their owners: Gamble the butcher, who wore a blue coat and a straw boater, Leadbetter the joiner, the Smith family fishmongers, of whom more later. Mainwaring was a gardener, Hesketh the painter.

At Mr Ashe's grocery and bakery, you queued in a narrow space for different provisions. Wearing his white coat, he weighed out the sugar and tea from a large bag, or, with two wooden spatulas, slapped the right size butter pats into shape from a large block. Nothing was pre-packed. Service was friendly – and slow.

I can't put shops to other names – Tuson (pharmacist?), Maguire, Ashton (all, I think, Methodists, at least theoretically), or names to the shoe mender, the haberdasher (habby, dealer in 'small wares of dress'). I was never allowed to ask for anything in a shop.

In the Village, one generally paid directly to the server; sometimes, and mostly in the big shops in town, money and bill were put into a little container on a wire above one's head. The assistant would then pull a cord and the metal box would shoot along the wire to the cashier, who, in small, privately owned shops, was often the wife of the proprietor. Produce was carefully put into the tough thatch-type shopping basket, usually rectangular and with a handle – no plastic bags. Woolton's shops were not exciting emporia, but stocks were ample, the rooms were clean, the owners chatty. Not one that I remember exists today. There are still shops, but they look isolated, as if trade were passing them by. An occasional visit was paid to Garston market on Fridays.

Two buildings in the Village were out of bounds. The murky swimming baths were suspected of harbouring and hatching unmentionable diseases. The prohibition suited me fine, as I have always feared swimming, mainly because of terror of the unknown, partly because, without glasses, I could see so little. I read recently that one-time Beatle Paul McCartney had gone back to see the baths; they must have changed since the War. The second prohibited place, strangely enough, was the original Wesleyan Methodist Church, then, perhaps still, a library; again, you didn't know who might have touched the books.

Apart from Friendly Benevolent Societies, such as the Oddfellows, there was the minute cinema; the nickname of the 'fleapit' was probably justified for once. Yet my cousin Leslie, eight years older than I am, was allowed to take me to children's matinees (the word correctly used for once) on Saturday mornings when he was staying with us during school holidays. He had to sit upstairs, I had to sit downstairs. I am surprised now that we remained friends until his death; the first film that I recall was the tear-jerking *Little Women* with Katherine Hepburn; he had to walk back home with a sobbing, red-eyed child. Were all films like this? I asked him. I still weep more at the cinema, theatre or television than in real life situations.

There were, still are, small side streets of little terraced houses, often back to back, often grim, their front doors opening either directly on to the pavement or on to three or four steep steps down. The names indicate their dates – Gladstone, Cobden – for many of these houses were built quickly out of local quarry stone for the influx of Irish labourers, some of whom worked in the docks at Garston, which is now not distinguishable from other suburbs. Castle Street harks back, Pitt Place commemorates the clay pits. Perhaps the inappropriately named Rose Street represented hope. The great sandstone quarry, hence Quarry Street, at its most productive in the third quarter of the nineteenth century, gave its distinctive colour to the houses.

Although the Black Death had passed Liverpool by, here, with severe overcrowding and abysmal sanitation, were still pallid, shoeless, knickerless children sewn into winter garments just as there had been in Liverpool 8. 'Street Arabs,' sniffed Mother. One historian describes the set-up as moral and physical degradation; a poor diet and too many offspring certainly meant that TB was rife. An agent called each week at many houses as women paid for clothes on the never-never. One may criticise the men who frequented the pubs (once there were forty; I remember only two), but at least it did mean one fewer in the tiny house. Local girls worked in shops, or, later, in the Bear Brand stocking factory. The only work opening for older women was in domestic service.

Some manorial houses remain on roads leading out of the Village. At the top of the 254' ridge is the imposing St Peter's

Church (1887) which replaced an earlier one which had become too small. The Congregational (Conger) Church of 1865 is further along the High Street.

SIX

Churchgoing

Wesleyan Methodists

We now come to the whole essence of my parents' life and so of mine.

> The Methodists were a class apart.
>
> Flora Thompson

> I think that I died and to Heaven did go.
> Where do you come from, they wanted to know.
> And when I said 'Woolton', oh, how they did stare!
> 'Come in and sit down – you're the first one from there.'

Methodism was often regarded as the poor man's religion; that may have been true for some districts but certainly not for all. It was born in song. Charles Wesley, described as the poet of the evangelical faith, contributed many hymns. Woolton had no truck with canticles or psalms; passages with responses were considered too automatic, too unthinking; the Ten Commandments were rarely mentioned. At the back of my Thirties' hymn book was a warning: 'It cannot be sufficiently stressed that in order to obtain good psalm-singing, regular practice is essential both for choir and congregation.' This contradicted the local desire for spontaneity and emotion; with only the Fishy Smiths and myself in the choir, it would also have been unlikely. I still remember most of the words and tunes of over 100 of the 984 included, we sang them so often.

Although no life story is completely unique, mine, in the religious aspect, is very different from that of all my many relations and from that of most girls then and certainly now.

Once caught at the head of my father's side of the double bed, muttering incoherent baby talk, I tried to explain that I was saying prayers like Daddy does. I was chastised for 'mockery', a word, indeed an idea, totally foreign to a five-year-old. Prayers at bedtime were compulsory, but at least were private and not *en famille*, although mine were supervised for many years.

For Dad, the Church was his real life, from the January Covenant service, when he renewed his commitment, through to Christmas Day service, which was the most joyous. Communion gave him especial spiritual refreshment.

Church ruled our lives, affecting our words, even our fun. Each child joined their hands, back to back, fingers entwined, then turned the hands over, so that the right thumb protruded:

> Here's the church and here's the steeple.
> Open the door and see the people.

A teller of tall stories – that is, lies – was Ananias. A serious speech of admonishment was a pi-jaw, short for pious. With me, Mother felt she needed the patience of Job.

It had been a great wrench for Dad to leave Trinity but he soon found his niche at St James', Woolton. Round the corner from the tramlines and on the corner of the High Street and Church Road, St James' was the Wesleyan Methodist equivalent of Rome or Mecca. Opened in 1866, it faces the Sunday School on the opposite side of the little road. It is now Methodist and United Reform, which must have caused some turning in graves. I remembered it as small and intimate; strangely, when I revisited it for the first time in over fifty years, it seemed, with its sort of turreted tower, much larger and more ornate – and much grimier.

Peter Owen has written that he spent much of the day on Sundays walking to and from church; so did we, on Shanks's pony (that is, on foot), as Mother said, three times the one-and-a-half to two miles there and three times back, because we must not be employing people, or expecting bus drivers or conductors, to work on Sundays. This was a lot to ask of a small, growing girl.

The only exception was when the charming if elderly Mr Barkla fitted four or six or even eight into his sturdy but seemingly even more elderly motor car. Fortunately, there was no limitation then on the number of passengers; seat belts had not been invented. I don't remember its make; I do remember that the starting handle was not always effective. An Austin 7 in 1938 cost £122.

His was no Tin Lizzie, although it lacked trafficators; he cranked up the engine, squeezed the horn and held out his hand to denote that he was turning right. Cars were often given names; they lasted so long that they became members of the family.

Mr Barkla was interesting on three counts: his name was unusual; he suffered virtually overnight from alopecia and lost his silver mane; and he gave me a hollow bird's egg to encourage me to collect them. This always seemed unfair, quite apart from the fact that I never found any. He later gave me a lovely mahogany chest of coins (what happened to it and them?) which I carefully catalogued. They were presumably his duplicates because I went subsequently to see his collection.

Sundays

Sundays meant no gardening, no sewing, no knitting, no cooking, no cleaning, no games, even no homework until I had to face public examinations, at which point the rules were bent. No newspapers, although Dad was honest enough to admit later that it was Monday's edition that ought to be eschewed. Illogically, shoes were cleaned in the morning, always his job. This was rationalised as being appropriate to appear shining in God's house. One could aspire to cleanliness even if godliness were out of one's reach.

Clothes: Sunday best (glad rags) were bought with religious observance in mind, for we had to be 'as neat as two pins and as bright as a button'. We togged up for Sunday and saved clothes for best, a habit which dies hard.

For me, shoes were a bugbear; in pre-War days, all shoes were too narrow, so that corns or chilblains inevitably resulted. For summer, it was black, non-malleable patent leather, which squeaked when new, and always raised blisters; some of today's problems result from this constriction then unavoidable. In winter, boots or gaiters, fastened by skin-pinching buttonhooks and later by laces crossing over the button on one side and across to its opposite number, seemed to keep the cold in rather than out. When trying on shoes in a shop, I was given no choice as to type or, more importantly, fit. Ankle socks in summer, turnover tops in winter (that is, to the knees and then the top turned over) meant that 'pull your socks up' had a literal as well as a figurative meaning. I had my own superstition of putting the right shoe on before the left.

Many springs and autumns saw a new topcoat suitable for the coming season, sometimes ignominiously and obviously let down for the growing girl the following year for daily wear. For many years, the only concessions to the cold were muffs, with a cord round the neck or wrist so that I wouldn't lose them. One never, not even on the hottest summer day, went to church gloveless.

The hat, similarly obligatory, was of velvet or wool in winter, and, bought at Easter for the summer, of uncomfortable, ear-clipping straw with flowers round the base of the crown. None ever fitted.

I cannot visualise dresses (velvet in winter, with detachable and unsuitable white washable collars) very clearly, although I recall vividly and still with the same blush of shame the telltale line where one had been lengthened. Which was worse, that or a garment made to 'allow' for growth?

I do recall a purple dress with flounces below the waist: was it voile? The distaste remains after at least sixty-five years as it does for my first petticoat (never called an underskirt, and always with built-up shoulders), a restrictive garment, necessary for an inappropriate yellow floral affair; it caused a day of sobs. Was the fact that I was a hoyden, very unfeminine in my detestation of anything flowery, connected in some way with Mother's desire for a boy, and/or my love of my father? For some bizarre reason, red was frowned on as too brash. Blue was favoured for summer, brown for winter.

Sometimes, one's vest, whether of summer or winter thickness, showed at the neck. Clean underclothes were essential if one went anywhere – illogically not for school – in case one was involved in an accident. A hobbledehoy, a scallywag, I was not a good clothes horse.

Mother had little or no dress sense. In summer, it would be a coatee (hip length) or an edge-to-edge coat over a dress (a frock was for housework) made of art silk (I never twigged that 'art' in this context meant artificial and not artistic) or crêpe de Chine (pronounced as one word, so that I didn't grasp its significance either), or, once or twice, of tussore or Macclesfield silk. As a V-neck was considered immodest, it was worn with what was known as a modesty vest, a sort of pocket handkerchief or tucked lace insertion, secured inside by tiny gilt safety pins, and spoken of without even a smirk. She had a best and a second-best dress, and her washing frock, often beltless and waistless in the Thirties. There was no choice: length was decided less by fashion than by age; she had escaped from ankle-length to remain at calf-length. Knees must always be covered once you were no longer a child; otherwise you might look like something the cat brought in.

For winter she wore either a heavier dress or a suit, always called a 'costume', hardly dressed to kill. Elizabeth Jane

Howard has written relevantly of the classic navy blue coat and skirt which were supposed never to date – but did. A blouse (coloured, because white showed the dirt) and modest jewellery such as a brooch or a locket, or, later, pearls with a twin set, completed the outfit. Fashionable at one time was a bracelet worn above the elbow. A lace-edged hanky was for show rather than for nose-blowing. Her prized asset was a fur tippet, mothballed for winter because it must not get wet, round her neck, with the fox's head sporting hooks to keep it on; the tail dangled. The fact that it had once belonged to a live animal never occurred to her. What a relief that it did not survive the War.

Her underpinnings were formidable, although whalebone corsets did give way to Spirella corselettes, much later. Unchanging in shape and style, they did nothing for her increasing flabbiness. Underwear was flannelette in winter, winceyette in summer. Knickers had elastic at waist and knee.

For many years, she wore bar-strap shoes, and court shoes (that is, no strap or laces) for best, over wool, or in the late Thirties, lisle, stockings.

Dad had spats especially for Sundays. He gave up formal wear for a three-piece suit; the bottom button of the waistcoat, for some weird and wonderful reason, was always left undone. His watch chain across his thin tummy fitted into the pockets. Braces held up the trousers which had turn-ups. Socks, usually knitted by Mother, who had had much practice in the Great War and one of my few hand skills, were kept up by a form of mid-calf garter. To avoid any suggestion of flashiness, they were erroneously called sock suspenders. He wore a body belt round his middle for much of the year as he felt the cold.

Shirts, always white, came with two detached stiff collars which were kept in a collar box. They were attached by collar studs; cuff links fastened the sleeves (two holes, no buttons). These small items were kept in a stud box. Attached soft collars came after the second War. No one 'decent' dreamed of going without a tie, but tiepins were vulgar.

A bowler then, daringly, in the Thirties, a trilby (my father's pate was virtually hairless), leather gloves and usually a long-handled brolly completed his outfit. In summer, he wore a flower, always from the garden, so that it was truly his flower worn to the greater glory of God; it was held in a tube of water behind his lapel. He always wore a signet ring on his left little finger; he wasn't wearing it in his wedding photograph and I was too shy to ask, so I don't know if it had any matrimonial significance. His nails were always beautifully clean and clipped.

Inside the Church

Thus accoutred, we were ready for church. Mother did not usually attend the 10.45 a.m. service, on the pretext that she had to prepare lunch, which, as you now know, was minimal. From the age of seven or eight, I accompanied Dad.

Along with the usual rousing general hymns of praise such as:

> All people that on earth do dwell,
> Sing to the Lord with cheerful voice;
> Him serve with mirth, His praise forth tell;
> Come ye before Him and rejoice.

Or, with its swooping tune:

> Let all the world in every corner sing:
> My God and King!
> The heavens are not too high,
> His praise may thither fly;
> The earth is not too low,
> His praises there may grow.
> Let all the world in every corner sing:
> My God and King.

There was a lot of repetition, and a fair number of Alleluias. There was also a hymn considered suitable for children:

> Father, lead me day by day
> Ever in Thine own sweet way;
> Teach me to be pure and true,
> Show me what I ought to do.

That was more practical than most, which now seem impossibly sentimental:

> Jesus, tender Shepherd, hear me;
> Bless Thy little lamb tonight.

And, worst of all:

> Gentle Jesus, meek and mild,
> Look upon a little child.
> Pity my simplicity,
> Suffer me to come to Thee.

Meek, mild, pity, simplicity, suffer – words all off-putting to a lively child. Even less relevant was:

> Death and decay in all around I see,
> Help of the helpless, Lord, abide with me.

Evening service was at 6.30 p.m. No pew rent was paid, because that smacked of commercialism. Although that meant that the open pews were free for all, there was an atmosphere if anyone intruded without invitation, rather like my present irritation, even though we haven't a car, when someone parks in front of our driveway. Our pew was wooden, covered with hard and inadequate blue matting, had a ledge for hymn books and was the fourth away from the pulpit. No one sat in front of us. It was, therefore, embarrassingly obvious when Dad took out his watch – that same tooth-bitten gold watch I mentioned earlier. I have it still. Both parents considered twenty minutes quite adequate for a sermon; a longer affair indicated that the preacher was showing off.

In my *Treasury*, poems which now cause a cringe of disbelief hint at the contemporary religious atmosphere. I'll let you off with just one.

> *A Laugh in Church*
> (From *Our Dumb Animals*)
>
> She sat on the sliding cushion,
> The dear wee girlie of four;
> Her feet in their shiny slippers,
> Hung dangling over the floor.
> She meant to be good, she had promised;
> And so, with her big brown eyes,
> She stared at the painted windows,
> And counted the crawling flies.

Her thoughts wandered to bees in cherry trees, puppies asleep in a basket and which she could cuddle…

> Then a sudden ripple of laughter
> Ran over the parted lips,
> So quick that she could not catch it
> With her rosy finger-tips.
> The people whispered, 'Bless the child,'
> As each waked from a nap,
> But the dear little woman hid her face
> For shame, in her mother's lap.

Unbelievable, isn't it?

After saying a prayer in the vestry with the Society (that is, Methodist Society) Steward, usually Dad, the minister came in to stand at the reading desk. He wore a black suit, black shirt

front and full clerical collar. Nobody knelt for the opening and
subsequent prayers, even though hassocks (tuffets, or buffets,
pronounced similarly) were on the floor, for that would have
been ostentatious, nay, idolatrous, because Roman Catholics
did that. Actually, it would have been impossible for several of
the elderly members. Closed eyes and bent heads showed
respect rather than abasement.

The minister prayed, read a lesson from the Old Testament
and chose a couple of hymns. We didn't sing Amen to these.
Mother sang contralto, Dad tenor, from hymn books in Tonic
Solfa notation. This verged on magic as, standing between
them, I struggled to stick to the 'right' tune in, say,

> Yield not to temptation,
> For yielding is sin,
> Each vict'ry will help you
> Salvation to win.

Or, more loudly, as it had a rousing tune:

> Guide me, O Thou great Jehovah,
> Pilgrim through this barren land;
> I am weak, but Thou art mighty,
> Hold me with Thy powerful hand.
> Bread of Heaven! Bread of Heaven!
> Feed me now and evermore.
> [or 'Feed me till I want no more']

The last line was repeated. More pleasing was the modern and
understandable,

> For the strength of the hills we bless Thee,
> Our God, our Fathers' God.

I am still conditioned to the Victorian stereotype of Thee and
Thou rather than You, and to the Victorian tunes. Whilst I can

no longer accept the sentiments, these retain an emotional appeal.

Then the Collection was taken, by two men of course. The 'best' people had envelopes into which they put their covenanted (guaranteed) weekly sum, which remained confidential. I had to put my penny on the plate, wishing that it were a bag as in the C of E. The Steward did the accounts after the service.

In the meantime, the parson crossed from the reading desk in front of the rail which separated the Communion table from the congregation – no genuflecting, no making the sign of the cross, no bowing – and climbed the three or four winding steps into the pulpit to give his sermon, read any notices, announce the final hymn and say the last prayer.

One hymn at evening service sums up the day:

> The day Thou gavest, Lord, is ended,
> The darkness falls at Thy behest,
> To Thee our morning hymns ascended,
> Thy praise shall sanctify our rest.

One knew who was preaching from the notice board outside and from the published quarterly plan which covered the six or eight churches in the circuit. He could be professional or lay, that is, a Local Preacher. Whilst it was felt that they were not quite the real thing, these men (no women) were admired for their devotion but criticised for their tub-thumping.

Mr Little from Roskell Road was one such; he believed in extempore prayer, as the spirit moved; the trouble was that the spirit did not seem to know when to stop. An uncompromising and literal-minded fundamentalist, he was a thorn in my father's progressive approach.

The churches could not have survived without them. In the four years 1935–1939, forty-five different ones are named in my diary. Generally, my highest praise was 'not bad'. One poor man was 'very conceited as usual… awful as usual'; another was 'ghastly, did his best, I suppose'; a third had not only a terrible voice but 'painful conceit'; a fourth was unforgivably long-winded; a fifth 'mouldy', whilst with a sixth, I was 'bored stiff for fifty minutes'. A few were clearly favourites: Thoran Singha 'marvellous', Travis 'funny as usual' and Johnson 'exceedingly good'. Subsequently, two brave women were merely noted. One Sunday each year was given over to the LPMA, the Local Preachers' Mutual Aid. A neophyte had to preach a trial sermon before being accepted on the plan, but recruits were always needed to make up the necessary numbers. Dad was not a local preacher, partly because he was shy and partly because he preferred to work with people, but mainly because it smacked of vanity. He did not include in this criticism his much-loved brother-in-law Fred (who had actually introduced him to his future wife), a sincere Christian, who was a Methodist lay preacher and, by special dispensation, a respected Anglican lay reader.

When there was Holy Communion, more generally called the Lord's Supper, about once a month, the Poor Steward summoned the pewfuls in turn. Most knelt at the rail in front of the Lord's Table (a few could only lean) and closed their eyes for prayer. They received from the parson (it had to be a 'proper' one) a knob of white bread (cut up by the Poor Steward's wife; what was left over was thrown to the birds) and an individual goblet of non-alcoholic Communion wine, also prepared by the lady. Even in the year 2000, alcohol was still not allowed in Communion wine, nor, indeed, on church premises. Having drunk the wine, communicants replaced the goblets in holes in the rail. Lady members took it in turns to provide flowers.

Attending one's first Communion, after a few classes, took place when one was about thirteen and indicated a step towards membership and religious maturity. Although at the time I was impatient to join in, to be in the swim, I am now sure that the age is too low. There was no Confirmation.

The usual hymn confused me, both as to meaning and possibility:

> Take my life, and let it be
> Consecrated, Lord, to Thee.
> Take my moments and my days;
> Let them flow in ceaseless praise.

However, it was less combative than:

> Stand up, stand up for Jesus,
> Ye soldiers of the Cross.

One hymn remains attractive to me even now. It makes sense whether you regard God as a personal deity or as a moral sense. It has no known author and is taken from a book written in 1558.

> God be in my head,
> And in my understanding;
> God be in mine eyes,
> And in my looking;
> God be in my mouth,
> And in my speaking;
> God be in my heart,
> And in my thinking;
> God be at mine end,
> And at my departing.

On occasion, there was a Retiring Collection, voluntary on leaving the building as distinct from the compulsory contribution – for Basque refugees, for example, for hospitals, the Poor Fund, or to provide baskets of fruit for the sick or for some other similar worthy cause.

One Sunday morning when I did not go to morning service

remains vivid. I was left at home because I had been stung by a wasp, or 'wapsie'. I thought that this was a child's version of the words but it is apparently dialectal. The accepted treatment, a blue bag, had no effect whatsoever, and my arm swelled badly. Dr Warner, a young probationary doctor, happened to be in church and was told of this. He dashed to Hunts Cross and was lancing under my arm when my parents returned home. He saved my life, bless him. He died of old age in 2002. I was stung again when I was older; my arm was put in a sling and I missed school. I'm warning you that now I have to be rushed to hospital; I always carry emergency pills and ointment in the wasp season.

The church had a single, central, wide aisle, which was considered perfect for weddings. A grated grille (for umbrella drainage? holding walking sticks?) ran down each side of this aisle. We knew nothing of the other architectural or hallowed features – what was an apse? which was east or west?

The organ, played by Mr Barkla or, on rare occasions, by Neil, was activated by bellows worked by a lad – was it a penny a service or sixpence a month? I forget. He half crouched in a Black Hole of Calcutta behind it. A door led to the gloomy vestry; by it was an extremely tiny and filthy lavatory – no washbasin, no light.

Two pews sideways on to the aisle and in front of the organ constituted the choir which was mainly (entirely?) composed of the Fishy Smiths, always immaculately turned out. The father (bass) was the epitome of the adjective 'gnarled', being so crippled with arthritis, presumably because of his trade, that he was confined to a prehistoric wheelchair and so was an object of considerable curiosity. Enid (soprano) the youngest, my class teacher in the primary or beginners' department of the Sunday School, was a model of decorum. Herbert, a tenor who wrung his hands and showed white cuffs below his jacket sleeves, taught in the Juniors. Bea, contralto, wasn't always there; she spent time, I think, in a TB sanatorium. Edmund, the eldest, who always wore a straw hat in the shop, was the only one not to participate in St James' affairs. I have realised as I am writing that nothing was ever said about the mother; she was never seen, so presumably she had died.

My parents said that they smelt of fish. This was the first intimation that I had virtually no sense of smell; it's probably why I was welcomed into the choir when I was twelve or thirteen! I have since wondered how long the fishiness remained in the shop, or, for that matter, in the choir pews.

A rare practice was held before an event such as an anniversary or carol service. In my diary I noted not only that I sang solo in 'We Three Kings', but that I was 'very good too' – I had to blow my own trumpet!

The Church celebrated its anniversary, which was followed by a tea (1/-) and enjoyed rousing tunes, if not always suitable words:

> Let us with a gladsome mind
> Praise the Lord for He is kind,

with its chorus:

> For His mercies aye endure.
> Ever faithful, ever sure.

This, incidentally, was distinctly more cheerful than the seemingly endless poems which we read in English lessons such as Milton's *Il Penseroso* or the sad lines:

> When I consider how my light is spent
> Ere half my days in this dark world and wide,
> And that one talent which is death to hide
> Lodged with me useless…

and concluding in his blindness that:

They also serve who only stand and wait.

We also sang John Henry Newman's

Praise to the Holiest in the height,
And in the depth be Praise,
In all His words most wonderful,
Most sure in all His ways.

More hot-gospel type was an eighteenth-century one, especially written with a tune which allowed plentiful repetition.

All hail the Power of Jesu's name.
Let angels prostrate fall; let angels prostrate fall.
Bring forth the royal diadem
And crown Him, crown Him,
And crown Him Lord of all.

More belligerent, lovely to bellow unthinkingly, but upsetting to my father after the Great War, was that by Julia Ward Howe, a nineteenth-century American writer and philanthropist:

Mine eyes have seen the glory of the coming of the Lord:
He is trampling out the vintage where the grapes of wrath
  are stored,
He hath loosed the fateful lightning of His terrible swift
  sword:
His truth is marching on.

Other warmongering hymns such as 'Fight the good fight with all thy might' and 'Soldiers of Christ arise and put your armour on' were simply not in Dad's repertoire.

St James' participated in the anniversaries of the other churches of the circuit and in that of the Congers further up the High Street.

High Days and Holidays

There were special Sundays at Woolton. I was never allowed to attend the strangely named Watchnight Service, which saw in the New Year. The first Sunday in January was Covenant Sunday, for the annual renewal of vows. That also saw Promotion Day in Sunday School, a popular event, although the upgrading depended mainly on age.

I wasn't allowed to go carol singing, neither on my own because 'You don't need the money', nor with the choir because I'd be out too late. Hotpot suppers for various celebrations were not for me either.

For Harvest Festivals, the pulpit and reading desk were draped with corn stooks in the shape of a loaf, and the aisle ends on the pews were garlanded with flowers and we sang:

> Come, ye thankful people, come
> Raise the song of harvest home:
> All is safely gathered in
> E'er the winter storms begin.

or:

> We plough the fields and scatter
> The good seed on the land,
> But it is fed and watered
> By God's almighty hand.

Not that many of the congregation knew anything about farming. Also, too often, hymns lost their meaning through the verse form, for a breath was always taken at the end of each line regardless of sense, as in that second harvest hymn.

Easter meant fish on Good Friday (smoked haddock, boiled and rare, because of the expense), hot cross buns and chocolate Easter eggs on the Sunday. Relatives, especially my Auntie Florrie (she of the music book), strove to find bigger and bigger eggs with smaller eggs inside. Mother disapproved of this conspicuous spending, sure that her sister could not really afford it. Needless to say, I adored them, both gift and giver.

Strangely, both parents were against giving up anything for Lent; but it was pronounced a good opportunity for Joan to give up being a naughty girl. I think now that they were against the tokenism.

The hymns were peculiar:

> There is a green hill far away,
> Without a city wall,
> Where the dear Lord was crucified
> Who died to save us all.

Why was it worthy of note that a green hill had not got a wall belonging to a city? No one explained this archaic use of 'without' to me at the time.

Even more problematic was:

> When I survey the wondrous Cross
> On which the Prince of Glory died
> My richest gain I count but loss,
> And pour contempt on all my pride.

Are you thinking that I am putting too much emphasis on hymns by quoting so many? You see, they were such a large part of one's life; they help to give the feeling and atmosphere not only of church but of daily routine. There were hymns for every conceivable occasion, most of them written by either the Wesley brothers or nineteenth-century ladies, unmentioned in any reference books which I've consulted.

Half a dozen were addressed specifically to sinners, although many of the worst showing a morbid preoccupation with sin and death were not used at either Trinity or Woolton. For example:

> Oppressed with sin and woe
> A burdened heart I bear.

or:

> Rescue the perishing, care for the dying
> Snatch them in pity from sin and the grave.

Some were certainly incomprehensible to, and most unsuitable for, any young person.

> Rock of Ages, cleft for me,
> Let me hide myself in Thee…

written by an eighteenth-century gentleman with the marvellous name of Augustus Montague Toplady, or,

> Art thou weary, art thou languid, art thou sore distressed?
> Come to Me, saith one, and coming
> Be at rest…

to which the short answer was 'no'.

These hymns bound me to the church emotionally because I enjoyed belting them out, but at the same time repelled me because of their emotionalism, their terror and their illogicality (although I wouldn't have been able then to express it in this way) and particularly by their incomprehensibility and irrelevance to my own life.

> When I tread the verge of Jordan,
> Bid my anxious fears subside.
> Death of death and hell's destruction
> Land me safe on Canaan's side.

On Palm Sunday, everywhere was garlanded with catkins.

Weddings brought forth a crop of clichés. 'Happy is the

bride the sun shines on' (neither you nor I had a good start in that respect, did we?). 'Change the name and not the letter / Change for worse and not for better.' A bride should wear 'something old, something new, something borrowed, something blue'. Less cheerful was, 'Always a bridesmaid, never a bride', and more vulgar, 'Here comes the bride, / Large, fat and wide.'

Most evenings had some activity. Teacher-training class, taken by Dad, aimed to ensure that the volunteers not only knew what they were supposed to be doing and saying but that they understood it as well. There was once a Circuit Teachers' Conference. In due course, having enjoyed the classes, I became a primary school teacher, although my diary suggests that I 'had a terrible time at SS. Pandemonium' – good practice for my future career, perhaps? Anyway, I seemed to get the knack of it quite quickly. Dad kept himself up to date, with, for example, a convention at Ambleside, Bible classes, class meetings of members of the Society (that is, church members), which were sometimes acrimonious, and lectures and rallies within the circuit.

The Band of Hope functioned at circuit level as did the Quarterly Meeting. I never thought of this occurring every three months; it was simply what it was called. The Circuit Steward, a sort of liaison officer, was the most important of the three lay officers, above the local Society (or single church) Steward and the lowest of them all, the Poor Steward. Endless appeals and disputes made up a vigorous way of life.

The Wesley Guild held a weekly meeting, occasionally using the latest technology of a 'magic lantern', and an annual rally. An Intermediate Guild held a debate as to whether Christians should fight in wars. It appears that, aged fifteen, I addressed it during its Bottled Sunshine evening, with a description of our holiday at Castleton in the Isle of Man – more of that another time.

One reference, dating from 1934 or 1936 remains obscure

to me: 'Daddy went to Mrs Elizabeth Clarke's storytelling affair. He had to stand up. I was going but had homework – not fair as did want to go.' Not fair – the lament of children of every era.

Back to St James'. There were no youth clubs, although there was a Boys' Brigade, run by Mr Coulson (?) and viewed by the older generation with grave misgivings. I found their birthday party 'a good do'. The Scouts were frowned upon; perhaps the disapproval had something to do with the fact that, together with cousin Kathie and her husband Eddie, we were squashed on the ferry going over and I was trampled on subsequently by its members at the 1929 World Jubilee at Birkenhead. I was not allowed to join the Guides, especially upsetting as my school friend Mary was a member. This may have been in part because Dad, after the Great War, was fundamentally opposed to uniformed organisations, indeed to any uniform. In any case, the church was considered to provide for all needs. The baby version: 'Brownies, on your toadstools hop: one, pause, two', did not attract.

For Mother, there was the Mothers', later Women's, Bright Hour on Wednesday afternoons, 2–5 p.m., a get-together (for 'gassing') with tea, buns, cheap china and an uplifting address, and the Ladies' Sewing Meeting, with more delicate teacups and saucers, on Thursdays. Note the nice social distinctions. The former had an annual outing, once as far as Morecombe; a photo, taken probably at Southport, shows Mother carrying gloves, handbag and one of Dad's cases for sandwiches. She was wearing her bar-strap shoes, hat and a long crossover coat with buttons low down.

The sewing meeting existed mainly to make things – cross-stitched, braided aprons, patterned cushion covers, lavender bags, kettle-holders, pincushions – for displays, bazaars and sales of work. The number of aprons, pinafores, overalls and duchess sets (for dressing tables) must have been astronomical. Mother was reckoned to be a dab hand with her needle; she used a modern, that is, non-treadle but of course non-electric, Singer sewing machine. 'I'd like to make Joan an apron, but she'd never wear it,' she wailed years later. Once, I 'threaded three necklaces of beads for Mrs Griffiths for her brother in Jamaica' – probably to give to the 'natives', rather than for his own adornment. I also, once, did a lot of sewing – actually the hem on a green frock, 'beautifully done'! At one of their Christmas parties, I recited… as well as demolishing four jelly creams.

An imposing lady of independent means and with a gammy leg, Miss Wilson, who kept house for her bachelor brother, ran it with Mother in the upstairs schoolroom. Ladies took off their coats but kept their hats on as in *Last of the Summer Wine*. For years, having got to Woolton on the tram, I had to call on my way home from school to wait for her and we walked home together. However carefully I climbed the wooden stairs, I always shuddered to be greeted by the same remark from Miss Wilson week after week after week: 'Here comes Fairy Feet' to sycophantic laughter from the assembled eight or nine ladies. She wondered aloud why I didn't join in the laughter and never realised how much it hurt and depressed. I loathed Thursday afternoons and resented this regular humiliation.

I have since wondered much about Mother's concept of religion: did it mean more than these good works, busy-ness, even filling in time in a small world, a certain smugness, a lifeline to an insecure person? It seemed to have no deep spiritual root.

For sales of work and/or of cakes and sweets, as for parties, long trestle tables covered with white cloths were arranged in a large rectangle with one gap for entry and exit. Again, thick, dry, white sandwiches, buns and cakes formed the main attraction. Bran tubs, 3d and 6d, rarely yielded treasures.

Rummage sales were more exciting; the vast and unbeliev-able sum of £50 would be collected in amounts of ½d, 1d, 2d,

3d, rarely more, for the most unimaginable rubbish. The last remains were sold to dealers, and we all had baths to get rid of the ticks.

SEVEN
Sunday School

This deserves a letter to itself.

The commodious school building on the opposite side of the road, difficult to clean and heat, was built in the same exuberant style as the church. On the outside wall there recently seemed to be a State of the Finances' Appeal to turn it into a community centre. When we peeped inside, the floors and walls looked as if they were made of somewhat dirty concrete.

Through the door to the left was the smaller room for the juniors, up the stairs and above it that for the primaries (and the sewing meeting). The seniors functioned in the large schoolroom to the right on the ground floor.

Sunday School began at 2.30 p.m. Dad was the Superintendent, or Super; he loved it and the wider Sunday School Union in Liverpool and throughout the country. On the spot, it involved unhappy dealings with the caretaker, Smith (no relation of the Fishy Smiths), and his pasty-faced youngsters.

As well as having responsibility for all the organisation and all collections and distributions of money, he was in charge of the seniors. When old enough, I occasionally mishandled the wheezy harmonium for him. He leaned over backwards not to show favouritism, which meant, in fact, that he sometimes penalised his daughter, for example, in respect of prizes.

Numbers remained good; the only exception was the annual recurrence of Jump Sunday before the Aintree Grand National only a few miles away, when people walked the course. This generated much high spirits and betting as well as absenteeism.

Two maiden ladies were also involved. Miss Bertha Hopkins took the beginners, Miss Lilian Bridgewater the juniors. Hops and Lilac (or Lyle as in Tate and Lyle, not that any of us dared to call her thus) lived together in Stuart Avenue, a social step above Roskell Road and were therefore regarded as somewhat snobbish, especially Miss Bridgewater, who had independent means and did not go out to work. Hops was a more cheerful, less censorious soul who worked in town. Spinsters, of whom there were a great many after the unimaginable slaughter of the Great War, frequently shared accommodation; often one was dominant, but there was no hint – even I was old enough to sense – of anything 'funny' or 'improper' between them, especially not of these two. Fond of Miss Hopkins, frightened of Miss Bridgewater, I was more interested in their elderly black spaniel, Rags, and was often indignant on his behalf when he was taken for granted or told to behave. Kay Barkla, also unmarried, helped out occasionally.

Sunday School consisted of a hymn, a prayer and an address by the respective Superintendent. Dad took enormous trouble with his preparation. Children then dispersed to classes; they encircled their appropriate teacher who mulled over a Bible story (according to national instructions) in the hope of extracting a moral, or did 'expression work', namely drawing or writing to illustrate the story.

The return to the three full assemblies meant a collection (½d or 1d), a final hymn and prayer. The Sunday School hymn book must have had some suitable hymns, but few remain in my head and I haven't traced a copy. Perhaps the most encouraging was Bunyan's 'Who would true valour see / Let him come hither'. Some words bewildered: 'This our sacrifice of praise', 'The Lord's my shepherd / I'll not want.' No one saw the need to explain.

Christmas parties were hearty, noisy affairs, with games such as Sardines (to see how many could be crammed into a small space), Oranges and Lemons, Tug of War (too dangerous for me to be allowed to participate) and Blind Man's Buff; Postman's Knock gave a great sense of naughtiness. The meal was eaten at endless trestle tables. There was usually a nativity play. Incidentally, we always wrote Christmas in full; 'Xmas' was near blasphemy.

The Anniversary no longer meant a new and totally useless white dress as it had done for Mother's generation, although there was usually a new, or nearly new dress, one with disliked lace collar and cuffs. It did involve much practising of hymns, recitations and, for the Monday evening, a simple play. When I was fourteen, I copied out the play parts, read the lesson, acted and 'played' the piano. In 1938, Dad's last anniversary at Woolton, there was a production of *The Good Samaritan*. He kept the programme and almost all the names are familiar still: George Baker, Walter Cliffe, Jimmy Radcliffe, the Wilson boys, and, in *The Pearl Merchants*, Vera Griffiths, Betty MacDonnell, Audrey Poulter. They remain fixed in my mind as they were then, sixteen and seventeen years old. Where are they now?

A Young Methodism Rally and a Young People's Sunday also took place.

The annual Sunday School Treat was held, first in Woolton Woods, later by train or charra (charabanc) to Ainsdale – more select than Southport, which, anyway, was boring when the tide went out about a mile. It involved races, plain and three-legged, and French cricket on the extensive sands, but not paddling or bathing (too much responsibility, probably), then a one-mile trek back to the stark local Sunday School for mugs of tea served from huge urns and sandwiches of potted meat which Mother helped to make and prepare. She took no other part in Sunday School.

In 1937, we took the train to Garston, walked to Allerton station, 'talked to all the boys. In carriage with JR, walked to Frodsham Hill'; amongst attractions other than J, there was putting and a ventriloquist. One year, an intermediate group went as far as Rhyl.

These were for long the only parties I knew. I was never invited then to private parties – I wonder why. The isolation of Hunts Cross? The overprotectiveness of Mother who would also not have wished to reciprocate? No one my age? Was I simply different? objectionable? or just odd?

EIGHT
Back to Church

Missionaries

Church and Sunday School were often visited by missionaries to 'the heathen' or 'lesser breeds without the law... in foreign fields'. They sometimes spent a night or two at our house. They worked unceasingly and with the best of intentions, but the attitude now seems to have been patronising, not unlike that of the most considerate rich towards their servants.

I kept two letters from Harry Buckley, from Mission Protestante, Dahomey, West Africa, now Benin. The first, dated February 1934, was typed, as he had a stiff right arm. After good wishes to my parents and hopes that Christmas was a happy time, he expected that I would be back at school, 'working hard and learning all sorts of things... Well here I am far away in Dahomey, over 200 kilometres inland – I wonder if you can change that into miles. I think if you multiply by five and divide by eight you will get the number of miles I am away from the sea' – and from the nearest missionary also.

Dassa was almost a town, and had a King, Abissi, whose rule had been curtailed by the French government, 'which is a good thing for many of his people'. He explained paganism, fetishes, charms and sacrifices in clear and satisfying detail – 'they are very superstitious. That is a long word isn't it, but your Dad will explain it to you. Perhaps you know what it means'. Heavens, I was already twelve! Christmas brought together about a thousand people for service, a dinner (roasted bullock) and games (races, climbing up a greasy pole), somewhat spoiled by a fire which destroyed six huts. Life was strenuous, as he had twenty-seven churches to look after, some a hundred miles away.

The second letter is dated almost exactly a year later. He sent greetings to all. 'What a lot of questions you do ask' – such as what the Sahara is like (too far away), native missionaries (none), the King (not really intelligent and lets other natives advise him wrongly). He gave news of the opening of four more churches built of a sort of mud, and sent photos of youngsters and family. Best of all, he sent weird and wonderful stamps for my collection.

He wrote another letter from the Gold Coast; Mr Moritawa included his name in Japanese symbols.

A distinct glory was attached to being a missionary, although I wondered aloud, and in her hearing, whether May Myerscough's skin had turned yellow when she was in China with her blind husband. Friends from Trinity days, they were deeply admired for their physical and emotional courage. She, interestingly, wrote in Mother's autograph album:

> The thing we long for, that we are
> For one transcendent moment.

We sang:

> From Greenland's icy mountains,
> From India's coral strand,
> Where Afric's sunny fountains
> Roll down their golden sand,
> From many an ancient river,
> From many a palmy plain,
> They call us to deliver
> Their land from error's chain.

We thought of the hills of the North, the isles of the Southern Seas (coral again), the lands of the East, the shores of the utmost West, and felt that in the

City of God, the bond are free;
We come to live and reign in Thee.

When I was thirteen, I answered a matriculation question of thirty-five minutes on Dr Grenfell of Labrador, having received his book as a Scripture prize. The essay contains no original material or thought. 'There are few men who have done such great work that they are recognised in their own day and generation as being real missionaries and apostles of peace', and, even more prosaically, 'a very interesting book for those who wish to know more is his autobiography, obtainable at 7/6 and an abridged edition at 3/6'. I don't suppose that you have ever heard of him. I concluded with Robert Louis Stevenson, for we were encouraged to quote – you may have already noticed that this recommendation at least has stuck!

Home is the sailor home from sea
And the hunter home from the hill.

At a general rally, we heard speakers such as Mr Joshua on Evangelism Abroad, and saw films including *On Trek Through Central Africa and China*. At one such, I was asked to take up the collection – a proud moment.

Another proud moment for Dad came when I was the youngest presenter of purses (that is, of monies collected) at a church garden party on the outskirts of Liverpool.

There was also an annual Missionary Sunday held in one's own church.

Fund-raising

To digress slightly: I had three specific church tasks, which I undertook initially with enthusiasm and eventually tried to avoid through embarrassment, with shame at being importunate, almost blackmailing. The first was a Missionary Collecting Card; on it were listed the names of regular subscribers who had promised to pay a penny or even a ha'penny per week (4/4 or 2/2 per year) or threepence, or, the few 'rich', sixpence. Paying an annual lump sum would have been so much easier and more profitable. I had to go round and ask them on Saturdays and Sundays.

If £5 were collected in one year (that is, 1,200 pennies), one received a sort of brooch on a ribbon. Similar amounts in succeeding years were rewarded with a dated metal medal slipped over the ribbon which was worn on the lapel at the annual Missionary Rally in the Central Hall. No other badges or symbols were allowed at home. Something big, I've forgotten what, was promised if one achieved ten such rewards. I, fortunately, gave up the whole business after nine. My first effort in 1931 netted £5 4s 11d; amounts rose steadily to reach £11 6s 10d (at what a cost) before falling back heavily.

The four-page lists of Liverpool medallists for six years was printed by the Wesley Press, New Ferry. Collectors varied in number between 101 and 198; a handful were grown-ups, the majority girls. Amounts varied too between £5 and £55; we felt that this last didn't really count as the collector was an adult (Miss Cissie Bate). The average annual total was about £1,300; the Thirties slump caused an average drop of about £200. There was most un-Christian rivalry throughout areas, circuits and churches, St James' being as guilty as any. It was most unfair to compare the 'top', Wallasey in the Wirral, with the 'bottom', Everton Road.

The second 'good works' also involved money, but was mercifully only once a year. Daisy Day meant shaking a collection tin at all and sundry on behalf of the NCHO, the National Children's Home and Orphanage, considered vastly superior, because more religious and less commercial, to Dr Barnardo's, which catered for all sorts of riff-raff. Even some of their collectors were regarded as not above suspicion. I have no way of knowing whether there was any foundation for these views. There were also NCHO envelopes to distribute and collect.

I found an NCHO letter from the YLU (Young/Youth?

League? Union?), Highbury Park, London, N5, dated 25 February 1929. I reproduce it as it was written.

DEAR JOAN

THANK YOU EVER SO MUCH FOR THE SILVER PAPER YOU HAVE SENT TO ME FROM ALL YOUR FRIENDS AND AUNTS AND UNCLES. I AM VERY PLEASED TO HAVE IT AND WE HAVE NOW GOT ONE THOUSAND AND TWENTY POUNDS FROM SILVER PAPER. ALL GOES TO THE YLU HOSPITAL. I WISH YOU COULD COME DOWN AND SEE IT SOME TIME. YOU WOULD ENJOY SEEING ALL THE WEE GIRLS AND BOYS BEING MADE WELL AND STRONG.

BEST LOVE

YOUR DEAR FRIEND

GEORGE A. PARKINSON

On the other side of the page is a postscript:

MY LOVE TO ALL THE AUNTS AND UNCLES AND BEGINNERS, PRIMARIES AND JUNIORS. TELL THEM ALL TO 'KEEP ON KEEPING ON' COLLECTING FOR US.

Less frequently, one collected money for the Sunshine Home for Blind Babies, or goods suitable for Parcels for the Poor.

The third involved taking sweets, but mainly chocolates, usually on Saturday mornings, to various houses, Mother having got her stock at discount prices. This hateful chore, another blackmail, was in aid of church funds. In my memory, Mars bars were tuppence each, Kit Kats one penny or two; also in the box were Aero, white chocolate (regarded as a miracle), Caramello, Rowntree's, Terry's and Cadbury's bars and slabs, Rolo, Quality Street and Crunchie bars.

Better by far was the occasional Mile of Pennies; no harm there, no distasteful jobs, and a splendid sight.

Scripture examinations

To return to Sunday School matters. The National Sunday School Union ran Scholars' Scripture examinations, for which I possess two large and ornate certificates, that for 1935 ('best paper') having vanished. The first, dated 9 March 1936, has the details framed by a picture of Jesus, a child with loaves, and expectant multitudes; the second, a year later, has Jesus and the Roman centurions. Each certificate is signed, legibly, by R. T. Annesley, Hon. Sec. Examinations Committee. Examiners, two to each grade – Lower and Upper Junior, Lower Middle and Intermediate – are named. Over the years, there were seven Reverends and two Esquires.

The 1936 subject was 'The First Missionaries of Christ', for which I received the Certificate of Merit, First Class, despite 'feeling very shaky on Paul', never a favourite, 'and the whole bang lot'. 1937 concerned Jesus the King, a similar certificate, but with Honours, actually with 100%. Surprised?

939 candidates for first- and second-class certificates and prizes collected 835 awards one year; they included Baptists (213), Congregationalists (75), Methodists (139; I was the only one from Woolton), Presbyterians (363) and unusual groups such as Bankhall Mission (79). A. C. Mitchell Memorial (47), Protestant Reformers (only five but all passing) and Hebron Mission (13). I doubt if I knew even then what they were.

Several Prize Distribution programmes survive. In May 1935, at the YMCA (Young Men's Christian Association) Large Hall, Mount Pleasant in town at 7 p.m., the Lord Mayor (Alderman F. T. Richardson) presided and his wife distributed the prizes.

O Lord of Heaven and earth and sea
To Thee all praise and glory be;

How shall we show our love to Thee
Who givest all?

This opening hymn was followed by a Scripture reading and prayer (Rev. W. Bramwell Jones, MA), then another rousing hymn:

Fling out the banner! Let it float
Skyward and seaward, high and wide.

I wonder now what banner.

The examination report by the Hon. Sec. was followed by Oak Vale Sunday School Choir's 'selected item', the Chairman's address, and, at last, the distribution of prizes. Two more selected items were divided by the inevitable collection, then followed the presentation of the Mrs John Lee Memorial Shield to the winning Sunday School, yet another selected item, the presentation of packets of certificates to school officers, thanks (President and Rev. Nichol Grieve, MA, Chairman Examinations Committee) and the finale was, it now seems, a most inappropriate hymn:

Oft in sorrow, oft in woe,
Onward, Christians, onward go.

A value-for-money evening.

1937's programme was almost identical in format. The Lord Mayor was Alderman W. Denton and this time the choir came from Richmond Baptist. They sang 'Skye Boat Song', 'Lass with the delicate air', 'Come, see where golden-hearted spring' and 'I vow to thee, my country'. Hymns were 'Praise, my soul, the King of Heaven', 'Ye fair hills of Galilee' and 'God bless our native land'. The second verse of this last has an antiquarian charm.

O Lord, our monarch bless [that is, George VI]
With strength and righteousness
    Long may he reign!

His heart inspire and move
With wisdom from above;
And in a nation's love
    His throne maintain.

The religious newspaper report revealed the regretted absence of the Lord Mayor, but his spouse made a speech in his stead. Mr Heyworth, President, 'maintained a spirit of good-natured chaff throughout the evening... The scholars' applause was, as usual, irrepressible, and the dainty singing of the Choir was an added grace.' The examiners, 'and all upon whom the work of the Examination had fallen', were heartily thanked. Liverpool regained the Ogden Challenge Shield, so 'the examination season of 1937 closes with congratulations to all concerned'.

People

The bigwigs of Woolton village, the Atkinsons, did, I believe, rent a pew. They lived in the big house, the grounds of which they magnanimously lent for an occasional sale. He wore pince-nez and at one time was Society Steward. Although, or maybe perhaps because, I was once invited for tea, they did not fraternise, so were snubbed as snobs. At this distance in time, I cannot blame their wish to keep themselves to themselves. Mr and Mrs Bernard Stott also were not short of a bob (a shilling); they were intelligent and kind to a hobbledehoy, but this time Mother felt securely superior: they had no children. Hannah Fawcett was one of the church mice just as Bea Helms had been at Trinity.

Ken was a grown-up young man from Hunts Cross. He was, therefore, much to be envied, indeed pursued. He worked in the Sunday School although it was felt that he lacked self-discipline – he smoked. He it was who saved his cigarette cards and their relevant albums for me, which caused me great excitement. My mortification came when Teddy was mentioned to Ken – who laughed. Relations were never the same again.

The name Duggie haunts me: was it he who worked the bellows for the church organ?

J. was my first boy friend (not boyfriend) since the play-mates in Liverpool 8. Giving me Egyptian stamps (he must have been a junior in some trading firm in town) – fine, but he made the unforgivable mistake, poor lad, of buying me two presents: Evening in Paris perfume, and, more rewarding, Black Magic chocolates. These purchases seemed a cheeky assumption of proprietorial rights – and that was the end of J. I trust that he found a more responsive girl.

My parents made friends with the ministers, who, after being invited to give a sermon, were, if the result was considered acceptable, offered an appointment for three years, although this tenure could be extended, with the agreement of all the other ministers in the circuit, to five or, the maximum, seven years.

Dad approved of Maude Royden, fifteen years his senior, who had done social work in Liverpool and worked for women's suffrage. Although an Anglican, she became minister of the City Temple for three years, but the first woman actually ordained into the Methodist ministry came only in 1973. He applauded this innovation, Mother did not – woman's place, etc.

I was not charitably disposed to the senior minister in the circuit, the Rev. Gordon Edge, 'gobbly, voluble', although conceding that at times he was 'quite good'. He once fell over (clambering into the pulpit? crossing the aisle?) which, to a heartless youngster, made an entertaining change.

I remember several at St James' – such as the Bacons, the

same Rev. F. Paul who had officiated at my parents' wedding in 1917. He once gave a lecture on 'No New Laws for Life', which I described then as just Mr Baconish. Dad was slightly envious (not jealous) of the couple's intellectual compatibility. He made two entries in Mother's autograph book; the first before the Great War, from Robert Louis Stevenson:

> Keep on looking for the bright, bright skies,
> Keep on hoping that the sun will rise,
> Keep on singing when the whole world sighs,
> And you'll get there in the morning.

The second, almost twenty years later, in 1932, was from Samuel Johnson:

> If the man who turnips cries,
> Cry not when his father dies,
> 'Tis a proof that he had rather
> Have a turnip than a father.

Even then, although I could not have expressed it, the logic seemed faulty.

His wife, Evelyn, wrote a lengthier contribution on New Year's Day, 1932. The author was unknown:

> When I feel in the blues and am down in the mouth,
> When I'm stuck in the North and I want to go South,
> When the world seems a blank and there's none that I
> love,
> And it seems it's all cloud with no sun above,
> When I feel discontented with all that's my lot,
> I think of the things I am glad I am not.
> A bird in a cage, a fish in a bowl,
> A wolf in a trap, a mouse in a hole,
> A bear in a pit, a bell on the door,
> A fowl on a spit, a mat on the floor!

> When I think of all the things I might be
> I go down on my knees and thank God that I'm me!
> Then my blues disappear when I think what I've got,
> And quite soon I forget all the things I have not.

I like the realism of 'quite soon'. I wonder if this was chosen especially for Mother? Evelyn was a 'jolly good' lay preacher.

The Rev. William Hurtley (Nobby) Clarke later performed the same marriage ceremony for us. An engaged but shy bachelor in his first church, he was a good man. Rev. C. J. Dugard, a Channel Islander I think, came with his new wife. He was replaced by Rev. and Mrs A. J. Stanbury, whose house was immediately burgled. They were the most frequent visitors and I enjoyed greatly their hospitality to me, which perhaps coloured my approval of his preaching.

Others are just names in a diary now: Moralee, Wesley Sainty, Le Poidevin (another Channel Islander, pronounced Pedvin and meaning, they said, 'unrecognised', but I suspect something more vinous), Ravenscroft.

Congregation members may have criticised the ministers' actions, their choice of wives or their discourses, but there was enormous respect for their sacerdotal functions.

Occasionally, there were visitors such as the Cliff College Fundamentalists, 'hot' preachers, although we didn't know the term. They took over for a whole Sunday and terrified most of us with their stories of Hellfire and made us feel uncomfortable by their lack of reticence. Most revivalist hymns were strong on repetition but somewhat short on substance.

> We have heard a joyful sound: Jesus saves!
> Spread the gladness all around: Jesus saves!

Margaret Drabble has aptly called such meetings 'emotional binges'. The effect was transitory as they did not really belong.

We put up the occasional travelling preacher or evangelist for the night.

Effects on daily life

V. S. Pritchett commented that 'the forms of Protestantism among which I was brought up taught one to think rigidly in terms of right and wrong'. I wholeheartedly agree. One's whole life, in trivia as in big things, was affected by it. Always in the background was the off-putting title of Wordsworth's 'Ode to Duty', 'Stern daughter of the voice of God'.

Newspapers, Monday to Saturday: Dad read the *LDP*, the *Liverpool Daily Post*, to give it its full title, usually after the evening meal. The evening *Echo* was deemed common; I can still hear the newsvendors' cry – 'Last City Ekker' – the voice dipping on the 'Ekk'. The *Manchester Guardian* would have meant having ideas above our station; workers (that is, manual) bought the *Daily Herald*. For weeklies, Dad enjoyed the then successful *Punch* (1/-) and *John O'London's Weekly*, but didn't buy them regularly as he did the *Sunday School Chronicle*, the *Methodist Recorder* and, once we had a wireless, the *Radio Times*, the only means then of knowing what was going on. More lively periodicals such as *Picture Post* and *Lilliput* belonged to the future.

Even school work was affected, so that, in English, I wrote 'A Modern Parable' when I was fifteen. Two brothers were trudging along the sea cliff. The boaster praised his own self-confidence, the lowly one felt poor, weak and helpless. But who saved the rabbit in the trap? 'Poor brother's eyes were lit up with joy at having been of service to one of God's little creatures. Rich brother turned round and tears ran down his cheeks. "Oh, brother mine! Clothes do not make the man." ' Oh, brother! Oh dear!

Raffles (but not bran tubs), buying on the never-never and betting were all sinful. One dreadful day, Dad had agreed to put his sixpence into the office draw on the Grand National. It goes without saying that he won. He wept, Mother wept, I wept because I feared that he had bought a first-class direct ticket to Hell. The prize was handed on to whoever came second in the sweep. He should have known better as he had once been persuaded into buying a raffle ticket for some good cause; after all, the chances of winning were slim. Of course, he won – a Christmas turkey, which had to be returned to the good cause. Some girls at school ran an illicit sweepstake; fortunately, it was well beyond my comprehension.

In this atmosphere of intense and narrow respectability, even the idea of being a farthing in debt was abhorrent, the idea of wasting anything equally so. On the good side, I learned the value of thrift.

Strong Drink was abhorred as the root of all evil, of all moral degeneration, of all broken or unhappy marriages. It was always the man's fault, needless to say. Even medicinal brandy was refused, as partakers would end up in the gutter. In this atmosphere, I 'signed the pledge' at an absurdly early age, eleven or twelve. It surprises me that such an anti-alcohol pair as my parents should not have joined the Band of Hope – possibly because it was open to non-Methodists. The first question about any newcomer was 'Is he TT?', that is, teetotal. 'My drink is water bright.' I wrote many a lurid story against the demon drink. Temperance Sunday was celebrated with gusto.

Smoking was nearly as bad – not for reasons of health, but because it was a waste of money and made a mess. I never smoked in their house or in their presence. Swearing was, of course, out of the question.

The general rigidity has been well expressed by H. E. Bates when referring to his father as not merely devoted to the Methodist faith, but positively locked in its uncompromising straitjacket. For too many, it was often un-Christian in its scorn for other denominations or weaker brethren.

Whilst chapels, Bethels, tin tabernacles and sects were considered the *social* inferiors of the Church of England, so, as there were very few rich Methodists, there was a tremendous sense of *personal* superiority, a fearsome and irreligious smugness, that of the minority elect. After all, the Wesley brothers had had to leave the C of E, hadn't they? John Wesley's bicentenary in 1938 was a great occasion for belting out his hymns and listening to his praises. The C of E had vulgar bells and advocated 'churching' after a birth and ten to fourteen days' rest, to 'cleanse'. As for Catholics, the hatred was extreme, although for my father, only for the institution, its set-up, ceremonies and doctrines and not for the misguided worshippers.

Minorities had to be respected – but not too much. Baptists believed in total immersion, so they were up to no good. The Sally Army – surely God did not like uniforms, and they were always asking for money. Congers were acceptable on sufferance as being undemanding and 'almost like us'. Unitarians – well, what did *they* stand for?

The Wesleyans were even a step above the Prims (Primitive) and the United members of the Methodist Connexion (I wondered why the spelling differed from connection, as in trains) – both of them were unimportant and slightly renegade. 'United' implied that compromises had been made somewhere along the line.

We were with God; this was exciting to a lonely, only child. According to different age groups, reactions differed towards belonging to a scorned minority, to being a direct descendant, in a sense, of John and Charles Wesley; obnoxious pride as a youngster, calm confidence as a grandparent, acceptance, indifference or the shudders in between. The whole set-up stifled enquiry, especially of the basic, fundamental kind.

What is left for me is a residual fear of abandoning it all, strong willpower, an insatiable desire to question and the Protestant work ethic.

Despite all this, I learned my first ribaldry, albeit mild, through church and church connections on holiday.

> We three Kings of Orient are,
> One in a bus and one in a car,

> One on a tricycle,
> Sucking an icicle,
> Following yonder star.

And:

> While shepherds washed their socks by night,
> All seated round the tub,
> A bar of Sunlight soap came down
> And they began to rub.

It had to be Sunlight because that was manufactured at Port Sunlight, 'over the water' in the Wirral.

My diary notes that 13 August 1939 was 'MY LAST TIME' at Woolton after 'a fight with Chris' in Sunday School, a protagonist and drama now totally forgotten.

The Hinchcliffe Family, possibly 1910.
Back row: Amy, Ethel(?), Edie(?), Florrie(?), Gertie(?), Beattie, Fred.
Front row: Bert, Granny, Charlie, Granddad.

Amy and John's wedding, April 1917

Granny and Granddad in the garden of 12 The Mount, early 1920s

Joan, 1923

Joan, Carrington Street, 1923

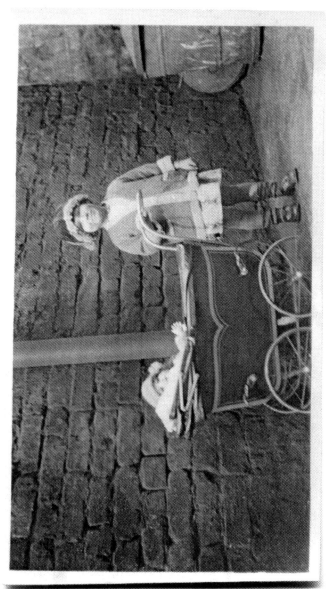

Joan with Dorothy Green in the pram, Normanby Street, 1924

Granny in her best dress, 1926, aged seventy

Mother and Leslie, mid-1920s

Joan in her best dress, 1923 or 1924

Skipper Sardine at 12 The Mount

Dad, camp at Marshbrook, 1926

A not-untypical birthday card from Aunt Edie, 1920s

Dolls' tea party, Roskell Road (notice Wilfred with the ears and black doll), 1927 or 1928

Mother, Miss Amy and Joan, 1927

LEWIS'S
YO-YO
CLUB

Miss Joan Cherry

has been elected a Member
of Lewis's Yo-Yo Club,
having passed the preliminary
three tests.

LEWIS'S Ltd.

Yo-yo certificate, early 1930s

Sunday School Union certificate, 1936

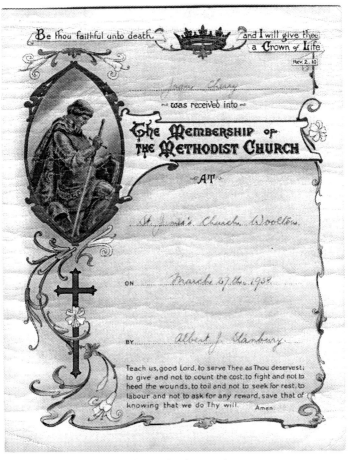

Church membership certificate

School garden party, 1935

Holidays: North Wales, mid-1930s

Holidays: Saltburn, 1935

THE SILVER JUBILEE, MAY 6th, 1935

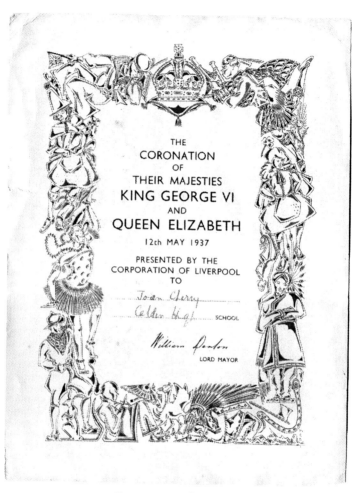

THE
CORONATION
OF
THEIR MAJESTIES
KING GEORGE VI
AND
QUEEN ELIZABETH
12th MAY 1937

PRESENTED BY THE
CORPORATION OF LIVERPOOL
TO

Joan Cherry

Calder High SCHOOL

William Denton

LORD MAYOR

Coronation certificate, 1937

Sixth form, Calder High School, 1938
Back row: Helen Guthrie, Jean Monether, Greta Pearlman.
Front row: Betty Davidson, Peggy Sharp, Joan Cherry, Mary Dunn, Biffy Smith.

Miss Macrae, Calder High School

Sixth form, Calder High School

Prefect, Calder High School, 1938

Mary, a visitor and Joan.
Garden party, Calder High School, 1938.

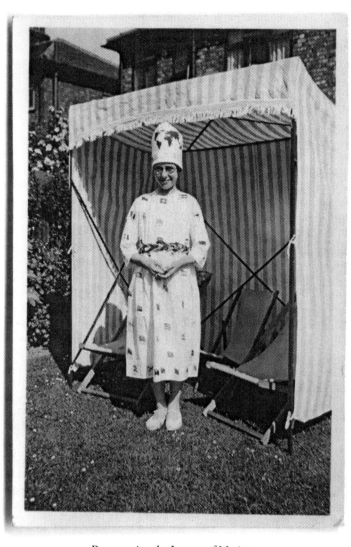

Representing the League of Nations.
Another garden party, Calder High School, mid-1930s.

Stratford, 1936

Three generations, 1937

In Kathie's garden, Shropshire

In Normandy with Domi, 1938

NINE

Fairlie

Getting to school

There was another high feature. Above all, I had only the village acquaintances, mainly older and, let's be honest, dimmer, to play with, no one I could call 'our kid', only myself to talk to, so I longed with passion mixed with terror to go to school. There was no compulsory early starting age then.

The tiny local one was attached to the C of E, so that could not do. Woolton had a free elementary school, but the rough children of workers in the stone quarry or Garston Docks would be there, so that wouldn't do either for this tiny, nervy and so unsociable child, made uglier by heavy gold-rimmed spectacles, with their clumsily constructed bar to spare the growing nose; they were torture as well as being conspicuous. 'Look at old four-eyes, ha ha!' Later tortoiseshell frames were better, but three cheers for modern plastic. Freckles too were an embarrassing point of amusement when compared with attractive dimples.

So it had to be a private establishment, although it cost a guinea each term, which seems, in retrospect, to have been daylight robbery. It was the best start my parents knew and could manage as, although I didn't know it at the time, Dad's Inland Revenue post had meant a marked drop in salary.

The only possible institution, then, was the Kindergarten Fairlie, with the emphasis on the second syllable. This meant catching the 8.33 a.m. train from Hunts Cross. The then awe-inspiring station house with its oil lamps on strong metal

chains was boarded up when, in 1997, it was put up to let.
Mother conducted the six-year-old me daily, except on the
awful occasion when the alarm clock failed and both parents
woke up late, as Mother had had a bilious attack. Dad picked
up the weeping mass and carried it to the station for the 8.39
and pleaded – in vain – with the Headmistress that I should
not receive a 'mark', as it was 'not the child's fault'. The fact
was marked on the end-of-term report and never forgotten by
Mother: just one more proof that she couldn't leave anything
to anybody.

Normally, clutching my contract (season ticket) Third
Class (now called 'standard'), I crossed the bridge to the
platform of wooden planks for the Liverpool Central train, not
that there was any other possible destination on that side. Our
dim little halt, at which only the local trains stopped, is now a
clean new terminus. As the train shuddered in, the platform
shuddered too. Then the stationmaster or a fellow traveller
would help me to pull down the heavy handle to open the
door of the Ladies Only carriage, and give me a hand up the
two steps. The porter on the platform blew his whistle and
waved a proper flag. Each separate compartment took three (or
was it four?) on each side. If such a designated carriage did not
arrive at a point convenient to where I was standing, I had been
instructed to get into one with a lady in it; I often wondered
why – another grown-up notion, no doubt. Mother's sole
sexual advice and instruction was 'Don't let them touch you',
which did not help later with teenage physical and other
problems. Anyone who began to mention physical parts or
reactions was stopped by a curt 'Not in front of the child',
varied, incomprehensibly, by 'little pitchers have big ears'.

A few minutes later, at the next stop, which was Garston, I
had to crank open the door, clamber down the two steps to the
platform, close the carriage door, display my contract to the
ticket collector, walk through the booking hall, climb up the
steps, cross the bridge with its trellis-type sides and, still

blinded by the smoke from the engine, struggle down the steps to the opposite platform, cross an alley – and there was the house.

A hectic beginning to quite a day for a protected six-year-old.

Learning

It was really a Dame School, although this name was no longer in use. Schools such as Fairlie were bought in the same way as shops. We always said Preparatory in full. It was all positively Victorian.

The Headmistress, Miss Edwards, was a lady of comfortable size and dress, well-intentioned, but qualified only in the sense that she owned the building. She spoke and wrote pleasantly – it was hoped that this would rub off on us. She could strike awe into a tiny tot.

Gold-bespectacled Miss Blacklock, the senior of the two teachers, had ginger hair twisted into ear-plaits, or earphones. She did most of the instruction, such as it was. I now suspect that while we copied out our Tables, she was getting one or two sums ahead of us. Still, she came from Wesley Avenue, so was deemed acceptable.

The other lady, thin as a beanpole, was known by us as Miss Wigwam; her real name (Wigram, perhaps?) is lost in the mist of time. She took the babies. Like the piano-teaching Miss Jones, she too was youngish, black-haired, permanently wore drooping black and had a dewdrop on the end of her nose. She sniffed her way sentimentally. There was also an elderly, noisily snuffly maid – Bessie, I think. Such were my first human contacts on my own.

The school accepted all ages, although it could not cater for them. There were three rooms. Forms (not the plebeian classes or standards) I and II (the school proper) shared the same one; this made chorus work agreeably useless.

Like H. G. Wells, I was one of those fortunate youngsters

who take readily to schoolwork. I was put with Miss Wigwam into the kindergarten that September, and given a slate and ear-damaging slate pencil. My ears still wince at the memory of that shrill scraping. Mind you, the chalk on the one and only blackboard squeaked. I was instructed to draw. Unable to draw, I began to write – so I was put up into the Lower First within a week. When Miss W. who, economically, looked after both classes, discovered that I could also read, she washed her hands of me and I was promoted to form I. When I could add up simple numbers and as I was hopeless at hemming a handkerchief, I reached form II – all this before the first Christmas! All very 'umfadoodlum' – or bewildering.

There were five of us in my new – and final – form. A boy with cropped dark hair and a sombre countenance – was *his* name Duggie? – had a desk to himself on the left. He wore a little grey suit and a school cap. Long trousers came only with youth. A four-seater, four inkwell-holed desk, with pen grooves, was shared by four girls, each with our own bit. I remember nothing about the three of them. We had no contact with any other pupils, nor with each other out of school.

Miss Blacklock stood with a book in her left hand, a long ruler in her right with which she pointed to the blackboard. Previous pupils had had the joy of a cane; I recall no physical punishment, although it was uncomfortable to sit, and stand when required, with our hands crossed behind our backs.

Writing: fortunately, we soon graduated to paper and, wisely, pencils. We first learned with curved strokes, then copperplate in copybooks with lines comparable with music staves. I could write but these copybooks retarded the process as I couldn't keep to the lines – hence, I blotted my copybook, so I wasn't as bright as I thought I was. In fact, I was just a nuisance. There was a plain sheet on which we drew horizontal lines with the aid of a ruler; mine refused to go straight – they still do. Joined-up writing, or cursive script, came later. If one's writing leaned backwards, that was bad; it apparently indicated a somewhat shifty nature. If anyone started with the left hand (known in our house as 'left kek') as I did, the pencil or crayon was firmly transferred; the secondary meaning of gauche persisted.

We progressed to a pen, a longish wooden instrument, which could accommodate two kinds of nib: a pointed one, which too often crossed, and a rectangular one, the latter called a relief nib. Both spattered, so that we needed pen-wipers. China inkwells were filled, often overfilled, weekly from a jug. This was a recipe for disaster. Blots were on paper, exercise and reading books, desks, floor, blouse and person. Pens, pencils and sharpeners of varying designs were kept in long, narrow pencil boxes; the lid either swung open or was slid off to reveal two or three tiers, with a special hollow for a rubber. I later left a beloved pencil bag (Woolworths, 6d) on the station platform. Moved by my utter misery, my indulgent father retrieved it from Lost Property – cost: 1/-.

Reading: most important. I cannot remember when I couldn't read, so I daydreamed through the reading lessons. There were blissful periods of silent reading – when a teacher couldn't find anything else for me to do.

Arithmetic meant sums. We learned, I'm glad to say, our multiplication tables by heart, rules which have stuck, so that, although a calculator is a convenient time saver, it isn't essential. I still have Thomas Parry's *Model Table Book*, in a new edition of 1928, 'Enlarged and Improved, Entered at Stationer's Hall and sold by Philip Son and Nephew Ltd, 20, Church Street, Cost One Penny'. It is still covered in brown paper, with my name inside on pages 1 and 12, which was customary. Actually only 12 of its 21 pages give arithmetical data, 'Adapted to Weight and Measures Act, 1878'.

Arithmetical signs (=, +, −, ÷, ∴, @) precede notation and extended notation (up to 905,061,000), addition and subtraction ('Note This Table may be applied to Subtraction by reversing it e.g. 1 and 1 are 2; 1 from 2 leaves 1), multiplication (and division similarly tackled) and table of factors (learning of which 'will facilitate the use of the Multiplication Tables'). This starts with 14 = 2 x 7, 15 = 3 x 5, up to 144 = 12 x 12. I was at sixes and sevens with all this. Why these numbers? Why not sevens and eights? It was an odd use of numbers to indicate confusion of mind.

Matters now become of more historical interest. The money table gives the coins which were in current use: Gold (Sovereign, Half Sovereign), Silver (Crown 5/-, although the word was used only for Half Crown, 2/6, Florin 2/-, Shilling, Sixpence, Three-Penny piece) and Bronze (Penny, Halfpenny, Quarter Penny or Farthing). The value of farthings was noted up to 400 which equalled 6/3. Unusual amounts formerly used have unusual names: Gold (for example, Mordore 27s, Carolus 23s or Angel 10s, Noble 6/8), Silver (Tester 6d, Groat 4d).

Nothing was left out: avoirdupois weights (from drams to centals and tons), long measure (rod, pole or perch, although we are warned that barleycorn and league are illegal), miscellaneous lengths (all illegal such as 3 inches = 1 palm, 5 feet = 1 pace), measures of surface when 144 square inches = 1 square foot or 0.092900 square metres, whilst 4,840 square yards = 1 acre = 0.40467 hectares). It would be both tedious and pointless to list all the details of cubic or solid capacity, time or calendar months and their meanings, but the little rhyme has always been useful:

Thirty days hath September,
April, June and November;
February has twenty-eight alone,
And all the rest have thirty-one;
But leap year coming once in four,
February then has one day more.

Mother added to this with such as 'February fill-dyke', or:

March comes in like a lion
And goes out like a lamb…

and the perennial:

> March winds and April showers
> Bring forth the sweet May flowers.

Then came leap years, those 'which are divisible by 4 without remainder'. The example given is 1876; soon it will be 2008. Quarter days are still used in come commercial work. Aliquot parts (money) showed the relation of 10s to £1 and included such small examples as $\frac{1}{4}$d = $\frac{1}{960}$ of £1, $\frac{1}{480}$ of 10s, $\frac{1}{360}$ of 6/8, $\frac{1}{240}$ of 5s and $\frac{1}{48}$ of 1s.

There's even proposed decimal coinage, ahead of its time and not as we know it today: 1 ml = 2/4; 1,000 ml = 100 cents = 10 florins = £1).

Whilst Mr Parry did not forget apothecary's or troy weight, fluid measure and weight (20 grains or gr = 1 scruple), matters become even more complicated and, let's face it, almost useless for most of us in the 21st century. Commercially, 24 sheets of paper equal 1 quire, 12 articles equal 1 dozen; it is less well-known that 13 articles make 1 long dozen. We can legally ignore pounds, barrels and packs, 'which should be invoiced as centrals'. Marginally useful is Roman notation, its strange examples include 1–15, 18–20, 49, 68, 99, 1000, 1880 and 1928.

In the final section of figures come metric tables for length, square, capacity, cubic or solid measure, weight and money. 'N.B. The franc is worth about 2d since the 1928 Act'. Other facts are ale (firkin, kilderkin, barrel and butt); wine (hogshead, pipe, tun, all essential for a teetotal household); wool (clove, stone, tod, wey); cloth (Flemish and English).

Whereas a dollar was about 4/2, the Old Testament silver shekel was 220 grains or about 2/3½; New Testament coins were both copper and silver. Biblical measurements of length are given as digit, palm and furlong and of liquid as log and epah, helpfully translated into pints, quarts and gallons. A weekday's journey equalled 30 miles, but only ½ mile on Sabbath.

Common abbreviations we used (e.g. AB = Bachelor of Arts, Able Seaman; AM = Atrium Magister, Master of Arts; a.m. = *ante meridiem*, before noon). Also used are such as CIF (Carriage, Freight and Insurance), HP (Horse Power), PGM (Past Grand Master) – there are seventy-five in all!

I could learn the dates of the sovereigns of England according to lineage: Saxon and Danish, Norman, Plantagenet, Houses of Lancaster and York, Tudor and Stuart lines, Hanover or Brunswick lines up to George V, son of Edward VII 1910 (which is not the only date I altered), plus explanatory notes of relationships.

Among the important dates are Caesar's landing in Britain, the Battle of the Standard 1138, the Barons' War, the One Hundred Years' War (the odd dates 1337–1453 have always stuck in my mind), the Wars of the Roses (including ten battles), the Civil War (mercifully only seven battles here), Jamaica taken 1665, the Trial of the Seven Bishops 1688 and a mixed lot of five more battles, eleven wars and such riveting dates as that of the Disestablishment of the Irish Church.

Inventions, discoveries, etc., all eighty-two of them, go from horn lanterns to submarines crossing the Atlantic 1916, via glass windows in houses 1180 and the first corridor train in 1887.

Famous men, not women, come in two groups:

a)   Authors, 78, from Bede to Masefield.

Richard Hooker 1554–1600, an English theologian, gains his mention as the author of eight books of the Laws of Ecclesiastical Polity. Initials only are given except for Thos., Wm., Jer., Robt., Chas., Mat., Al. and Jon.

b)   Statesmen, artists, all 131 of them.

They ranged from Dunstan 925–988 to Sir John Silcock, the first, with Sir Arthur Brown, to make a non-stop flight of the Atlantic in 1919. The names of fourteen of these men elude me now. Such is fame.

What unexpected riches! Heady stuff for a child of six – and all for one penny!

Everybody's Pocket Companion, all eighty small pages of it, 'Interesting and Useful to Young and Old' came later – possibly 1935, as this is the year given for postal information: letters not over 2 oz, 1½d, parcels up to 3 lb, 6d, and rates for all parts of the globe.

This second compendium added population figures, countries with their capitals, form of government and ruler, colonies, League of Nations Mandates, British Empire and Islands, counties and county towns, USA states and capitals, the Earth, seasons, solar systems, principal rivers, lakes and mountains, interest rates, months and special days of the year, Zone Standard Times, races, languages, speed of light and sound, freezing, fusing and boiling points, ranks in the Services, the world's biggest things, the contemporary royal family, birth stones (did you know that yours is jasper or bloodstone?), various trigonometrical formulae, the barometer, thermometer and heat, elements, orders of chivalry, railways, the Seven Wonders of the World, group names (kindle of kittens, broad of grouse, wisp of snipe), pronunciation of some surnames (Mainwaring = Mannering), largest ships, canals, bridges, tunnels, 'curious' facts about the Bible, sport and speed records, literature, history and geography dictionaries, first aid, wedding anniversaries, bells on ships, foreign phrases in everyday use, mythology, electrical terms and, more banal, how to read the gas and electric meters. Believe it or not, I've left out several pages.

Between the two booklets, everything was surely covered, even if the 'facts' are no longer valid.

And Fairlie itself? We even learned a few words of French – truly of *la plume de ma tante* variety; indeed, the textbook opened with this phrase. I recall little else, although school reports suggest that we 'did' Scripture (there were no Assemblies), English, Geography, History, Art and Singing. Nature

Study did not merit a comment. Miss Edwards did present me in 1929 with *Tales from Shakespeare*, with stories, carefully chosen, printed in large type with wide margins and in language suitable for those of tender years and interpreted by Victorian pictures.

No games? No, because there was only a small yard in which we congregated in the middle of the morning for Bovril or hot milk brought on a tray by the cook.

On Friday afternoons, we were shepherded to the local swimming baths. I didn't like the dun colour of the water, the un-private cubicles, slithering on the slippery duckboards, my restricting swimming costume, the squeals and screams hitting the high roof, the taste. 'Buck up, Joan', that is, metaphorically, pull your socks up; I never was bucked up for swimming. It did not help that Mother found nits in my hair, which was tantamount to being branded as dirty. Swimming caps were essential as you never knew who or what had been there, although recent research suggests that nits prefer clean hair, so this shame has been removed and the shibboleth overturned after seventy years. It provided ammunition against my desire for a pigtail. My confidence ebbed further away. Our wet clothes were dried round an open fire. Slipper baths were advertised – this seemed odd. Washing slippers? in public? Strangely, my friend Mary and I went later several times, but voluntarily, which made all the difference.

We did endure occasional Drill, even several Dancing, lessons (tap dancing was considered inferior, albeit more cheerful) on the sparkling floor of Garston Drill Hall, used for the abominated Masonic functions. My clumsiness eroded what confidence was left.

Rules were few – in fact, I can recall only one. We were supposed to walk everywhere, as running made the chandelier in the schoolroom shake. I was once punished for this offence – either by lines, or, more likely, standing in the corner facing the wall – whilst stubbornly and meretriciously maintaining that I hadn't been *running*. We were allowed to rest our heads on our desks if we felt poorly.

A few stayed for lunch, called dinner. They were much pitied, although it was hardly fun doing the train journey twice more between 12.30 and 2 p.m. Round glasses over her short-sighted eyes, the cook – was she called Maggie? – had one speciality: treacle toffee, 1d for a vast sticky slab on the last morning of term.

We girls wore a white blouse with a round collar, and a green and gold striped tie. I hadn't fully mastered the art of tying a tie when I left secondary school twelve years later, although shirt blouses did make the task easier. The rest of the uniform consisted of a little green gymslip, thick brown woolly stockings (I bought a pair of these in one of the cold winters of the Nineties), held up, less rather than more, by suspenders (which I thought were called conspenders) attached to a Twilfit liberty bodice or stays. The adjective liberty was presumably to distinguish the straight up-and-down garments from Mother's boned corsets. There were vests of different thicknesses for summer and winter (Chilprufe); in the latter season, there were itchy com(b)s or combinations. I cannot now work out how they functioned; on the face of it, it would seem to involve undressing to go to the lavatory.

Brown bar-strap shoes; metal toe and heel pieces were economical, but the noise gave you away. Galoshes (gollies) fitted ill over shoes. A green coat with a velour collar and the strangest of headgear, made of itchy woollen material and fitting closely to the head with two ear-hugging flaps and coming to a point in the middle of the crown: this in green with gold piping completed the outfit. The colours were considered most distinguished. Uniform gave a sense of belonging, of not being different or set apart.

Although intensely proud of this unbecoming garb, I had to change out of it immediately on arrival at home in the late afternoon, as it must not be dirtied. Johnson's, the cleaners, was not yet acceptable to Mother.

There was one excitement in those two years, which none of us understood at the time and probably have the wrong end of the stick now. One pupil was a beautiful girl, with dark curly hair down to her waist, much envied by those of us with pudding-basin fringes. She seemed nearly as old as Miss Wigwam, so she must have been ten or eleven. One Friday evening, the few boys were putting their satchels round their necks and we girls were closing our tiny attaché cases before making our way to the station. Suddenly, a man and a woman came from opposite sides of the road to meet our heroine. One took her left arm to pull her to the left, the other did the same with the right. The girl screamed and screamed. The 'husband' yelled at the 'wife', the 'wife' yelled at the 'husband'. My form, all five of us, settled on the railway bridge to watch this tug of war, mouths hanging open with delight, curiosity, envy and a lovely tingling of fear. But adults always spoil the pleasures of the young. Miss Wigwam was despatched to see us on the next train, but not before we had learned two things: a new word, kidnapping, and that some people had an aunt and an uncle instead of (not as well as) a Mummy and a Daddy. My next school provided much more fun overall, but never matched this spirited episode.

Less agreeable was the visit with singing, dancing and poetry recitations, to the Home for Incurables in Upper Parliament Street – an annual torture. The name can't have done much for the inmates' morale. One old lady screamed spine-chillingly whenever anyone touched her, others slobbered and wobbled. This searing experience made us loathe looking at deformities.

One of our bizarre pleasures was sending one or other to Coventry. In the morning, a decision was made jointly by the five of us as to who should be thus treated, so that no animosity would be felt. It was my first taste of teasing which, deep down, I could not take as I had no means of distinguishing between real and false, between animosity and a game. When the railway carriage door was opened and I was put on the top step before Hunts Cross station was reached, I was terrified and could not work out how to react to give myself a feeling either of safety or of reassurance. The inevitable tears encouraged the tormentors. I wonder now whether it was at Fairlie that my pathological fear of frogs began – was I chased by someone holding one, or was I made to touch one?

I never breathed a word of these troubles at home. I realised something that I didn't know before, probably because I was a not over-strong child of parents with elderly attitudes. I learned that people could tease one, and if one couldn't both give and take teasing, it could easily turn into cruel mockery and, occasionally, physical violence. This must be more easily recognised when there are more children in the family; then no one has an exaggerated sense of his or her own importance. The bubble of self-importance is soon pricked by brothers or sisters.

However, although I didn't know the word, I was bored in school.

TEN
Liverpool

Travel

What a thrill it was to go 'down to Town'! We never took the train. Was it too expensive? Certainly it would have been much quicker. We walked to Woolton tram terminus. There, the long metal pole going from the vehicle to the overhead wires was taken down and refitted at the other end.

We preferred the 5W to the 4W. The latter took a less pleasant route. The 5A and 4A (it dawned on me only recently that W probably stood for Woolton and A for Allerton) turned round at Penny Lane, then, as now, a roundabout with a waiting room on its island. Every Beatle fan has heard of Penny Lane, now an 'attraction' on the tourist circuit, but there is truly nothing unusual or intrinsically interesting there.

I had until recently bits of a blue tram ticket. Friday is written in red across some now illegible notes referring to bye-laws.

TF 2177

Transfer	Ticket
AM 2d	PM
5	2
6	3
7	4
8	5
9	6
10	7
11	8

12	9
PM	10
1	11

Reverse side:

> OUTWARD JOURNEY – For routes and Transfer Points, see notice in Tram Cars.

I also had until recently a small piece of a beige 'Day Ticket GENTLEMAN'; times of use must have been on the back and marked with the days of the week; all that is visible is 'not after 12–0 midday' and 'not transferable'. A 'Scholar's ticket', valid for four journeys, cost 1d. Probably the reason why these survived so long is that we collected tram tickets in those days. Those ending with the number 7 or whose four numbers added up to 7 (or a multiple of 7) were especially lucky, so 2177 gave four points and was a precious possession. The conductor had a ticket machine held in a strap over one shoulder. Buses came later, at first with an open top deck.

When we returned last, we were confronted by the age-old problem of not knowing the routes as there are still no indications either on the vehicle or on the stops, just a notice saying, for example, Zone C. At one such stop, a passer-by warned us, and not entirely in jest, that the buses ran once every twelve months and had already gone that year. Our three journeys gave us the reactions of that special, ruggedly individual breed of Liverpudlians.

On the first, an elderly woman (real Scouse women look permanently drained, dry and sardonic), heard us ask the driver for the Childwall Arms. She proceeded to give us detailed instructions as to where to get off, where to cross the road and which road to take for Childwall Abbey. After she had clarified this several times, a woman from further back could stand the strain no longer. We were completely ignored as she disputed these directions. It was Childwall Priory that we needed; she ought to know as her daughter lived there. The two went at it hammer and tongs; so absorbed were they that the second one missed her stop and got off in a terrible huff. You won't be surprised to hear that we got lost, thinking that they were both wrong. It subsequently became clear that each was thinking of a different pub. The irony is that when we did find the Childwall Arms three-quarters of an hour later, it was being stripped of all its furniture and so was closed.

The second was on the way back to town after this *débâcle*. A wizened man with shudder-making tattoos had heard our request for Victoria Street. At two-minute intervals, amid a cacophony of coughs and sneezes, he gave us not only positive instructions as to what we should do, but also a list of things that we should not do. Such was our confusion that, although we got off at the correct stop, thanks to the driver, we had to ask the way again.

The third was our taxi driver. Hearing of my quest for the Liverpool I once knew, he took us, out of the goodness of his heart, on a guided tour. The road to Hell is allegedly paved with good intentions, but a Scouser's heart is in the right place.

For a child, the most exciting outing was to go down to the Pier Head and the Liver Buildings, with the two eighteen-foot-high statues of the Liver Bird. The 'i' in Liver is pronounced as in tie. Before it was installed, the clock face, Britain's biggest, apparently served as a dinner table for forty, one seated every minute and a half! I once read that no waterfront in England was more impressive. We certainly thought so then, and the transformation of the Albert Dock has extended that impressiveness. The dock system to the north (showing its nineteenth-century origin by its names – Princes, Victoria, Trafalgar, Nelson, Wellington, Huskisson) now lacks the bustle of my childhood. There was the permanent raucous sound of seagulls; frequently there were foghorns; always the hooters of boats and ships. A man tried to sell hot chestnuts from his cart.

At the Landing Stage, we could watch a Mersey Ferry boat (the *Royal Iris* or the *Royal Daffodil*) go 'over the water'. This steam service, the oldest in the world, had begun over a century earlier in 1817. Better was to travel; you went down a wide sloping tunnel with dirty glass sides, stood on the shifting quay, squawked as the boat thudded against it and the quay lurched then one concentrated as chains were thrown round the bollards and the gangplank flopped down. The first stop was Seacombe; our destination, New Brighton with its pier and fairground.

As well as those of the Elder Dempster and Holt shipping companies, there were the big Cunard liners. The New York service had been launched a little later, in 1840. Occasionally, through office or church contacts, Dad had a pass or an invitation to go over a liner; once, we were invited to tea in the Captain's cabin. I don't remember why, but it was awe-inspiring. The names have a magical ring even now: *Aquitania*, *Mauretania*, *Samaria*. They took rich travellers First Class, and emigrants to America, usually steerage. Among these last was Mother's youngest brother, my Uncle Charlie, whom I loved dearly until he sent me a postcard from the *Franconia* saying that he hadn't fed the fishes yet. As a five-year-old, I took this omission seriously and thought him unexpectedly unkind. We and several members of the family saw him off on his way to Crossing the Bar – an unhappy phrase as when it occurs in hymns it signifies death. I didn't know about such matters then. He was one of those who made good, becoming a State Senator for Iowa.

I could dream, with Masefield:

> I must go down to the seas again,
> To the lonely sea and the sky.

Or, more realistically to look at the

> Dirty British coaster with its salt-caked smokestack.

There were the railways too. The Overhead ran alongside the docks. The Underground, the first in the world in 1884 and electrified nineteen years later, took us to the Wirral, to Hoylake and West Kirby. There, when the tide was out, the best was to ride on a donkey, or walk, to Hilbre Island, a lovely place for a picnic, but an eye had to be kept on the tide, otherwise you could well be marooned. Many Liverpool children enjoyed the delights of the white sand, whipped up when the wind blew.

This was early tourism, but the word was not used as it is today.

Nothing seems to have changed in these parts. There were, and are, some posh houses. Mother's favourite brother, Fred, lived at Parkgate, a charming and unspoiled spot – possibly because his most agreeable wife had money from her lovely mother, Granny Clegg; my insecure mother felt that Fred's wife was hoity-toity.

This uncle once completely fooled me. We went down to see him in his GWR (Great Western Railway) office opposite, I think, St James' Station. He spoke to me. Nothing unusual, you think. But he was in one room and I was in another! I held something black to my ear and his voice came through that. This frightening magic was, of course, a telephone conversation.

The Liverpool to Manchester railway was opened way back in 1830. I've still not been to Liverpool's rival, Manchester, deemed to be even wetter than Liverpool. Altogether, there were four town stations: St James', Central, Exchange and, for London, Lime Street. Two other mainline railways serving the North were LNER (London North Eastern) and LMS (London, Midland and Scottish).

One accepted, as a child, without a second thought, that Liverpool had important and imposing buildings. I've already mentioned St George's Hall with its 3,000 seats and many free concerts; the Cotton Exchange was a reminder of past trading;

the Picton, opened in 1860, was the first public library in England; the Lyceum was a Gentleman's Club; the exciting new Philharmonic Hall in 1939 replaced an old 1849 building.

Liverpool became a city only in 1880. Edward VII laid the foundation stone of its C of E Cathedral way back in 1904. Backed appropriately by Hope Street and consecrated in 1924, it took some seventy years to be completed to the plans of Sir Giles Gilbert Scott. They say that it is second in size only to St Peter's in Rome. Two well-known characters were Canon Raven, the Chancellor, professor, lecturer, Great War army chaplain, chaplain to King George V and writer, and the Dean, the Very Reverend F. W. Dwelly. The Anglican Cathedral is now complemented by Paddy's Wigwam, or the Mersey Funnel, built on the site of an old workhouse and officially known as the modernistic Lutyens Roman Catholic Cathedral, bordered on one side by Mount Pleasant – a slight hill, yes, pleasant, no. Its stone was laid in 1933, but the War delayed its completion and it wasn't consecrated until 1967.

There is now a Liverpool Heritage trail. Some of the erstwhile slums now boast listed buildings. Evocative street names still exist: Tithebarn, North John, William Brown, Myrtle, Hope (its hall became the Everyman theatre), Swan. Canning reflects history.

There was the Market. Women sold art (artificial) flowers from huge baskets on the quayside. Behind were second-hand bookshops where I bought the Everyman edition of *Cloister and the Hearth*, still unread, for 2d. Just past the then posh Adelphi Hotel, publicised nationally by a television series, were the Penny Bazaars.

There were, still are, peaceful oases of parks, though the noise of traffic immediately outside is deafening. Wavertree Playground is known as Wavertree Mystery. Why? Simply because the donor wished to remain anonymous.

Historians write of the importance of class in the Thirties. I don't recall that the word itself was much used. It was all much more subtle than can be encompassed by a single word. Although most true Liverpudlians are anarchic and have a proper sense of their own value and place in society, Lord Derby was still regarded as the feudal seigneur. When, in full fig, he led in his Grand National winner and doffed his hat to the crowd, this was deemed right and proper behaviour for a Lord.

This is not to deny the importance of job status. This affected how and when men travelled. A cheaper Workman's ticket on train or tram was issued before a certain time – was it 6.30 a.m. or later? Booked and paid for in advance for a specific period of time, a train contract indicated that the owner was non-labouring and in steady employment.

In First Class, each of the four seats on each side bore a white cotton headpiece. On long-distance trains, each carriage was separate, but a door opened on to a narrow side corridor which led to a WC, usually indescribably dirty. A small child travelling alone might be put in the care of the guard in his van. All trains, without exception, were filthy as the smuts blew back from the coal-burning engine. When travelling any distance, as on holidays, one wore shabbier, older, even one's oldest clothes. You had to have a platform ticket, 1d, to see anyone off or meet any arrival. Exiguous fires burned in minute grates in station waiting rooms – if you were lucky.

Dad felt privileged to have a good, steady, permanent, pensionable post with four weeks' total annual paid holiday, although he worked three out of four Saturday mornings, or four out of five, depending on the month. He was all the more relieved for family reasons. Two of his wife's brothers and four of her brothers-in-law worked on the railways and so wore a uniform; true, one held the responsible job of a signalman and the two brothers both became stationmasters. Admittedly, railway employees benefited not only from the provision of their working clothes but also from free travel, regular paid overtime and, if porters, tips. Worse, his own brothers in

Northern Ireland found it almost impossible to get work; several lived on the 'beru' – bureau; that is, the dole.

From Hunts Cross on the CLC (Cheshire Lines Committee) line, he caught the 8.11 a.m. (8.40 on Saturdays) which took him to Liverpool Central, where shoeblacks, often negroes, plied their trade hopefully. He then walked down to India Buildings. The service was, to us now, incredibly frequent and reliable. He came home the same way, the train stopping at St Michael's, Otterspool, Cressington and Grassendale, and finally Garston, between 5.50 and 6 p.m. His monthly contract involved precise calculations around summer holiday time. Otterspool once had an old dock for coal-carrying ships at anchor in the river, but then had a little zoo and, after the Second War, a proper promenade.

On rare occasions, he brought home chocolates or biscuits; the same lady who sold fireworks supplemented her income thus.

To the office, he always took his attaché (pronounced attachie) case containing the *LDP*, his freshly cut sandwiches wrapped in greaseproof paper, the book whenever any new Finance Act necessitated amendments, and, in the early days, cuff protectors. Nothing gives such a clear record of the passage of time as clothes. His office jacket, the dying remains of a suit, or, much later, an ancient 'sports jacket' had reinforced cuffs and often leather elbow patches. It remained on a hook at work. On the journey, he wore during the week a three-piece suit, possibly one that was no longer good enough for church, or else a cheaper one. Whilst Frisby Dyke was one man's shop, he usually had his suits privately tailored, for such bills were generally modest.

Even so, collars and cuffs were often turned as an economy measure. A Harris tweed jacket and grey flannel trousers, sometimes referred to as 'flannel bags', were allowed on Saturdays. Many of his rank still wore black jackets and striped trousers like Captain Mainwaring in *Dad's Army*. Belts came in during the Thirties; they were first deemed suitable only for 'bounders' or for wearing with 'slacks' or non-suit trousers. The fear that they might not hold up the trousers gave rise to the phrase 'with belt and braces' to indicate someone ultra-cautious. A bowler gave way to a trilby in the same period. As soon as Dad reached home, he would change into carpet slippers. I was proud of my father and his job until I was not so sure when fathers of girls in school were in the professions or management. That is adolescence for you. In mitigation, I knew nothing of his background then. But that's another story.

Before I went to school, there was little real excitement until he came home. One day it was raining, so, with sharp advice and dire warnings from Mother, I was despatched to meet him at the station with his umbrella. This involved going to the bottom of Roskell Road, turning the corner past a detached bungalow and a house, crossing Stuart Avenue and there was the station – a walk of three to five minutes. And it goes without saying really that I broke the brolly. As Mother repeated over the years: 'I knew she'd break it, I told her she'd break it.' This theme went through my childhood and adolescence – Joan will fall/tear it/mess it up/break it (as I did with the lavatory chain in a friend's house before a party). I was the one bound to tread on the newly washed kitchen floor. I was clumsy to start with and such assumptions made me even more prone to catastrophe and being labelled a 'chump'. Even now, on the relatively rare occasions when I have a disaster, I revert to being a nervous child.

Shops and the like

As local shops in Woolton, Garston and later Allerton provided all that we actually needed, a visit to town meant excitement, although it inevitably involved the agony of new clothes or, worse, new shoes. One didn't take a basket as each shop wrapped up goods in brown paper with string – no plastic bags, remember. On arrival home, the string was carefully untied and the brown paper smoothed out, both for reuse. The shop assistant addressed a customer as Miss, Madam or Sir.

Early closing on Wednesdays was strictly observed; it came as a surprise that some towns and villages closed on Thursdays. That seemed almost like breaking the law. None opened on Sundays, smaller ones closed on Saturday afternoons.

Most thrilling were the cafés and milk bars: the rivals ABC (Aerated Bread Company) in which I discovered on his death that Dad had had a few shares, and Lyons (of Corner House fame) where the highlight was a Knickerbocker Glory.

More decorous and suitable for parents and aunts (at least during the day) included Reeces Café, which in 1939 advertised in theatre programmes, as did others, 'a delightful meal in town [as] the perfect complement of charming company and a good show'. Meals were also served 'a [sic] la carte' on both floors. 'After the theatre, light meals and refreshments are served until 10.30 and in the Grillroom there is an extensive menu and informal dancing until 11 p.m. to Bert Pearson and his Band.'

Not dissimilar was the Kardomah Coffee House, where one was served by waitresses (only restaurants for toffs had waiters) who wore black skirts and white, long-sleeved blouses or black dresses, black stockings and shoes, frilly white headgear and inadequate or token frilly white aprons, and carried trays.

Such outlets expanded in the Thirties, but they were nothing like today's proliferation of sandwich bars.

We didn't frequent Cabbies' Pull-ups for mugs of steaming tea, nor did we go to the Stork Hotel which proclaimed itself 'the perfect rendezvous for husbands and wives after shopping or before the theatre'. A three-course business lunch cost from 6/-.

Eating lunch in a big store, or, as a very special treat, at Coopers, the shop which sold coffee (with the grinding machine in full view) and exotic foods such as salmon and watermelons – that was truly super-duper, spiffing. The standard meal was fish and chips, or chipped potatoes, if the menu was being elegant; the Thirties' equivalent of French fries. This meal was perfectly acceptable when eaten sitting down in a café.

Cod was the cheapest, plaice a step up, even more luxurious were halibut and smoked haddock. I thought that this last had most taste. Salmon was out of our range and, in any case, rarely on the lunchtime menu, unlike today. Coopers boasted 'the choicest foods gathered from the markets of the world, examined and checked with special care, and as a final protection we place our stocks under the searching scrutiny of our analysts, thus leaving nothing to chance'. A final touch of class: Telephone Royal Six Thousand.

There were lovely specialist shops which dealt in coins, old books, stamps, maps, antiques, leather, wool, engravings. For new books and stationery, one went to Philip Son and Nephew, for music and instruments to Rushworth and Draper, for glass and china to Stoniers, for watches to Boodle and Dunthorne ('A trusted Jeweller is essential when the occasion arises to purchase precious gems'), for furniture to Ray and Miles on London Road or Waring and Gillow, Robinson and Cleever for less interesting household linen, for shoes to big stores or Timpson (Dad had some POW connection with the owner), for men's clothes to Watson Prickard rather than the Fifty Shilling Tailor. It's obvious what Macfisheries sold.

Liverpool's Woolworths (Woolies) was the first to open in England. Its maximum price was 6d. Paradoxically as it now seems, the store was considered 'better' and more reliable than cheapjack Marks and Spencer. Mind you, almost everywhere was then considered better than M and S – even Blacklers and T. J. Hughes (both clothing emporia), C&A (coats an' 'ats), British Home Stores and, for shoes, Freeman Hardy and Willis.

For clothes, it actually was a matter of area and purse. London Road was cheap in both senses of the word; Bold Street was for the likes of those who had accounts at Henderson's, which, together with its customers, was considered top-notch or la-di-da, dependent on your point of view. George Henry Lees was next best. The general run was Owen Owen's in Clayton Square (it's just struck me how Welsh that name is!), opened in 1925 when old shops were destroyed, and 'still the store for PLEASANT SHOPPING', and the Bon Marché (we never thought of it as French for it was always called the Bonne). It advertised its 'gay French Restaurant' and bade:

MADAM

BE FAMOUS

FOR

YOUR CLEVER LITTLE LUNCHES

'Delightful food – deliciously cooked. Four dainty courses with Coffee for 2/-, or Special School Holiday Roast Chicken.' In another theatre programme, it promoted its Fashion Calendar, Parades of School Clothes, Palmistry and Beauty Shop (from 5/-, for removing tired tan 6/6), offering, for example, 'Shampoo, Waves and New Set 4/6', and its suits ('enchanting pastel angoras... heavenly colours' which included 'glorious scrambled yellow' and jackets 'which hug you as they love you') from three to thirty-three guineas, namely £3 3s 0d to £34 13s 0d.

The big store, Lewis', now seemingly full of concessions, was where most of our clothes and later household linen (brand name Standex) were bought, the last usually in the scuffle of the January Sales. Unbelievable escalators succeeded slightly frightening lifts. Lord Woolton, future wartime Minister of Food, was on the board, eventually becoming chairman.

193

Where are the shops and where are the helpful assistants of yesteryear? Church Street, Lord Street – they might now be in any town's pedestrianised area.

My parents had an ingrained mistrust of all building societies, of all estate agents and of all solicitors, except the Glass family and the wonderfully competent Miss Rooke of Harris, Rooke, all connected with Wesleyan Methodism; everyone else was considered as untrustworthy as insurance companies, except the North British and Mercantile. Martin's was the only acceptable bank. In one quirky branch of the Midland (now HSBC) which took it over, you still go up in an ancient creaking lift to be served in a small room on the first floor. One had no confidence in the Corpy, or Liverpool Corporation. Because of thieves and pickpockets, the warning was 'If it isn't nailed down, sit on it!'

This feeling of dubious dealings doesn't completely leave one's gut.

On my returns to Liverpool, both when my parents were alive and on my last, and final, visit in 1997, I've been saddened. Perhaps one shouldn't go back, but a sense of unfinished emotional business made us go. I wonder how you have felt about Kittle?

Liverpool remains a foreign place which cares little for the outsider and, more distressingly, apparently for its own. Upset by the dirt and the grime, the sheer inefficiency, especially at the main station, the poor housing conditions of so many families, the loss of the personal element, I was reminded of the external effect of the Blitz.

I am only a first generation Scouser, but Liverpool was, is and, I fear, always will be, my town. To go back was human and necessary; to go back again could well be overwhelming.

ELEVEN

Calder High School

Getting in

Life when one is young is split up by a series of interviews and examinations. The first interviews were with the doctor and the eye specialist – much later came the brain specialist, so don't say that you haven't been warned!

Calder High School (CHS, or Calder Hot Sausages – don't ask me why) was an unattractive but well-maintained building. We thought nothing of the cold outdoor lavatories, and we were inured to the totally inadequate heating system. Now its entrance is open to trespassers, its fencing is dilapidated. Opposite, in front of Calderstones Park entrance, there were six irregular stone slabs forming a rough circle, known as the Calder Stones. I think that they were discovered in the mid-nineteenth century and put in place shortly before I was born. Were they druidical, part of a burial chamber? No one seems sure. They are now hidden away along with a few limp bits of greenery inside the park in a locked and rusting greenhouse.

Next door was the boys' grammar school, Quarry Bank High School (QBHS). One student later complained that a frustratingly unscaleable wall separated their lustful eyes from those Calder girls next door playing tennis in short skirts.

First, there was the interview, or oral exam, to get in. As I was only eight and going into the first form as a fee-paying pupil (was it four guineas a term? I think so, but that seems a lot of money), I suspect that it was mainly to check that I was clean and not mentally retarded, and that my parents were respectable. High schools looked down on Elementary schools.

Until then, I think that I simply accepted and stored experiences partly unconsciously; with Calder, I was actually pushing ahead and beginning to learn the rules of the survival of the fittest in several spheres.

Miss Irving was in charge of forms I and II, the pre-entrance examinations forms. Fairlie was repeated; after one week in form II, I went into form III at the tender age of eight, so joined what would later be called the II-plus girls, those who had taken the SCHOLARSHIP (for it was always articulated in capital letters) when I was just nine. Being two, even three, years younger than anyone else had different and unexpected consequences.

I was first in Lower, then in Upper IV, when I sat for the Junior City Scholarship. I remember it two years running as a result of inability to master it sufficiently the first time. These scholarships for fee-paying pupils were limited in number and subject to a means test. The exam took place in the fearsome Education Offices in the City. On the first occasion, when asked to spell movement, I put an unnecessary 'u' into it (French spelling already). I realised the error just as I was closing the door behind me, opened it again and called out that I'd made a mistake and gave them the correct spelling.

A similar difficulty occurred on the second occasion. This time, it was arithmetical, concerning the numbers and sizes of bricks. I got the answer this time when I was already in the corridor, rushed back and yelled 'twelve' at the already deliberating committee. The janitor removed me forcibly, but it seemed to work this time and I secured my scholarship, which reduced my fees to three, then to two, guineas before wiping them out altogether in the Sixth form. The certificate, 44 cm x 33 cm, is too big to fit into any file or sit on any shelf, but it is a splendid glorification of Liverpool.

The Director of Education, Mr C. F. Mott, wrote an impersonal letter addressed to my father:

6 June 1934

Dear Sir (or Madam)

I beg to inform you that your son/daughter Joan H. Cherry has been awarded a Junior City Scholarship at the Calder High School.

He enclosed a leaflet of explanation on white paper and two forms on blue paper 'for your use'. Full particulars of financial circumstances had to be given, and an unspecified undertaking; this presumably was to keep his daughter at school. He was 'particularly requested to read the explanatory leaflet before completing the form' and was given a week in which to comply.

The Headmistress

Then, more than now, the Staff – although we always called them the Mistresses, never the teachers – dominated our school life and none more than its first and sole Headmistress, as CHS had opened only shortly before I was born. Miss Florence A. Macrae, always known as FAM or Fanny Mac, was MA, Oxon (Somerville, I think).

She seemed to be everywhere. In a small school with a two-form entry (once in the third year, there was an extra form), she had to be everywhere. She signed all prizes and certificates and taught, as was the custom for Heads, Scripture. You might know the subject as Religious Instruction, or, more probably, as Religious Education. Scripture more accurately described it then. A broad-minded Unitarian, she made her lessons exciting, although she didn't always turn up, so that we often gained an extra prep period. She shared an infectious enjoyment in all the extra-curricular activities of school life.

The only rule which bore her personal stamp was that there was to be no speaking to boys, not even to a brother at QBHS next door. Home and school were at one with this segregation policy. The prohibition disappeared with the War and evacuation.

Like many headmistresses of the period, she urged parents at every Prize Giving to send girls to bed early. Her report, reproduced in full in the magazine, had it in capital letters: 'THEY ARE NOT GETTING ENOUGH SLEEP. All the physical fitness campaigns in this country are going to be worthless if the children of this country are not getting enough sleep.' This too went down well with Mother. Below the Fifths or fifteen-year-olds, the Headmistress said that girls should be in bed by 8.30 p.m., and juniors even earlier. This stricture did not go down well with us.

She took daily morning Prayers from the platform in the hall-cum-gym. Each Form Mistress conducted her form in silence along the corridors; we were lined up in forms, the smallest girl (me) at the front, the tallest at the back. The Mistresses stood down the side by the rib-stalls (sturdy, polished horizontal bars of wood between upright posts, a bit like a five-barred gate) by the First form. The Sixth were over by the windows and the grand piano.

I later discovered that there was a daily Jew duty rota, for Liverpool had a goodly number of both Scouse and posh Jews, but this phrase seemed most disrespectful. I felt sorry, maybe unnecessarily, for them filing in conspicuously for notices. Thirty years later, I tried, quite illegally, to atone by making my own assemblies relevant to all faiths and to none.

There were no Houses, for she was averse to an over-competitive spirit; perhaps there was not enough of this stimulus. The Form was the unit; I was glad for it was small enough for survival.

She was ahead of her time in holding a parents' meeting; I was packed off to the minister's to do my homework. She also asked parents of the Lower Fifth (that is, the year before first public examinations) to come and talk to her about their daughters' careers, preferably making an appointment as she would not like them to hang about.

I owe her much. She was impressed by my father's probing mind and innumerable questions (often an embarrassment to his daughter, who has, however, inherited the same approach), so took on the challenge of convincing my terrified parents that their daughter ought to try for Oxford, and specifically go for St Hilda's, as the friendliest, most welcoming of the four women's colleges. She was absolutely right in this. She subsequently recalled my father's 'understanding sympathy over the difficult business of evacuation'. Her concern was all the more remarkable because she publicly sent me out of Prayers on the last day of one term for taking the Merit half-holiday the previous afternoon when I had a Bad Mark which ruled out this privilege. She also gave me a detention for making a noise in prep. This must have been when our Fifth form room adjoined her study.

She retired only in 1947 after a quarter of a century and moved to Ditchling in the country with a view of the Downs. 'I have two guests' rooms and I shall be very pleased to welcome old girls (and their husbands) if they are ever in the neighbourhood.' She recalled enjoyable coaching for University entrance, my 'spirited' dramatic work, and signed, as was the custom, 'Yours affectionately'.

When she died in the Sixties, I sent a farewell note to the *LDP* which printed most of it. I repeat parts as it gives you the flavour of the lady and her school as I remember both:

> Life does not seem quite the same this year to those of us coming home for Christmas who were in the care of Miss Macrae, to those of us for whom CHS means FAM. To us, that ugly building of mixed architectural styles on Harthill Road was always presided over by her, for she made it into a school of which we were affectionately proud.
>
> Before the War, she was at the height of her many and varied powers, when the school was still small enough for her to

know each of us, and to know more about us than we thought at the time... She remains for me the upright, rather austere figure of my youth – white-haired, long-nosed, dignified, but with such a sense of humour in her blue eyes... I remember being sent to her in my second year to show her my inky fingers and filthy Mathematics 'best book'. She mercifully forgot this episode. For each subject, we had a rough book and a best book; can you imagine being sent to the Head in a big school, or indeed any in these days, for such an offence? Instead of the punishment and the cold words which were my due, she tried to instil a sense of pride in work well done, and of shame in falling below one's best. Although old-fashioned in the matter of early bedtimes and long black stockings, she allowed us to run our own magazine one year free of Staff interference.

She was most interested in individuals; in the over-studious, she was pleased to see signs of healthy mischief, in the naughty girls (naughty by the standards of the day), she loved to stimulate the mind in her own fascinating lessons... [Those] on Browning in the Sixth form were unorthodox and ranged widely, so that we felt that we really understood what the poet was aiming at... Her Staff speak of her with deep affection and pleasure.

A general inspection must have tried her patience; even we girls found it nerve-racking.

The other Mistresses

As far as I'm aware, there was no prospectus; names and qualifications were not printed in the magazine as they were in your mother's school. Sadly, not one of them was of her calibre. Were good teachers not available in Liverpool, or was she, or the Education Committee, an unskilled picker? I still have the autographs of twenty-two of them, collected over the years.

Miss Macrae shared a house with Miss Dorothy M. Riddell (with the emphasis on the second syllable), much to our surprise as the latter was a more prosaic and earnest character who taught lower school English, such as parsing (which failed to fascinate then, but has proved invaluable since) and, more immediately useful, that 'i' comes before 'e' except after 'c'. She once gave the whole form a 'Collective Bad Mark', yet we congratulated her on her birthday. My diary tells of a row with her during a prep – I wonder what that was about.

Together, they spoiled for me a family visit to a Gilbert and Sullivan opera – simply by being there. Two worlds clashed.

Actually, at least four 'couples' lived together. We used to wonder who did the cooking, who made the bed and so on, but thought this sharing of accommodation perfectly sensible and normal. As I've told you, Mother felt, instinctively – certainly not rationally – superior to such women. Most were 'wedded' to their profession, which they had to leave on marriage.

Auburn-haired Miss Pyke and Miss Scott, neither of whom signed my book, also shared. The former was the senior mathematician. We were well grounded in arithmetic, but I found geometry 'ghastly'. I found the three subjects distasteful despite the stimulus of a geometry set. I threw out the protractor and other bits and pieces only the other day. I could not fathom any reason to be concerned with a square root or the equality of the sides of an isosceles triangle or the square on the hypotenuse. Why did they matter? We never questioned; she never explained. I've managed quite well without that knowledge. Algebra was likeable because it was just a game, although I don't seem to have risen above a 'B', and 'absolutely collapsed' in one exam.

Miss Scott took Art, so that her pseudo-lessons were doomed to fail. A diary note shows that for two periods we washed jars and jugs and talked. She once set 500 lines – 'I must obey orders' – a futile and wasteful punishment. Did you ever suffer such a counterproductive absurdity? I still sympathise with my fourteen-year-old self who commented 'The cheek of it!' We struggled, unsuccessfully, to speed up the process by writing with two pens at the same time. The lady also provided 'small and unsatisfactory paint brushes', and made us read 'uninteresting art books'. There was no question of appreciation of great artists.

Miss Winifred Brett (Latin) shared a house with Miss Margaret McGregor (History), our Form Mistress in Upper IV. I remember mnemonics: for example, '1492, Columbus sailed the ocean blue', which was a trifle unhelpful as '1493, Columbus sailed the deep blue sea'. We enjoyed that lovely word, antidisestablishmentarianism.

She, and we, were handicapped in that Upper and Lower VI had to be taught as one group, so that alternate years had to begin the syllabus in the middle. We ploughed through the Renaissance and the Reformation, Castlereigh and Canning ('Ugh!'), the Industrial and Agricultural revolutions. With the help of cadged cigarette cards we learned the tables of the Kings and Queens. We struggled through the Reform Bill.

She set 'one awfull [sic] exam paper' (although I received a B) and a matriculation question was 'not very nice', and she sent my friend Ruby out of a lesson, yet she was kind and thoughtful to me during college vacations, inviting me to walks and meals in the Wirral.

She would have been happier in a freer age and in a higher professional environment. Staff knew us well in lessons, but had very little awareness of us as individuals with lives outside school. MIM was the only one who made any long-term effort to find out.

Miss Brett was too intellectual for us; our relationship was stormy. She once told me that I had got a bit of taste – a remark as incomprehensible today as it was then. Results in the lower forms were 'worse than awful', but in matriculation and subsid (subsidiary, a lower level than full Higher School certificate in the Sixth) were 'quite good'. Again, a lack of clarity. I now remember a test on Catiline, and two statements:

Ego sum Claudia (it had to be someone beginning with C to match my surname of Cherry) and:

> *A ab absque pro prae de*
> *Corum sine cum ex e.*

Did they all take the ablative case? Unfortunately, Latin was essential for both entrance to and first term examinations at University. Somehow I survived. When Miss Brett had a year off for travel, Miss Coomber took over and stayed on after her return. The lady herself transferred to the Foreign Office during the War.

Miss Edmunds (did she take junior maths?) shared with the Geographer Miss Houldsworth, always thought of as 'sarky' (sarcastic). Asking for the hymn 'Holy, holy, holy, Lord God Almighty' brought us to the heights of hysteria. 'Holy' kept me in for the equivalent of a whole lesson once – for laughing! I doubt if it was from her that I learned Toulon and Toulouse – like a pair of sailor's trousers, but I did acquire a short-lived interest in the *National Geographic* magazine, but little sense of direction. To this day, I can read a map only if it is facing the way I am going. East must be cold because an east wind always was.

Mr Edgar C. Robinson, from Liverpool Cathedral, came every Friday morning. Apart from not-much-enjoyed hymn practice for the following week's Prayers, we rehearsed songs for Prize Givings, the Coronation service (on which he gave us an illustrated lecture) and other such festivities. The choir had an extra dose later on in the morning.

For the annual carol service, an afternoon presided over by FAM, Canon Jordan of All Hallows, Allerton, gave the address, usually on the lines of urging us to be interested in people rather than in things and to spread the Christmas spirit of goodwill. The *LDP* commented just as regularly on our excellent singing of the old favourites. I was chosen to give two solos when I was fifteen.

We were not always kindly disposed to Mr Robinson; I suppose the modern expression would be that we took the mickey out of him on occasion. Poor man, he couldn't win, but he was kindness itself. He gave us a recital of music by Schumann and Bach and conducted a party round the cathedral.

The choir in the upper and middle school were coached by him, the one in the lower school by Miss Degge, who also encouraged an orchestra to support a dramatic performance. She taught Music when the subject became an integral part of the curriculum – not, incidentally, a word we knew. For us, it was just another lesson. She initiated the music society, along with Miss Houldsworth and Miss Greig; our papers on the lives of such composers as Johann Strauss and Edward German were followed by solos or extracts. Each form had a free choice one year, unaided by grown-ups. This resulted in Schubert, Great War songs, sea shanties, comic opera and gypsy music. Miss Degge took practices for the *Toy Symphony* and composed incidental music for school plays. In my mind's eye, she was exotically dark and well dressed.

Others have left less impression. Miss Harkness took Elementary Mathematics; she became School Secretary; we all, uncharitably and without a shred of evidence, assumed this was a demotion for poor performance. Poor Harky!

Miss McQuarrie took Biology and Hygiene, ran the science society/field club, and, together with Miss Nettleton, took a party of – wait for it – four girls from Upper VR and VI to spend a biology weekend at Yealand Conyers Friends' Guest Cottage. Students also visited Evans' Biological Institute and heard a talk on medicine through the ages. Who taught Chemistry escapes me now; was it Miss Ibbotson, our Form Mistress in IIIR? Yet I mildly enjoyed it, which is surprising as we had extra lessons after 4 p.m.

Miss Bell? – some form of Craft? Anyway, after two years, she presented two vases. Miss Eagle? – a one-time secretary?

Miss Moffatt? Miss Thomas? They were there as I'm looking at their signatures, but nothing comes to mind. Miss Hill? – Maths? Miss Moat's Craft classes made costumes for plays and garden party items but I had no contact with her. How many of your teachers have you forgotten?

The first Games Mistress was Miss Roberts, who seemed old to be wearing a gymslip, even if it did have a velvet border. She tirelessly trained us for days for the annual Saturday Garden Party – no small undertaking as each form and every girl did something. Juniors performed country dances, a gavotte, a Jewel dance, one year wearing 'attractive and colourful print dresses and peasant aprons'. Seniors gave a gym display, in Coronation year wearing white shifts and tricoloured hair ribbons, with a tableau at the end, having a crown in the centre. The only activities which I remember vividly are: Second form Maypole Dance, which sticks in my mind, no doubt, because I snarled the whole thing up by going under when I should have gone over and, probably, vice versa; when I wore a long white dress with silk flags (from Kensitas cigarettes) representing flags of all nations sewn on; the year when 1,800 ice creams were sold, Mary and I selling 300 of them; the cricket match, which followed 'Jerusalem' and 'God Save the King', between girls and fathers, the latter usually winning, one year by five wickets and 112 runs. I remember the statistics as Ruby and I kept the score. For the unathletically gifted, there was the Display of Work.

The Gym Comp. (always thus abbreviated) was an annual purgatory, 'such a bore'. My form won it once; the following year, we were third from the bottom. All was made worse by the insensitive gift of a previous Head Girl (was it Helen Guthrie?) of a trophy for the form with the Best Deportment. Wearing gym shoes, we performed on ropes let down from the hall ceiling, we played pirates on forms, we struggled up and down the rib-stalls along the inside wall (it was more fun during wet dinner times when you had to escape without putting a foot on the ground), we vaulted (most of us) over horse and buck and suffered sore bums; we marched endlessly. What *did* we do with beanbags? Off the record, what a thrill it was when one girl could do the splits. The only physical skills I had were eyebrow and ear wiggling, and making believe that my thumbs were double-jointed.

As Editress, I had to write the tribute to Miss Roberts when she left after eight years to become a PT organiser. The best that I could come up with was that she had come to be regarded as part of the school! She gave a shelf in the corridor for cups and trophies – no need then to lock them safely away.

Her successor, Miss Green, was a more roly-poly person than her straight-up-and-down predecessor. She won approval by playing lacrosse for the North v. South International trials – 'marvellous'.

Miss McGregor Cookery – to distinguish her from Miss McGregor History – would have interested you more. The subject then embraced cookery (pastry needs a light hand, use the tips of your fingers, wash all your utensils) and needlework (run and fell seams). I'm not sure when Miss Kitty Cox came, but I think of her every time I wash a hairbrush according to her demonstration. Was the subject called Domestic Science in your schooldays? Now, it's Home Economics.

English

I enjoyed English; I longed for elocution lessons, but there was a firm maternal 'No', perhaps because of the cost, more likely because she thought it swanky or uppity. The lessons would have been unnecessary as both parents spoke beautifully.

Sixth-form English was a delight; a hatred of shoddy grammar has, often uncomfortably, remained. Miss Goyne, flat-chested, black-haired, with slender spectacles and addicted to green suits, taught us well, although I grew to hate some of the set books: *Eothen, Twelfth Night, Cranford, Barchester Towers, Idylls of the King, Mirror of the Sea* ('desperately boring' for matric), even *Jane Eyre* and the Romantic poets in a way that didn't happen with French books. Perhaps I was simply too young. You may be lucky in coming late to books which have stood the test of time and can investigate in your own time and way without being taught them.

To her, I owe the delight of my first holiday without any member of the family. In the summer of 1936, she took a group of about ten of us to Stratford, an awkward journey. I can still name every girl on a photo taken outside our boarding house. Our landlady could not have been more kindly. Miss Macrae came down to show interest, but, perhaps wisely, stayed in a nearby hotel, although our landlady could not have been kinder.

Amazingly, we were allowed to wander round in twos and threes, even to go blackberrying; we were taken on excursions, by bus, but mostly on foot – Charlecote Park, Shakespeare's house and New Place museum, Shottery, Wilmcote ('walked about seven and a half miles'), all before the onslaught of mass tourism. I learned how to pole a punt, which came in handy a few years later, although Miss Riddell and Ruby both fell in just before we had tea on the river.

Apart from Sunday, when we went to the parish church ('not very nice') and Friday (our last night), we saw a different play every night and at two matinees: *Twelfth Night* ('wonderful', with lemonade to follow), *Taming of the Shrew* ('very good'), *Much Ado About Nothing* ('gorjus' on two birthdays, mine and Ruby's), *Hamlet* ('marvellous'), *The Merchant of Venice* and, the only slightly sour note, the 'not so good' *Troilus and Cressida*.

The main attraction was queuing up outside the stage door to get the autographs of the players. Our idol was Donald Wolfit (whose signature netted £2 recently!), who took us in completely with his anguished curtain calls, although we were saddened to hear that he was already married and had two children. His wife, Rosalind Iden, was less flamboyant.

Some of those who signed for me don't appear in later reference books, which doesn't necessarily mean a failure – Valerie Tudor, Donald Eccles and the magnificently named C. Rivers Gadsby. Others were at the beginning of successful careers on stage, in films, on television: Rosamund John (her first appearance), Pamela Brown, then only nineteen, Peter Glenville, a 24-year-old Romeo. Others had already had vast experience: James Dale who first performed in 1908, Basil Langton, Barbara Couper born in 1903, Buena Bent, five years younger, and Trevor Howard, perhaps the best known. It was most exciting.

The programme indicated that 'there is always space for Diner's Cars in the Theatre Car Park', that 'Refreshments must not be taken into the Auditorium' and that 'Smoking is not permitted'. Top price seats were 8/6 stalls; the gallery, unreserved, cost 1/3 – that is a little more than my then weekly pocket money.

After a visit to the Cripple Girls' School and a last look at the shops, we faced a tiresome homeward journey. Leaving Stratford after 'dinner', namely at 4.35 p.m., we had an hour's wait at Birmingham, left there at 6.10 and arrived at Woodside (Birkenhead) at 9.30, so it was 10.40 p.m. before I reached Hunts Cross. The happiness, the emancipation, the confidence boosting of that holiday remain. I bought a 6d 'silver' thimble as a present for Mother. I use it still.

Miss Goyne was also modern in that she invited a group to a play reading of *Pygmalion* at her house: 'good fun. Lemonade and Sausage Rolls', and took some of us to see T. S. Eliot's *Murder in the Cathedral*. The English Classical Players paid annual visits with plays by Shakespeare and G. B. Shaw – *Androcles and the Lion* ('awfully good'), and *Caesar and Cleopatra*.

She was responsible for dramatic work. In a form play, I was Shylock in *The Merchant of Venice* – at the tender age of ten. I recall three plays. Firstly, Lady Gregory's *The Dragon*, for which I sold programmes. Honesty compels me to wonder if my criticism, 'mediocre', had anything to do with the fact that I wasn't in it. In A. A. Milne's *Ivory Door*, in that important year of 1936, I was Bruno, Captain of the Guard, and received praise in the newspaper! The faded, marked copy cost the penal amount of 2/6. Copies were typed and handed round. The names of fellow actresses remain totally familiar – Elsie Jefferson, Marjorie Noel, Joan Postance, Freda Collyer – where are you all now?

The third, 'an old Chinese play', was *Lady Precious Stream*, first produced in London in 1934. 'The stage represented the picturesque garden of the Prime Minister [who was] wearing a long black beard which indicates that he is not the villain of the piece.' Well, well. Our 'stupendous success' was given in school on two evenings in December 1937. Humiliatingly, I had to be prompted once on the first night in my role as His Excellency Wang Yun. The *LDP* gave particular praise for my prime ministerial performance. No wonder I was thrilled with this form of escape which rewarded showing off. Performances were for the School Fund. I was so tired that my parents took me home in a taxi and I spent the next day in bed! This time, the flimsy handmade programme bore no names in a vain attempt to prevent us from getting swollen-headed and too big for our boots.

We took the play to St Athanasius' school in a deprived area, not for the pupils but for their mothers. The Headmaster, Mr Peach, talked about his school one morning after Prayers and the tiny children came for a party.

Less attractive, indeed boring me stiff, was the annual day-long Poetry Comp. Poems were usually chosen from Palgrave's *Golden Treasury*, much of which ('It was a lover and his lass') was out of our experience. Representatives from each form recited and were criticised, praised and awarded prizes in three categories – junior, middle and senior – by a generous Mr Dellar, disrespectfully called Dickie. He had married a former CHS girl and taught English at QBHS.

Some lines, particularly of narrative verse, have stuck:

> There's a breathless hush in the close tonight,
> Ten to make and the match to win...

and:

> It was a summer evening,
> Old Kaspar's work was done,
> And he before his cottage door
> Was sitting in the sun.
> And by him sported on the green
> His little grandchild Wilhelmine...

with its refrain:

> It was a famous victory [Blenheim].

All too often, the unrealistic (to us) Lakeland poets were chosen. We had never seen Shelley's skylark, and Wordsworth's daffodils hardly resembled those in the back garden, and we never wept to see them haste away so soon. We'd never known a tiger but Blake did stimulate our imaginations:

> Tiger, tiger, burning bright
> In the forests of the night,
> What immortal hand or eye
> Could frame thy fearful symmetry?

All too often, poets seemed obsessed with time passing quickly; one has to be grown-up to feel this personally.

> Gather ye rosebuds while ye may.

As for Coventry Patmore's tortuous effusion:

> My little son, who look'd from thoughtful eyes

And moved and spoke in quiet grown-up wise,
Having my law the seventh time disobeyed, I struck him.

Enough of that one.

Who else? Mrs Fish, appropriately, was cook. Mr Fearn, the caretaker, was a great support in all activities, with 'confirmed good temper'. Did he have a daughter at school? I think so. I think too that we admired her for having such a competent father.

French

Miss Evans, Form Mistress of II, nearly put me off French for life by teaching phonetics for a whole term. This was quite a different language; we then had to waste another term translating its symbols into 'proper' words. Why couldn't we get on with learning real French? Most confusing. I vowed subsequently never to teach French that way.

Miss D. A. Joyce Pindar (Pinny), UVR Form Mistress, dared to leave to get married just when we all had a 'pash' on her. She was 'ever so nice' and impressed us by asking how we were on our return from sickbeds. Fancy remembering that; it suggests that none of the others involved herself even thus far.

She organised a visit to The Playhouse to see members of La Comédie Française in *Gringoire* and *Le Médecin Malgré Lui* (the programme thoughtfully included English notes, but how learned we felt) and to the David Lewis Theatre to see French films of *L'Avare* and four of La Fontaine's *Fables*. In the Sixth, she taught some Spanish, which entailed a happy dropping of Maths and Chemistry. When exam results weren't brilliant, we felt sick at having let her down. Incidentally, she was the first, the only one to wear noticeable make-up. Professor Pears lectured on Majorca ('V. Gd!') to the Hispanic Society in Abercrombie Square.

Miss Foster (Fossy) gave a lantern lecture on Paris, and, with Pinny, took the first party of twelve to Paris in 1937. In this as in many other ways, CHS lagged far behind your

211

mother's school, their first, and by this time, annual trip to the Continent taking place in 1912. 'We are all very much indebted to [them both], who organised this expedition so efficiently. We must also thank Miss Macrae for her kindness in allowing [!] us to go to Paris.' Heartbroken at the time, I am now glad that I paid my first visit on my own to stay with French people.

Grey-haired Miss Greig, a graduate who referred to Cambridge as if that were her Alma Mater, took over VIA and most of the serious French teaching. I respected her expertise even then, but we didn't get on; a few rows ended with lectures on behaviour, or being sent out of dinner or disqualified from competition ('la [sic] diable'). She wore high-heeled slingback sandals and hitched her skirt up before sitting on the magisterial seat. FAM paid tribute at Prize Giving to 'our very unselfish and able Second Mistress'; she would now be known as Deputy Head. She took the few of us in the HSC group in her car to the Scala cinema in town to see a French film starring Louis Jouvet, *L'Entrée des Artistes*.

Uniform

School uniform was rigidly enforced and proudly accepted, although it was the done thing to complain from time to time about specific items. The aim was to blur financial disparities (not entirely successfully) and to encourage the corporate spirit (which it did). It also needed very little thought each morning, which suited me. Second-hand uniform was available for sale, but that would have brought shame on the family; even second-hand books were unacceptable. I wonder how Mother would have reacted to some of my excellent purchases from charity shops!

The velour hat, brown with the band in school colours of blue and brown, had purgatorial elastic under the chin, as did the ear-clipping panama in summer; together with ties, they were the items hated by all of us. No headgear was to be removed while the wearer was in uniform; the panama sometimes was. A navy gaberdine mackintosh, horribly long to allow for growth, or a brown blazer, with blue braid and the City emblem of the Liver bird encircled by the words 'Courage, Honour, Service', were the prescribed outer garments.

Uncomfortable bar-strapped shoes were kept in a shoe bag on our individual hooks in the cloakroom. They remained there overnight, as safe as houses.

Satchels, either with one strap and so worn over one shoulder and round the neck (from Garston Co-op) or with two straps and so worn like a rucksack (as my friend Mary had), carried lunch and books until we graduated to cases in the Sixth – a sign of seniority, but less practical on a bicycle, for it had to be strapped onto the carrier, and was more awkward in school as it left only one hand free. We carried a purse on a strap round our necks; it was commonly known as a peggybag.

Black gymslips (we never questioned this odd word), never tunics, were obligatory until the day when summer was, whatever the weather, officially declared. They were then exchanged for the blue cotton summer dress with its Peter Pan collar – white so that it was obvious to everyone when it needed washing. The gymslips originally had slack buttoned belts at the waist; we were all pleased when these were replaced by girdles, which could be tied tightly to give the impression that one had a waist. Colours, in the form of a shield, for games were blue with golden brown lines and the letters sewn in the space, and the whole thing sewn onto the left top. I still have mine with an L and a T (lacrosse and tennis) sewn insecurely and crookedly. The tunic had to be 4" above the ground when the pupil was kneeling, so that the bottom hem was often disgracingly bulky to permit letting down as the wearer grew. Box pleats wore thin and eventually split into holes and were then perversely cherished. I can still feel the prickly serge.

White shirt blouses attracted ink and therefore trouble. A V-necked sweater in school colours was allowed. Sixth form status was marked by the wearing of a white blouse and navy skirt and therefore light-coloured stockings. Most of us, perversely, preferred our old gymslips; perhaps we didn't really want to grow up, although we proclaimed the opposite. We disliked being conspicuously different. It also meant changing for gym and games.

Black woollen stockings often 'concertinaed' à la Nora Batty. We often wore ankle socks, or 'sockettes', underneath, giving an oddly lumpy effect. This was so that we could remove the long ones on the way home.

Knickers still had elastic at both waist and leg; white cotton linings were advocated, but Mother didn't even know what they were. She seemed to feel that such a suggestion invaded the parental domain. They were not truly bloomers, but were capacious and not made more elegant by having a pocket for a handkerchief, especially if a knot had been tied in that to remind the wearer of something. White cotton knickers would have been simpler.

Clothes were inspected periodically, nominally to see if they were marked. Bought Cash's name tapes were too extravagant, so there were two possibilities, both equally embarrassing: names were either written in indelible ink on a strip of cotton or, more often, flannel, which was stitched onto the garment or, worse, boldly embroidered on the article itself.

As at Fairlie, I changed out of uniform immediately on arrival home – not a freedom protest, but to protect it and make it last longer. This habit of changing persisted.

TWELVE

School

Day to day

Today's letters are the excuse for sentimental nostalgia. Getting to school from Hunts Cross took time and energy: walk/bus to Woolton, tram to Harthill Road, then a short walk. Mother joined me at Woolton and we walked back together. This was until I got my bicycle: what a liberation that was!

On the platform, Miss Macrae read out the new form lists at the beginning of the year; we then marched out in line to our new form room with our new Form Mistress. Sometimes pleased, sometimes disgruntled, we were totally dependent on this lady. A few stayed down, a dreadful ignominy; it is now called, less degradingly, repeating the year, but everyone knew, and knows, why.

After the preliminary first and second forms, there were usually two forms in each year in the school proper, sometimes only one, once three. Was that due to a particularly bright year or a bulge in the birth rate?

We were very conscious of the word 'form'; 'class' and, even lower, 'standard' did not belong to a High School! Generally, but not inevitably, Lower then Upper forms III and IIIR (for 'Remove' – but why?) were followed by Lower then Upper Fourths and Fifths, Lower and Upper Sixth (first and second years). We, in III, considered ourselves to be the good-at-exams (justified, just, by published results) and the Removes to be the duffers; they considered us to be the swots and themselves the good-at-games-and-nice-types.

The register was painstakingly read out each morning and each afternoon. Each girl replied 'Yes, Miss —'; many names still stick therefore, although I was usually thinking of something else by the time she was reaching the end of the alphabet. A number of them wrote in the ubiquitous autograph album. There were at least four Joans, a horribly popular name for those born in the Twenties; mind you, I was never called Joan by other girls, always Cherry from my surname.

Armorel Adams was the first name; pretty with fair curls, good at games and especially tennis, she went to France for a month's exchange – a pioneer. Joyce Ashe got her bike for £2 2s 6d; we once went down to town together to have a 'fuddle' in the shops – that is, to look at everything and to buy nothing. Emily Bell came before me, then Estelle Chesters, a tall girl who married early; Vera Colecliffe, lovely skin; Muriel Cresswell, another tall one; Ethel D'Arcy, of the glamorous surname, who had the unenviable job of opening bat – 'Pokes at the ball without swing and the result is a catch' (magazine encouragement!).

Betty Davidson joined later and was held in awe for her elegance. Her clothes were tailored and clearly expensive, so she couldn't have been Liverpool born and bred! She invited me to my first non-church party, 4 to 9 p.m. It was customary to take something.

Unfortunately and, of course, unintentionally, I'd thrown her present (a little brooch, doubtless an unwanted and rewrapped gift) on the fire! This was a major economic and behavioural disaster. I wrote 'not my fault, though Mother said it was – awful stew'. I don't remember how the matter was resolved, but I had a 'super, lovely time, royal sport', playing adverts, anagrams, treasure hunts and paper games, such as the one where one person draws the head, folds the paper over and passes it to her neighbour who draws the body, the third the arm and so on, with 'hilarious' results. I myself was not allowed to give a party until I was sixteen or so.

Athletic Mary was, as I've told you, my best friend. Having a best friend was terribly important, indeed essential. Was it so when you were at school? It was especially important for me as I had no other friend and needed someone to stick up for me. She has since told me, for we kept in touch until her death aged eighty, that she was sorry for me because of the *régime* at home, that I was nagged to tidy up and put things away. She shielded me from anything untoward as she did for her youngest sister Muriel (Billie), my contemporary, although this entailed rougher handling of the sister in the middle, Barbara. Mary adored her mother and disliked mine; she was less fond of her pharmacist father. We shared a school garden, although she did nine-tenths of the work. We never won the annually awarded gardening picture, our joint enthusiasm being too short-lived.

A garden is a lovesome thing.
Mine's not.

For obvious reasons, she came to our house less frequently than I went to hers, where I enjoyed sitting and talking on the stairs, and nice teas. I noted one quarrel in 1936; neither of us subsequently remembered its cause.

We still followed the incredible convention of the Coventry rota: 'Who aren't we speaking to today?' There was nothing personal, no bullying about it, quite the opposite; it was the same for everyone. It probably didn't last for more than a term or so. It saved feuds, alliances, groupings. We had our private signs: tapping the side of the nose meant 'I'm in the know'; thumbs on shoulders and wiggling the fingers meant 'I'm great'; thumbs to one's nose indicated that the third person was nasty.

Back to Mary and me. Tennis was the only game in which I was superior, for I was a complete butterfingers. We cycled ('spiffing time') and cleaned our bicycles together. Mine, despite its general inferiority, did boast a little basket on the front and a carrier on the back. On dark winter days, a sort of torch-lamp was fixed on the front.

The register continued with Norah Dunwoody, Primrose Easson (we thought she had a lovely name), Jean Emerson (another sporting girl), Joan Evans ('Juv') whose elder sister Nancy was a professional singer, which added glamour (she is probably the only Calderite to have had an obituary in *The Times*), Jean Flood, Joan Geller, Lilian Goodwin.

Ruby Gregson was the third Musketeer; this was a love-hate relationship, as Ruby was much more streetwise than either of us. She won the Poetry Comp.; I beat her at tennis by the impressive margin 6-2, 6-2.

Next came Eunice (pronounced by one Mistress as three syllables: Eu-ne-cy) Green, Marjorie Hall, Muriel Halsall, Joan Hallett, Joan Harding (both these Joans alarmingly tall), Jean Ibison, Ada Johnson, Renee Meachin (FAM always read her name as Runner Meakin), Greta Pearlman (I don't know that anyone thought of her as Jewish), Peggy Sharp (who had a marvellous fancy dress party) and Brenda Smyth (pronounced Smith and always known as Biffy), whose bowling was 'a trifle dangerous'. Her party featured Lexicon, ghost stories and trials of memory.

There were also twins. A problem of credibility arose because they were very different, one with black, the other with ginger hair. Could they really be twins? Was one Pat and the other Joan? One once had a magnificent nosebleed and gained status thereby. Mair Parry Williams' middle name was never omitted; that never seemed strange, such was the Welshness of Liverpool.

I was impressed by them all, especially as they seemed to have high jinks and I didn't. A few older girls counted: Lucy Myers (of the Myers family when I was tiny) who became a Liverpool University classicist; Freda ('Fred') Smith who had her name on the Games Honours Board; Amy Dooley, known as Billie; and Rose Leighton who became a respected member of my father's office.

The form rooms were old-fashioned. In most respects, they differed little from the single room at Fairlie: pen grooves along the desktop; in its holes china inkwells filled with Stephen's ink by the Ink Monitress (never me); felt pen wipers; a blotting pad but there were still smudges and blots which spelled trouble. A bottle of ink (1d each) to use for my homework stood on Dad's bureau; there is still a huge ink stain on my own bureau. Fountain pens – what a thrilling name – came in. They had a sort of plunger to enable them to suck in the ink. I lost mine, of course, which was a major family catastrophe until it was found somewhere. We sharpened pencils with a penknife or, preferably, a small metal pencil sharpener and took care to avoid any indelible pencil left lying about. We kept pen, pencils and rubber in the same wooden boxes. Incidentally, it was not 'quite' for a man to show a pen in the outside pocket of a jacket.

It was an unwritten and unbreakable law that you never opened anyone else's desk. Another crime was to sneak, to 'tell on' someone. It was incumbent on each girl to carve her initials on her desk so that successors would know from whom they had inherited it.

It was the job of the Chalk Monitress to ensure that each Mistress had an adequate supply. The Door Monitress, me one term, stood outside the form room door (for we were always taught in forms) waiting for the Mistress. Ahead of the lady's arrival, she nipped in quickly to quell any noise, then closed the door when the grown-up was safely in. At this point, we all stood up ready for the official greeting and our reply.

I was never Form Monitress, not even her deputy; these positions were held for a term as a result of a vote. I wasn't popular enough and, rightly, not considered capable, reliable or dynamic. Sad, but I was three years younger than most. I did become Head Girl, by reason of longevity and to give me something to do and to put on my CV, I guess. I then had to ring the bell for the divisions of the day – lessons, lunch, register and so on. I felt keenly the responsibility of checking the times.

A Conduct Monitress kept the tally of Good and Bad Marks. One crime, at which we were skilled, was passing notes in class – good practice for stealing sugar unseen in a café or restaurant in wartime and therefore regarded by us as virtually legitimate. Was it three or was it five Bad Marks which meant automatic detention? Another punishment besides lines was to face the wall with arms folded behind one's back – tiring.

We raised a hand to ask, 'Can I leave the room, please?' – the euphemism then in vogue for going to the lav, itself a euphemism, as are lavatory and toilet. A pedantic mistress might reply, 'You can but you may not.'

At Break and/or Dinner, ½d bought hot water for Oxo, 1d a cup of cold milk (at break, one-third of a pint was provided for ½d), 2d a cup of hot milk, 2½d a cup of Bovril; 1d equalled three biscuits. All these purchases were supervised by prefects. Fig rolls were sold through the kitchen hatch. The outside drinking fountain was impossibly dirty.

At the end of the fifteen or twenty minutes, we lined up in alphabetical order to march to the form room for the next lesson. Mistresses moved; we stayed put except for Art, Chemistry, Cookery and, obviously, Drill and Games.

We brought sandwiches wrapped in greaseproof paper inside a metal box (no lightweight plastic then) for dinner, about two tables of us sandwich-eaters to one table for eaters of hot dinners presided over by a Mistress who said Grace. I think that they paid 1/- a day, although I'm sure that it was for a time reduced to the unmanageable cost of 11d. There were free dinners for some but the system was insensitively run and the stigma was obvious. We paid ½d or 1d a day towards the provision of plates, washing up, etc. As seniors, we three Musketeers kept the account book, an awesome task of collecting the cash which did little for our digestive systems.

Afterwards, before we graduated to more orthodox games, we lay in the sun, did cartwheels and handstands and walked on our hands, played cowboys and Indians at the bottom of the main field in the trees and shrubs which sheltered the grass tennis courts, French cricket and 'tip it and run'. Wet days meant the Hall.

A merit afternoon holiday at half-term and end of term occurred on the Thursday afternoon before the Friday break-up at noon. The names of those who forfeited this because of their Bad Marks were read out publicly in Prayers, as were our final grades, A, B, C or D. Half-term Friday afternoons were usually used for school shopping, such as buying a new blazer in spring.

It wasn't a matter of 'teacher's rest, mother's pest' in our house; the Monday was eagerly awaited by father and daughter. Mother, mercifully for once, couldn't interrupt her routine. That would have made her all behind like a cow's tail. Dad took a precious day's leave; we set out for the whole day, usually going over the water to walk in the Wirral, eating our packed lunches on a beach or in a field, completely content to live in the present. Little was said on these occasions; there was no need to talk. Was it always fine?

Reports were important. I brought mine home in its sealed envelope, never allowed to open it, and had to wait until Dad came home in the evening and until both parents had read it and questioned me on my weaknesses – a thoughtless torture. Alas, all were destroyed for the War Effort, without any reference to me. Two B reports were copied: three As, one C (Geography), and all the rest were Bs – but I was 'talkative'; the second had four As and eleven Bs. As always, we felt that we had too much homework; we certainly had more than I ever set for my students.

A medical certificate, purchased from a doctor, had to be presented to the Form Mistress on the first day of each term.

The doctor had to sign that the pupil had neither had nor been in contact with any infectious disease during the holiday.

Medical inspection (termly or annual?) was much loathed. We stripped to our knickers and liberty bodices, and, in the presence of our mothers, were insensitively prodded and ignominiously poked by 'a ghastly female Dr'. However much we stuck up for girls' rights, a woman for us could not be a proper doctor.

CHS was health-conscious. Outside lavatories were considered much more hygienic than rows of them indoors, although there were no washbasins. Now, such an arrangement would be considered barbaric; they were extremely icy in winter, despite wooden seats. One pulled the chain to flush. There were, of course, no graffiti and I cannot recall any mess.

Remedials took place after Prayers with the Gym Mistress. Miss Roberts had a flaming temper at times. On Mondays and Wednesdays, those with round shoulders stayed behind, on Tuesdays and Thursdays, those with flat feet – like me. We stretched our ankles and wiggled our toes – we had changed our outdoor shoes on arrival at school. Some poor wretches suffered from both of these socially unacceptable conditions. It was demeaning to be branded officially as physically inadequate, quite apart from feeling silly performing such exercises which did me no good at all. The better-constructed majority suffered fifteen or twenty minutes of silent Scripture Reading.

We were instructed never to sit on radiators – which were never more than lukewarm – as we could get piles. As we didn't know what piles were ('piles of what?') and as our bums were frozen, we continued to sit on radiators when it could be managed discreetly. My piles took fifty years to develop, so the risk had been worthwhile.

The worst for me was, of course, my eyes. The Victorians (and Mother) believed that eyes could be strained by poring over books; possibly they were right, but for a different reason, namely poor lighting conditions. It was bad enough having to stand at the front of the line in Prayers because I was the smallest, but my desk had to be at the front because of my sight. This limited one's scope, but may have contributed to good results. It was difficult to be good at games – in addition to lack of coordination. Wearing glasses does affect one's self-esteem, doesn't it? You have been fortunate in that you can wear contact lenses. The saying 'Men seldom make passes / At girls who wear glasses' didn't do much for morale either; in addition I squinted, so unkind folk would claim that they didn't know whether I was looking at them or not. I broke the frames at least twice; Dad treated this sympathetically and had them mended. Golden Eye ointment was always close at hand. When plastic came in for frames and lenses, daily life became so much pleasanter.

Ordinary ailments continued to be coughs and colds – according to my diary, up to thirty-eight in one year alone, sometimes degenerating, with sore throats, into bronchitis and congestion of the lungs. Flu and tonsillitis also had a weakening effect, so I had several patches in bed. This susceptibility is lasting throughout my life. I was not unique; Liverpudlians of all ages were affected, and more than once the school day was shortened. Once we broke up early because of it. I was coughing too much to enjoy the extra time off.

Bilious attacks and indigestion were not infrequent. Miscellaneous problems included perpetually grazed knees, numb fingers (which Mother had too, so she was dismissive of my trouble), slashed fingers, a spell of chronic earache, a bandaged foot from a netball accident – indeed, feet were a nuisance with veruccas (caused by barefoot work in the gym?), corns (eased by a good chiropodist in Lewis' stores), chilblains and blisters; the last three are still a plague. I twisted an ankle in games on several occasions. I never considered myself anything other than tough, but my diaries suggest that I was not as healthy as I had thought.

Strength had to be built up, for most of us girls were anaemic. There was always the danger of outgrowing one's strength or of overtaxing eye or brain!

Games

Official games were popular on the whole. The general theory assumed that they built character and encouraged team spirit. On the other hand, we can't criticise succeeding generations for non-involvement when we read that 'the Captain's work would be lightened if girls saw to it that they were not kept in'. My friend Mary was in everything and 'inspired the teams with her own enthusiasm'. In such a small community, everyone was able, indeed encouraged if not actually forced, to join in; even clumsy characters such as myself did reasonably well and coordination improved.

Matches were fiercely, if too often unsuccessfully, contested and partisanship ran high. We played 'better' schools such as Huyton Ladies' College and Belvedere (Girls' Public Day School Trust), our rivals in all spheres Aigburth Vale and Blackburn House, Holly Lodge and Queen Mary High, the Bluecoat and La Sagesse Convent (pronounced Lah Sjess – we never saw it written) and ad hoc teams from the new Childwall High, Higher Tranmere, the Old Girls, even Merchant Taylors and the University – evocative names.

In the magazine, each team member was given a personal report, often shaming and certainly patronising. 'Steady Norah blocks, until the bowlers get weary, then she hits... Her batting is confident but rather lacks judgment... Her bat is usually straight... Many spoil their play by roughness which is the result of slow footwork and obvious dodging.' It was all 'play up, play up and play the game' in tone.

For most English schools, hockey was the winter game. We were different and played lacrosse, as did many Liverpool schools, altogether a more stylish affair. Even here, in a game I loved, I managed to break a stick. One great day, we left school early to go by tram to Central Station, then on the underground to Birkenhead Central, then by bus to play Birkenhead High School; after all that, we drew 5-5. I graduated from 3rd XI to 2nd, much improved, it would seem, by changing position from 1st Home (clearly a poor scorer) to 3rd Man, then to Point, a more reliable defender and hopeful that the ball wouldn't come too often my way. We played inter-form matches too, twenty minutes each way; our form won the trophy once. When losing in the final on another occasion, I recorded that it was most unfair.

A strange thing happened only the other day. At a lunch given by former students, I was their guest to celebrate my last book, *Onward Ever*, the story of your mother's old school. One spoke of my kindness to a girl going on to a Physical Training College who, in turn, had been kind to another girl and so on. She then disappeared among the mass of coats to return with the subject of my 'kindness' which had been found in an attic – my lacrosse stick, still legibly marked with my full name in indelible ink, returned after more than fifty years. I had totally forgotten all this; is it now to become a trophy on the garage wall or is it to remain in the hallstand to deter burglars? These Southerners felt that the game must denote a posh school; as you can see, it did not.

A 'useful Netball player', I captained the junior thirteen-year-olds and worked my way up to captain the school team, yet I didn't achieve my Colours. Odd. The Mistresses beat us 11-9, although 'the rules of the game were not strictly adhered to'; but a nice tea softened the blow. My form lost in the finals to Lower V, 'but it was most unfair. They disputed the result so we had to dispute and they made Miss Roberts say they'd won'. The more I read of me, the less I approve!

Rounders was an official activity only for forms I and II. After lunch, we played our unofficial game with the monotonous regularity so delightful at that age.

Against the University, 'School collapsed absolutely'. Cricket, not played by many girls' schools then, was less popular with me; I was too afraid that my glasses would be broken. Much to my relief, I never achieved a team place despite being 'promising' at one stage and 'outstanding in form games'. Discovery of this praise in a magazine astonished me; it must have been a triumph of persistence over limited innate ability.

I several times manned the primitive scoreboard. Tin numbers were hooked over nails to indicate runs, numbers of the current batters and runs made by the last one out.

My game was tennis, especially the lovely lazy games on the one asphalt court or on one of the ten or so grass courts. Wooden framed rackets then were orthodox in shape and, when not in use, were kept in a rectangular press tightened with four screws and in a plain zipped cover when rain fell. No one owned more than one, so it was a major catastrophe when a gut string broke and the racket had to be restrung, especially as it was taken to Jack Sharp, 'Expert Sports Outfitters, providers for Lancashire and Test Match XIs, Everton and International Football teams', in Whitechapel in the heart of the City. It was good fun, if you were quick enough to grab a court, after lunch or when public examinations were over.

Matches were played in short-sleeved white dresses which were replaced by a white aertex shirt (the idea being that sweat was lost through its 'holes') and skirt, the latter being exchanged for a divided skirt. This last was the most comfortable and gave the greatest freedom. Shorts were the final symbol of emancipation but were not as kind to an enlarging backside. My predecessors at school and the older women at the club had worn long white stockings; I was fortunately too young for such horrors.

Graduating from fourth to first team, I did manage to win the Junior singles when I was in the Lower VI. Magazine comments on the standard of play would suggest that this was no big deal. 'Perhaps more looseness would help... Serving appears to be a major problem, and until girls learn to throw the ball higher, they will continue to find this difficult. There is a general lack of courtcraft and general bad footwork.' I don't remember any lessons designed to remedy these basic problems. My own difficulty was then and remained the backhand; as for the rest, I didn't care too much as long as the ball went in and I won! The War put paid to any serious improvement.

I loved playing, partly at least because it wasn't a team game. One of the main attractions of matches was lemonade and biscuits afterwards – and not dreary Marie ones either, but custard creams (Dad's favourite) and fig biscuits.

Are you surprised by this erstwhile athleticism? Come to think of it, I have never heard you mention games!

Prize Giving

This was one of the highlights of the year, especially for swots like me. An extra attraction was a subsequent half-day holiday. Every girl attended.

Five programmes, 1934–36, 1938–39, bring it back. Each opened with the National Anthem and ended with the School Song:

> Glad Hearts adventuring, the Way is wide,
> Valour and Faith shall shield the pilgrim's side.

It then looks confidently if inappropriately to the hereafter:

> Constant and undismayed,
> Your journey past,
> Across the hills of Time Home lies, at last.

Finally, the repeated chorus:

> Glad Hearts adventuring, the city of God dawns far –
> Brothers, take to the trail again, Sisters, follow the star.

> *M. A. Macdonald*

We sang it with fervour because it was our song and had a rollicking tune, but I doubt if any of us took any real notice of the words.

This, together with three or four items, had been rehearsed and rehearsed, and, on a Friday evening in March at 7.45 p.m. (no early bedtimes that evening), was sung with gusto if little finesse. Words come rushing back of the hectic opening song:

> Welcome, Wild North Easter,
> Shame it is to see
> Odes to every Zephr,
> Ne'er a verse to thee.

I would not readily endorse the sentiment today.

> Drake is in his hammock an' a thousand miles away,
> Captain, art thou sleeping down below?

Or:

> Praise to God in the Highest

'Eldorado' is now remembered only as a series of repetitions of its title and the name of a particular ice cream.

Those rendered during the evening were gentler: 'The Fairy Queen', 'O'er the Valley', 'The Song of the Imp', 'Weep you no More, Sad Fountains', 'Know ye the Land?', 'Song of the Vikings' and groups of part-songs: 'Tramping', 'County Gay', 'The Song of the Harp', 'The Larchwood' and, with descant, 'Loch Lomond'. Apart from the last one, neither words nor tunes come back to me at all. Words were sometimes but not always included in the programme lest enunciation be less than perfect.

It was only when, as a prefect, I helped to prepare the sandwiches that I knew that the platform guests had a reception afterwards in the Head's not overlarge room by the front door.

Speakers were all local and connected with church, university or schools – again this narrowness of vision: Rev. Laurence Redfern, MA, BD, Professor E. T. Campagnac and Mrs H. B. Gair. Professor Porteous, the new occupant of the Chair of Education, urged the need to be alone and quiet to develop our gifts so that we could achieve independence of mind and the power of forming our own opinions. Perseverance and persistence had to be added to cleverness. This speech chimed with my own aspirations; otherwise, pious sentiments tended to be yawned away.

In 1938, Miss Potts, MA, Head of the College for Girls, Huyton, was billed but she was ill. She sent books, we sent flowers. Roles had to be exchanged at the last moment. Councillor, later Alderman, later Sir Sydney Jones, MA, LLD, JP, then in his sixties, usually took the Chair, but on this occasion, he moved up to Speaker/Distributor and Mr Mott, the Director of Education, presided. Sir Sydney began, acceptably enough, by telling us that whenever he called upon Miss Potts, she became ill; last time, she caught measles! He went on to suggest, however, that her love for children was clearly so great that she caught their complaints. Oh dear! He extolled the sense of beauty, be it physical, mental or moral, and looked to the women of England to uphold the standards and keep the menfolk up to the mark. He once admonished us about litter; his appeal may sound strange to you: 'I ask you not to throw tram tickets in the street but to put them in the fire when you get home.'

Tribute was rightly paid to him; no one had done more 'to make our School more beautiful, materially and spiritually'.

The Head's Report varied little. Apart from her emphasis on going to bed early, she commended the international interests of the girls and the OGs' Club for the less fortunate and told the parents of her pride in the results.

Over those five years, only seven external scholarships were recorded: two to Liverpool School of Art, two to Oxford and three for Junior City Scholarships for otherwise fee-paying pupils, one being mine. Your mother's school at this time had over twice as many pupils, but won seven or eight times as many awards in any single year. It is only since I have been able to compare CHS with similar schools, even with QBHS over the wall, that I have realised how low were the aims, the expectations and the achievements. Still, we didn't know such things at the time.

In the Sixth, the public exam of the JMB (Joint Matriculation Board of the Universities of Liverpool, Leeds, Sheffield and Birmingham) was then called the Higher School Certificate (HSC, the ancestor of your Advanced Level) and was taken by a mere nineteen candidates overall in forty-nine papers, with only three distinctions, French, Geography and History. Not much to look up to, but not too difficult to surpass. Eighteen who did not achieve HSC standard received a Subsidiary Certificate.

Exams now become confusing, even to me, with what were called Letters of Success. As some candidates attained a Principal as well as a Subsidiary result, I think that the sixty-one entrants from both Lower and Upper VI either did not reach or did not attempt the number of subject passes required for a complete HSC. My sole Letter of Success was for Latin. The range of subjects for eighteen Principal and 150 Subsidiary candidates was wide, including Latin and, surprisingly, Domestic Science.

School Certificate (SC) was equivalent to your Ordinary Levels – well, we enjoyed a lovely time unsupervised on the field after they were over. As most girls would leave at the end of the term, it was considered not worthwhile having any lessons. This was an opportunity missed for, say, secretarial, social or charitable work or an intensive course in a new language or in domestic subjects. In SC, you had to succeed in at least three of the four groups with a minimum of five passes, the aim being all-round competence. The fourth group included Art, Music and Domestic Science, so was not for me. The range of subjects and the marks obtained determined whether you matriculated, the first step for any higher education. In my year of approximately sixty girls, only twenty-three achieved SC and only five matric – Betty, Ruby, Jean, Ada and me. My success was mentioned from the pulpit in our church! A watch appeared on my next birthday.

Over these five years, only ten matriculated, twenty-four distinctions were gained and an average of twenty-four failed altogether. It may be that other local girls' schools fared as badly. Details were never published.

English was subdivided into Language and Literature; there were fifteen other subjects which included Greek for one girl. The only memory that I have of the French Viva (or Oral) is of missing quite a few lessons because of it.

Despite these poor results and although she professed to dislike meaningless statistics, FAM claimed that the success rate of 81–86% was better than the national average of 72%. The basis for such an assertion seems flimsy.

Prizes were given on examination results to Fifth and Sixth forms, a total of eighty-eight. Other form prizes totalled 114, a generous provision. I have several worthy tomes: *Oxford Book of English Verse* (Lower V, of which I'm ashamed to say some pages remain uncut to this day), *Myths of Greece and Rome*, *Forsyte Saga* (reread several times) and Stevenson's *Merry Men* (rather less appreciated). Heads always seem to have to fork out for a Scripture prize; mine was Basil Matthew's *Life of Jesus* – 455 pages of text, 9 of appendix, 16 of index plus a fold-out map. All are beautifully bound and stamped with the City's crest and with the school's name.

Success in Cookery, Needlework (Machine Sewing certificates in 1934), Art (poster competition RSPCA) and in unspecified subjects was also rewarded. Completely gone from my mind now are the prizes and certificates, distributed annually over the whole Liverpool district awarded for

Observation and Record by the Committee of Associated Learned Societies. Clearly, I didn't win; I hope that I didn't enter.

As well as all these trophies for work, shields and cups for form and individual prowess were presented – for all four games, for gym and, once, for discus throwing. Perhaps once was enough for this dangerous activity.

Leavers

'If possible, would you keep the girls at school to finish the five-year course.' FAM's plea was echoed by virtually every headmistress before World War II. Social and economic conditions in the slump and depression of the Thirties did not give most girls much of a chance.

When again I compare what leavers from Calder did with what they did from your mother's school in Enfield, we were an unenterprising lot. Why such a big difference? Was it to do with the North–South divide? Perhaps mistresses had too narrow experience or failed to stimulate them sufficiently? Was the attitude of parents and so of girls too restricted? Did Liverpool not have the openings for girls? Perhaps there was less general scope here and less spare money. Maybe some of the older establishments creamed off the 'better' pupils.

Some girls and their parents undoubtedly wondered what the point was of staying on into the Sixth or of acquiring professional qualifications when a woman would be forced to give up a career upon marriage. The boys of QBHS, opened at virtually the same time, showed a greater range and expectation of success.

A helpful article in the magazine and notes from FAM as President of the Old Girls' Association suggest that over 750 left before the War; the whereabouts of almost half were recorded. This does not indicate a strong loyalty to CHS. The Head wrote a personal letter to each leaver and the Association (annual subscription 2/6) claimed a goodly number of attendees, perhaps because there were so few meetings; socials with QBHS Old Boys, a dramatic group which presented two 'interesting' plays (a one-acter by Houseman preceded *Other People's Lives* by A. A. Milne), the odd jumble sale or whist drive to create a loan fund. Otherwise, it was mainly tennis and cricket teams which challenged present pupils. Members were invited to the annual garden party and ran a short-lived club for the less fortunate. The War finished the Association off by the time I left.

Teaching was the obvious and expected choice of at least sixty-five of the 'bright' ones; that is probably why I said that it was the last thing I'd do – which, in fact, is how it turned out! Few were high fliers; only nine were noted as University students – a geographer to Cambridge, an historian in the year before me to Oxford, the rest to Liverpool. Only one achieved a First, and that for Latin. More took Diplomas of Education or Board of Education certificates. Over forty others followed some course of academic training, whether in training colleges (again, all but two locally) or establishments for Domestic Science, PT, Gymnastics or Froebel. Of the ten who studied at Liverpool College of Art, one won a Travel Scholarship. A handful gained their LRAM. Known elementary school-teachers numbered thirty, again all locally, except for one in Egypt; ten worked in secondary schools, one as far away as Dublin!

About forty went into caring professions, mostly as nurses, whilst individuals included hotel caterer, restaurant food supervisor, dress maker, librarians, pharmacists or shop assistants.

The majority of the 150 remaining were either in, or training for, 'business', mainly as shorthand typists in, for example, shipping, factories such as Crawford's Biscuits – again the emphasis was on local work.

What happened to most? They married.

Thinking of these students has helped to make me realise

what a shock I must have given to all by wanting, indeed craving, and being determined, to leave Liverpool.

The War was to widen the scope enormously and give new ideas to those who had been stick-in-the-muds.

THIRTEEN
Not In Lesson Time

Magazines

Only three copies remain and they are far from intact. Successive Editresses (the term always used) must have shuddered when they received my repeated offerings. Having the first silly and improbable story printed when I was just eight clearly went to my head.

THE LOST GRANDMOTHER, Joan H. Cherry, Form II

Kennie is the name of my little brother, and my name is Jean. We had wandered away into the forest, a long way from where we live, and Kennie was frightened, so I told him not to be frightened, that now we had got out of the forest, to wait until we had climbed a big hill in front of us.

So we climbed the hill, and we saw a little cottage, and as we were very hungry we ran to it, and I was just opening the gate to go in, when I saw the person who owned it. She was a beautiful old lady, and was watering her garden. Then she looked up and saw us and she said: 'What is your name?'

I said: 'My name is Jean Robinson, and this is my little brother, Ken.'

Then the old lady exclaimed: 'I am your Daddy's Mother.'

Then I said: 'Oh, Granny! We were lost, and you found us. We have often heard Mummy and Daddy talk about you, and we have found you.' So Granny wrote to Mummy and Daddy, and when they knew they sold their house and came to live with Granny. And they all lived very happy [sic] ever after.

A psychologist would have a field day with that.

In my defence, I have to say that it wasn't much worse than many pieces by other girls, such as Mr Mole who hates spring-cleaning and quotes poetry!

Subsequent non-acceptance should have prepared me for a more recent pile of reject letters.

Three years later, Joyce Ashe and I offered *A School Alphabet*, from A is for Algebra to Xs and Ys, full of in-jokes and subjects. It was not printed, neither was a sentimental and ill-spelled contribution about gypsies.

That same year, I submitted a criticism of the magazine which now appals by its idiocy. The patient Editress's comments are in brackets.

Not only did I demand more humorous items ('yes, please, but I have to print what we get' and want only more original material), more interesting and amusing competitions such as collecting quotations about things – I was good at this kind of thoughtless but industrious pursuit (the idea was welcomed) – but I also requested less about school activities as we were all there and knew all about them (not very sensible as the magazine must be a chronicle). I didn't know how dependent on magazines I'd be when I was researching my last book. Similarly, there should be less about games and more original comments rather than the hurtful criticism, more illustrations (too expensive) and 'less [sic] advertisements'.

Hoist with my own petard, I became Editress myself for two years. There was one panic when I received an official document asking why no copy had been sent to the British Museum. I'm still unsure how I was expected to know of this mythical obligation.

My editorials were crisp and clear, but how I changed my tune! I encouraged Old Girls to give news of their doings and to write articles thereon; this would be 'interesting for those of us who are still at school', and would form a link with the outside world and might help with choice of careers. Another example of this need to reach out. There was virtually no original material; it was almost entirely a chronicle. I was advocating all that I had criticised two years previously.

I appealed for more support; the price was increased to 1/-, but the mag was to appear annually and not at the end of each term, so purchasers made a net saving of 6d. Even that was too much for some of us. I even asked all to patronise the large number of advertisers, for, like every comparable production, it had to be subsidised. Such a consideration had never previously occurred to me.

Advertisers paid 5/- (technically 25p, but comparisons are pointless) for one-sixth of a page, 9/- for a third, 10/- for half, 12/- for two-thirds and 15/- for a whole page. Actually no one took a full page in these three copies. Who advertised? Almost entirely local shopkeepers: chemist, newsagent and tobacconist, florist ('Bouquets and Wreaths Quickly made to order'), Irwin's, the grocer ('a treasure house of value [with] clean tempting goods... displayed at prices which make them genuine bargains'), Kirkland Jennings ('Confectioners, Vienna and Fancy Bread Bakers') which had seven shops in the suburbs as well as in town. Unique was Dr F. W. Dickerson, MusD, FRCO, LRAM, ARCM, who offered 'Lessons in Pianoforte and Organ Playing, Singing, Musical Appreciation, Harmony etc.'.

Somewhat thwarted, I filled two little personal magazines of collections of my own writings. The first was headed *Poems and essays*, aged nine to thirteen; the second, more ambitiously, *Poems, Plays, Stories and Puzzles*, aged thirteen to unspecified.

The first is written in very neat script; how *naïve* and derivatory they are!

The River

See how it rushes by!
Youth-like and merry, never to die.
The little fish inside it swim,
They too are gay and light of limb.
The seaweeds by the sunny shore
With rocks and stones are waging war,
The little shells, so small and sweet
Are where the water wets my feet.

There are three prose descriptions of morning, evening (a shepherd taking his flock back to the fold – something I could never have seen) and night (shops shut, and shutters pulled down over windows – these seen daily). I draw a veil over *Spidermonkey Island* (a boat trip – as if I'd be allowed to go with my friend Joyce on a boat!), descriptions of people (*The Charwoman* – as if I had any first-hand knowledge of such an individual), of Baby John, and a ghastly all's-well-that-ends-well story of an orphan, a tramp and her burglar father.

Others resulted from homework: *Cranford Society* ('this essay is original and from memory'), a parody on *A Case of Identity* by Conan Doyle ('done in a composition about mystery') and a 35-minute matric question on castles.

Strange to me, now, is *My Choice of a Career*. I had hoped at the age of twelve to become a teacher of French and English. 'I do not wish to leave school until I have passed all the examinations – also one to Cambridge.' My desires were based on enjoyment of parties and friends, hatred of domestic matters (I'd be out all day and the work would be done by the time I got home – perhaps I still believed in fairies), long holidays, respect from society and a large salary, after which I'd go on the Mission Field. Just how wrong can you be! I changed so much in a few short years.

In the second notebook, there's a pious and stilted defence of examinations ('necessary, but I do not think they should be the be-all and the end-all as they seem to be nowadays') which tortuously led to the bizarre conclusion that they made war less likely!

Parodies were in vogue, perhaps to help us to be aware of styles. So there's one of Hazlett (an autograph hunter), a sloppy modern parable, and *On a Punt*, after the Stratford holiday: 'If boating be the food of fun, boat on,' which ended, endearingly, 'the author finding this subject to be above the years she had when she wrote it (fourteen years, four days), and nothing satisfied, left it unfinished.'

Books

An essay, set by the Head, indicates my main interest. With which character in fiction would you like to spend a day in the country? Having mentioned that the country, like war, brought out the best and the worst in man, I would take Boots, Rudyard Kipling's creation in *Thy Servant a Dog*, but not Sherlock Holmes, not Meg Merrilees, not Bottom nor Chaucer's Host; perhaps the materfamilias of the Swiss Family Robinson as she would attend to the picnic, but she was a bit antiquated. No, it must be Lord Peter Wimsey. His man Bunter would have packed a beautiful and large luncheon basket for two. I extolled Lord Peter's character and enjoyed his interesting tales. FAM noted it as quite good.

V. S. Pritchett sums up the right and proper attitude to reading: 'Books have always seemed to be a form of life and not a distraction from it.' Philip Howard goes further: 'Life is OK, but give me a good book every time.'

Mother treated them with a mixture of scorn (to me, 'You'll ruin your eyes') and awe (to others, 'Her nose is always buried in a book'), as something outside her experience. With relations and with church folk, there was the risk of being taunted as a clever clogs and a show-off.

Dad revelled in them, although he was an exasperatingly slow reader. This was not for lack of intelligence or reading skills. He simply had to absorb everything. He read and reread his Bible and religious books, but loved, for example, Edgar Allan Poe (*Murders in the Rue Morgue*) and H. G. Wells. I became fascinated by the latter's life, but not by his writings; for Dad, it was the reverse. He chuckled over Herbert Smith's present of *Goodbye Mr Chips*, but he was not adventurous in his choices.

All public libraries, not merely the scruffy ones in Liverpool, were forbidden, whether because they were free, or the books were unsuitable or simply because they were bound to be dirty – literally, not figuratively. Boot's library, with a token sum payable for each withdrawal, was different. There was a children's section from which one graduated to the adult division. Later, Penguin books at 6d each were manna from the gods. The first, in 1935, was *Ariel*, the biography of Shelley by André Maurois.

As at Fairlie, textbooks had to be covered in brown paper, a task quite beyond me for the folds at the corners never stayed folded. Anyone who had lost hers could not claim as her own another girl's copy unless she tore out her name on the flyleaf *and* on page 12. In our own books, we wrote our names and made the address as long as possible by adding after Liverpool, England, Great Britain, Europe, The World, The Universe.

A book, or later a book token, was a sure-fire present, a visit to Philip Son and Nephew a special delight. Graduating to a higher position, I put the current reading on a chair seat and knelt down to read and, so they say, stuck my tongue out to aid concentration.

The Form Mistress distributed reading lists for both term time and holidays, not always easy to accomplish as Calder had no library, merely plans for one. Quantity was nearly as important as quality. I began lists: in 1936, I read thirty-nine; in 1937, thirty-six; in 1938, forty. One year, these included nine in French and three in Spanish. Many were of their period, their authors sunk without trace. Few have proved their worth except to contribute to my reverence for the written word and an almost physical shudder when language is ill-treated. To see my own words in print remains a thrill.

Poetry, as I've already told you, did not cast its spell. I read little voluntarily beyond A. A. Milne, calendars, comic verse, Henry Newbolt and the popular Robert Browning. Poems still need a rhyming pattern for me. What about:

> The Assyrian came down like a wolf on the fold,
> And his cohorts were gleaming in purple and gold…

and:

> Abou Ben Adam, may his tribe increase,
> Awoke one night from a deep dream of peace…

or the exuberance of:

> The year's at the spring,
> And day's at the morn,
> Morning's at seven,
> The hill-side's dew-pearled;
> The lark's on the wing;
> The snail's on the thorn;
> God's in his heaven –
> All's right with the world!

Even better:

> Hamelin town's in Brunswick
> By famous Hanover city;
> The river Weser, deep and wide,
> Washes its walls on the southern side;
> A pleasanter spot you never spied!
>
> But when begins my ditty,
> Almost five hundred years ago,

To see the town's folk suffer so
From vermin, was a pity.

Rats!
They fought the dogs and killed the cats,
And bit the babies in their cradles,
And ate the cheeses out of the vats,
And licked the soup from the cooks' own ladles,
Split open the kegs of salted sprats,
Made nests inside men's Sunday hats,
And even spoiled the women's chats,
By drowning their speaking
By shrieking and squeaking
In fifty different sharps and flats.

In my tiny (Blackie and Son) edition, the 303 lines are pre-ceded by information on the author and followed by three pages of largely unnecessary notes such as obese = fat, and 'notice the comic effect of the strained rhyme obese and robe ease', and 'sharps and flats = degrees of silliness'.

If only all poetry for children were like this stirring stuff! Too often, 'official' poetry caused a giggle.

Early reading was an escapist mixture of swashbuckle and sobs: Angela Brazil's school stories; *Huckleberry Finn* and *Tom Sawyer* ('grand fun'); *The Fifth Form at St Dominic's*; Baroness Orczy, a British novelist despite her exotic name, and her *Scarlet Pimpernel* series; the religious G. H. Charnley's *The Skylark's Bargain* and *The Enchanted Highway*. Bessie Merchant has disappeared completely from my memory and is not mentioned in any of our reference books, but I suspect that *The Gold Marked Charm*, *Sally Makes Good* and *Three Girls in Mexico* had religious overtones.

As time passed, taste mercifully broadened somewhat. You already know that R. L. Stevenson was popular in schools with *The Dynamiter*, *Dr Jekyll and Mr Hyde*, *Master of Ballantrae* and, of course, *Treasure Island*. So was John Buchan – *Midwinter*, *The*

Thirty-Nine Steps (subsequently a successful film) and *Hunt-ingtower.* J. B. Priestley's *Good Companions* occupied many happy hours as did the 1938 blockbuster by Margaret Mitchell, *Gone with the Wind*, which was not only filmed but, according to my diary, also provided my first recognition of a rude joke. I wish that I remembered what that could have been.

There was little true discernment: Ruby M. Eyres rubbed shoulders with Prime Minister Baldwin (*The Torch I Would Pass On To You*, lent by the Head), Lytton Strachey (*Victoria the Great*), Mazo de la Roche (*Jalna, Whiteoaks*) with Trollope (*The Warden*, 'boring'), Margaret Urwin's historical novels (*Royal Flush*) with Sapper (*Bulldog Drummond*) and with F. S. Smythe (*The Spirit of the Hills* and *Kanchenjunga Adventure*, the excite-ment based on a Christian attitude).

Dad's choice of *1066 and All That* by Sellers ('Aegrot. Oxon', which translated means a fourth class degree on the grounds of illness) and Yeatman ('Failed MA Oxon' – which is an impossibility if you have your BA Oxon first) showed how his schoolboy sense of the absurd appealed to his daughter then. For example:

> Test Papers: N.B. Do not attempt to answer more than one question at a time.
>
> Give the dates of at least two of the following: 1. William the Conqueror; 2. 1066
>
> What is a Plantagenet? Do you agree?
>
> 'An Army marches on its stomach' (Napoleon). Illustrate and examine.

What is also clear is a delight in detective novels, some still classics of the genre: Conan Doyle (*Study in Scarlet, Poison Bait, Hound of the Baskervilles*), J. J. Connington (*Death at Swaythling Court*), Agatha Christie, E. C. Bentley (*Trent's Last Case*) and the inimitable and prolific Dorothy Sayers. I wonder how out of date her books might seem to you – or, for that matter, to me now.

There was little pattern – Horace Annesley Vachell, Ernest Bramah, Phyllis Bottome (*Mortal Storm*), G. K. Chesterton, Aldous Huxley, E. V. Knox, Beverley Nicholls ('Just too naughty, my dear'), P. G. Wodehouse, Ann Radcliffe's *Mysteries of Udolpho*, Eden Phillpotts, Kate O'Brien, Shaw. Periodically, I intend to reread them to see what pleased me over sixty years ago, but there's the fear of shattering illusions – and there's never time. Perhaps I redeem myself by enjoying, both then and now, Virginia Woolf's *A Room of One's Own*.

I was all for possessing the 'right' books, the heavyweights, but they were not always read. One or two remain unread to this day. There is a noticeable lack of autobiography and biography; then, the need was to escape into another, wider, more worldly world than my narrowly religious one. Now, I'm so curious about what makes other people tick that 'lives' are my favourite reading.

Extra-curricular

I can't recall many organised activities outside lesson time. Magazines and programmes suggest a lack of enterprise. Maybe authority then felt that such were both the prerogative and the duty of parents.

A few clubs did exist. In addition to those for Music and Science, the most flourishing was the Literary and Debating Society. It came as a surprise to discover that I was its Secretary in 1937 and its President the following year. We read plays, ballads and papers on writers such as Barrie and Shaw, but most important were the debates, two of which in 1939 were with QBHS boys! This was growing up with a vengeance. A boy and a girl argued for each side. That the 'Modern Home' is not strict enough was lost by nineteen votes. It was agreed, would you believe, that it was better to be single than married.

After the time-honoured subject of sexual equality, which we found very daring, we 'had tea, warmed up and fooled around' – surely verbally rather than physically. I do wonder which side won.

Films, slides, photos and lectures were infrequent: 'Tea Picking in Ceylon', Cadbury's illustration of the production of cocoa. FAM took the lead with the Oberammergau Passion Play and with road safety (because a child had been killed). She showed slides and photos of the Tyrol and North Hungary; this was supplemented by Miss Czanthşa, who talked about the hardships of the Hungarian minority in Rumania: 'How ashamed we felt when we learned that [she] can speak eight languages.'

Outside school, girls heard talks on postage at the David Lewis theatre, on a Mount Everest expedition and on elephants, and saw films on 'The Growth of the Bean', 'Swimming and Diving', all in an exhausting morning at a local cinema. Grey Owl (an American Indian?) gave a lecture to eighty in the Central Hall.

These are the only ones mentioned in my diary. Was it perhaps the fault of the local education authority? Once again, all compares very unfavourably with your mother's school. Democracy came one year – and evaporated in the same year – when the Fifth forms were allowed a Council Meeting. Not for CHS a School Council or parliament, not even voting for prefects.

Six Mistresses did take ninety of us to Chester to see the dress rehearsal of a pageant, as an Old Girl played Princess Victoria. She rode in the actual carriage used by Queen Victoria on a later visit to Chester Castle.

What I do remember most vividly, even painfully, were two excursions to Lever Brothers' Sunlight Soap factory on the Wirral peninsula on the other side of the River Mersey. The township of Port Sunlight had been virtually founded in 1883 by William Lever. Each time, most of us developed very sore throats which ended in colds and coughs, so strong was the soap-filled atmosphere.

Like most schools of the time, we did our bit for charity, much less than in more affluent or responsive schools. An annual Cake and Sweet Sale in December aimed to raise £50 to support a cot in the Children's Hospital; the best year, 1935, achieved £67; our form came second once, making £5 15s 6d. Attendance by both parents at the sale, as well as at carol service and summer garden party, was automatic.

Highly enjoyable were the winter and summer parties given, almost as a rite of passage, by successive Fourth forms, for poor children. Once a Halloween party, for sheer pleasure, proved 'great fun', with the inevitable treasure hunt, producing 'music' with a comb and paper and such unexplained delights as 'Obstacles and Noses'.

FOURTEEN

Outside School and Church (or almost)

Holidays

I expect that you are wondering if there was any life beyond church and school. One activity which, for a time at least, bore little relation to church, although Sunday was punctiliously observed – a wet day in a boarding house was more than usually dreary – was a holiday. Going on holiday was regular and long-anticipated.

Whatever the destination, preparations were horrendous and extended; everyone was all of a tiswas. Camphor of mothballs impregnated the house as goodness knows what moths might get up to with the house shut up in a whole fortnight in August. Cases, heavy leather and wheel-less, for overnight or weekend family visits were taken out of their protective handmade material covers. Usually, a trunk was sent on 'In Advance' to await arrival. Did you know that the humped lid of an old-fashioned trunk was thus designed to take hats? My own sixpenny cardboard box from Woolworths lasted many years. The last days of a holiday were also a misery as the trunk had to be repacked and sent on ahead to arrive before Monday washday. Proper holidays, you see, began on a Saturday and ended on a Saturday.

The August migration was becoming the norm; those who had a fortnight (us) looked down on those who had but a week's leave, who in turn looked down on those who went out just for days.

One extraordinary year saw us at a hotel, Ballaqueeny, in

the Isle of Man at Port St Mary – superior to the trippery Port Erin. This was the only hotel I had ever stayed in until my honeymoon some twenty years later. The venue was not the brightest of ideas as Dad was seasick before the boat had left the landing stage. Milton's overlong 'Elegy on a Friend drowned in the Irish Channel' could not be taken seriously, perhaps because it was too close to us and surely no one drowned there. Much more likely and certainly funnier was the eighteenth-century tale of a favourite cat, Selina, drowned in a tub of goldfishes.

Otherwise, we stayed at guest houses, a distinct social step up from a boarding house, although indistinguishable in other respects. The seaside was chosen, undoubtedly for my benefit. Dad aimed at variety, from Torquay when I was nearly four when we discovered Buckfast Abbey with the sandaled monks, honey and, so I'm told, tales of Glastonbury (no hippies then; even the word was unknown) to Whitby with its very cold east wind.

St Anne's-on-Sea, to give it its full title, in 1932 was deemed more suitable than nearby Blackpool with its Big Dipper, its illuminations famous all over the country, its pierrots and mother-in-law jokes, its booths with the fat Bearded Lady.

One year, somewhere in Scotland, I secured the autographs of six golfers who were staying there too, a thrill at the time, totally bewildering now. Above all, North Wales attracted, although already in the Thirties, Butlin's was spreading there.

We usually travelled by train Third Class with booked seats at an extra cost – 1/-? I don't think that there has been a Second Class in my lifetime. All stations, and there were many, many more of them, were manned. The stationmaster called out the station's name as the train arrived. Dad used to wander off ('gone to Timbuktu') if he had to wait more than a minute or two for train or bus. I wondered then why this habit drove Mother up the wall. Had he, perhaps, once missed a connection? Did she simply feel insecure without him? I now share a little of her anxiety. Machines on stations could stamp out your name on a strip of metal. A ticket collector looked at your ticket at the barrier to each platform.

I'm baffled now how we knew the right platform as there were no automatic arrival and departure signboards. The man in the ticket office probably knew. Suburban trains went from their usual platforms at Central Station. Maybe there was a sign or a handwritten notice on a board at Lime Street, or did a man with a megaphone call out? I just cannot remember.

Local trains usually had no corridor and therefore no lavatory. On a long-distance train, there was understandable anxiety lest there might not be one. We later sang, sotto voce, to the tune of Dvorak's *Humoresque*:

> We encourage constipation
> While the train is in the station.

The lavatory could be used only while the train was moving.

For a child, the magic was in looking out of the window. When I was tiny, I slept in the luggage rack. We took boiled egg sandwiches wrapped in a cotton serviette or greaseproof paper.

What clothes were packed in the trunk? I remember few apart from my red and white check dress and school blazer. Dad had a series of home-knitted berets or 'tammy', short for tam-o'-shanter, which made me laugh, then, as I grew older, cringe. Still, they were an improvement on the handkerchief over the pate, with knots in each of the four corners to keep it on. Women wore hats even on the beach, although a beret or a hairnet was later acceptable. I don't think that Mother went out in the whole of her life without a head-covering. Eddie, a cousin by marriage, wore his bowler, braces and rolled-up trousers to go paddling.

My dress was tucked into the waist elastic of my knickers.

Dad sported long shorts when his khaki ones eventually wore out. I had a new pair of Startrite sandals (5/-?) most summers; rubber paddling shoes helped on pebbly beaches and in the water. I was often told that I wasn't the only pebble on the beach!

One undressed and dressed with difficulty under a large towel. Dad wore a long bathing suit with built-up shoulders to thrash about in the water; so did I. One was green and knitted. I can still see the mixture of purl and plain squares. You can imagine what it felt and looked like when it was wet! The swim hat was so tight that wearing glasses was impossible, meaning that I couldn't see what I was doing or where I was going. That, coupled with ludicrous water wings, slippy paddling shoes and the fear of jellyfish, made me happier on dry land holding a shell to my ear in order to hear the sound of the sea and repeating, 'She sells seashells on the sea shore.' It was helpful that no swimming, no bathing or even paddling was allowed until two hours had passed since the previous meal. Other parents dictated one hour: Mother had to make doubly sure.

All three of us burned in the sun. The soreness and the itchy unsightliness of heat lumps required uncomfortable sunhats; skin cancer hadn't been thought of and suncreams were for the rich and fussy. We sat in deckchairs under umbrellas hired by the day or half-day. Lilos came later. Once dressed again, one suffered the indignity of having one's face washed with spit and dried with a hanky.

I wasn't any good at skimming pebbles, but I did have a tin bucket and wooden spade, for which I was thankful as boys had heavier and hurtful metal implements. Sitting on the beach, one covered oneself with sand to the waist, then wriggled one's toes; it was a sensuous delight, although we didn't know it as such. A superior sandcastle – mine normally disintegrated – was often surrounded by sand pies, sometimes decorated with little flags of no particular significance. Still, one could then be king of the castle and of all that one surveyed.

On the prom (promenade), we ate ice cream, 1d for a cone, 2d a wafer. We sucked rock with the name of the resort right through it; Dad brought jugs of tea. Not for us the pier; not only might we lose our place on the sands, but would surely be tempted to waste money on the machines. Donkeys plied for trade, but parental economy and personal timidity combined to put them out of bounds. I did possess the almost obligatory shrimping net, but you won't be surprised to hear that I never caught anything – which was actually a relief.

Dad had his 5/- Box Brownie camera which took six (or was it eight?) snaps. A more sophisticated version expanded like a small concertina and worked on a sort of string. Professionals buried their heads under a 'dicky bird' hood. The results were, of course, black and white. Most have now, sadly, faded.

On Sundays, there was no bathing, no sandcastles, no ice cream and no shopping. One memorable day saw the display by the Sunday Sand Artists; more often, revivalists held a rousing service; Nigger Minstrels performed in Llandudno's Happy Valley.

Once, Mother and I went to Shrewsbury. Dad's sister Lily and her gentle husband Ben had stayed with and cared for Granny and Granddad Hinchliffe, and, after their deaths, had stayed for some time at 12 The Mount. Ben took me on several walks round the town to see the old buildings – the Abbey (our favourite), the Castle, the old market which no longer exists, Lord Hill's Column (172 steps) and the old alleys (known as Shuts or Passages, such as the now-developed Seventy Steps Shut), some of which, including St Julian's Shut, Bear Steps and Grope Lane, still remain.

Religion still ruled. We had to visit the cemetery to see the graves of my grandparents and of my father's sister, who had died two years previously. I'm sorry to have lost a collection of quotations from tombstones (wartime salvage?), for, even then, graveyards were interesting – 'Six foot in earth my Emma lay'. A fascination remains with inserts in the press, especially those which indicate a sureness that the defunct reads the local free newspaper.

I helped in the choir with the anthem, told a story to nineteen children and played the harmonium for Sunday School. The purpose of this visit was Mother's attendance at a niece's wedding. I don't seem to have been invited. I don't think that she ever saw that niece again.

Several Easters and summer fortnights were spent with my cousin Kathie, fourteen years my senior, and her husband Eddie, he of the bowler. They lived in Shropshire at Hadley, a small village near Wellington, once a busy market town in its own right and now absorbed into Telford. It was another awkward journey: train to Central Station, walk to Lime Street, then usually, but not always, securing a seat in a direct train taking about three hours to Shrewsbury, where one frequently missed the local connection to Wellington, where Uncle Ernest would join me to go to Hadley station where he worked. After tea at Auntie Florrie's, I'd walk round to Kathie's house in Brookdale.

Eddie had one enormous advantage over the few other relatives with whom Mother remained in contact – a car, into which he would dangerously pack up to eight family members. At least once, he and his wife came to fetch me, bringing Kathie's older sister, Queenie, with them. She was a great giggler like her father, to whom her mother, my aunt, was quite subservient. I learned, much later, that her father drank too much, although whether it was too much by family or by medical criteria is uncertain. He ran his allotment profitably. He wore heavy black, and went off to his work in his railway signal box, carrying an enamel jerry can of tea.

The two sisters had worked at the Chad Valley Toy factory which mopped up the local female labour; this was considered better than being in service. Eddie was at Sankey's, which did the same for men. It was whispered that Kathie and Eddie couldn't have children. This bothered me: they were married, weren't they? Two other pairs of childless relations came to visit; Dad's sister Lily and her husband, Ben, and Mother's sister Beattie and her husband, Frank. These last two and Mother remained at daggers drawn; I'm not sure that they ever met after Mother left for Liverpool, yet several cousins have commented on their kindness. Sad.

I enjoyed the liberation, but feared some of the happenings. Why, we listened to radio Luxembourg! – or, to be more accurate, it was on permanently. It was completely prohibited at home. Was that because it was foreign, or because of the morally debilitating dance music? We ate chips out of newspapers! Worst, or best, of all, we ate ice cream on Sundays! The initial terror of their damnation, and mine by association, changed to a faint suspicion that Wesleyans had not got everything right. These activities did not seem likely to do much harm to their immortal souls. Normally, I spoke without thinking of the consequences as the hymn dictated:

> Sins unnumbered I confess
> Of exceeding sinfulness…

but, as with the flasher, I instinctively did not tell my parents of these lapses from the straight and narrow.

We talked a lot, we walked a lot, we enjoyed the pianola and its rolls of music. At least twice I climbed the Wrekin, 1,335' and so only just a mountain, even once sitting in the sun and getting burned at the Needle's Eye. Local wisdom had it that if you could see the Wrekin, it was going to rain; if you could not, then it was raining. It also had its own saying: 'to go all round the Wrekin', the equivalent of the Scouse 'all round the houses', implied either a lack of straightforwardness or unnecessary complications to reach your objective.

There was church even here, but only once on a Sunday. I sometimes joined the Good Friday or church anniversary choir in the anthem or cantata; I remember only *Olivet to Calvary*. This was exhilarating when compared with Woolton's efforts with the Fishy Smiths and me. In my diary, there is one cryptic note: 'Trifle at Auntie's church.' Another year, it was cake and trifle for my birthday.

I didn't know until many years later that I was paid for. They were the only ones welcomed by Mother at home, although they never stayed a night; maybe she felt superior to them financially, perhaps she was grateful that they took me off her hands.

Entertainment at Home

The short-lived gramophone had to be cranked by hand; if you were careless, or mischievous, this affected the speed of speech or music. Steel needles too often skidded over the $33\frac{1}{3}$ records. I remember only nursery rhymes.

Virtually coinciding with my birth, the wireless was awkward with its heavy acid-filled accumulator and its battery which had to be recharged. It was, nevertheless, a great improvement on a crystal set with headphones. Was the fee (licence) 10/- a year?

When we eventually had one, it sat on an occasional table (another odd adjective to a child: what was it when it wasn't a table?), or on a pot stand near the window. Was it a Pye, or HMV? It was an upheaval to buy a 'proper' one as it necessitated an electrical point in the 'surround' (skirting board). Its use was allowed sparingly, and, as I've said, never on Sundays.

Whilst considering it a gross extravagance, but a necessary one, to buy the *Radio Times*, Mother tried to teach me various stitches – such as lazy daisy – to adorn hessian covers for it at home and for Christmas presents.

Children's Hour – the very term makes me cringe now – was a must until the age of twelve or thirteen, with real-life uncles and aunts. Aunty Doris and Aunty Muriel combined with Uncle Mac at 5 or 5.15 each weekday afternoon to give news of other children, suggest hobbies and be generally uplifting. The programme closed before the news with 'Goodnight, children, everywhere'. It was here that I first 'met' Romany, alias Rev. Bramwell Evans, a Methodist minister who talked about the countryside. At a public meeting in town, I later collected his autograph and that of his mother who signed falteringly 'Romany's Mother'. These have now gone to the Romany Archive.

The evening news was a regular must; six o'clock was an especial time as working families were at home for their meal. Stuart Hibberd was the chief announcer; it is said that he wore a dinner jacket to read the bulletins! Not that I knew what a dinner jacket was. In those far-off days, nothing was known of the private lives of wireless celebrities. Broadcasting grew in importance as it increasingly covered public events at home and abroad.

Wimbledon's breathless commentator was listened to with equally breathless and mounting excitement. In my lifetime, Great Britain had won only doubles, but in 1934 we had the first of Fred Perry's three consecutive singles' titles and the first of Dorothy Round's two. She was especially approved of in our house because she didn't play on Sundays. Whilst they won mixed doubles twice, the women's doubles champions were British on three occasions. How we cheered 'Bunny' Austin, who died quite recently! How patriotic we became! In 1936, only the women's singles title left these shores. Hard to believe now, isn't it?

Cricket coverage was great too and interest was stimulated by cigarette cards, featuring such immortals as Bradman, whose obituaries filled columns in 2001, Washbrook, Sutcliffe, Hobbs and Hutton, but the game was too slow for me.

Saturday nights (8.15 p.m.?) gave us variety shows; in my memory, Mondays did too: In Town Tonight, Bandwaggon,

Palace of Varieties, Variety Bandbox, Music Hall, Monday Night at Eight, Carol Levis and his discoveries (to bring in new blood). Some of the acts did not survive the War or the advent of television.

There was a wealth of Northern comedians; it's impossible to convey the attraction of so many of the double acts, one the feed, the other the foil, the Morecambe and Wise of their day. They relied on quick timing, wit, puns, maltreatment of the language, catchphrases, old jokes. Names come happily back; what most said and did is a blur, but the whole process was so new that the sheer novelty of it made us receptive to what now seems incredibly old hat: Revill and West (two women), Flotsam and Jetsam, Clapham and Dwyer (a bit more earthy), Elsie and Doris Waters, Flanagan and Allen, Leslie Holmes and Leslie Sarony, Bebe Daniels and Ben Lyon (the age-old argumentative sex gambit with an American accent), the Western Brothers ('I say, old chap').

Some transferred happily to television and films, some were less successful because the radio listeners were disappointed when the actor or actress differed too much from their audience's own imaginings. Arthur Askey (his catchphrase was 'I thank you', and his girlfriend Nausea Bagwash) and Richard (Stinker) Murdoch 'lived' in the flat above Broadcasting House. Was theirs the first comedy series we listened to? Arthur carried your godfather in his arms, having been at school with his father. How's that for fame? The great exuberant Tommy Handley, who first broadcast in 1925, with his signature tune 'It's that man again', gathered a cast in ITMA of comic actors and cheered everyone up so much during the War. His trademark was speed: 'Hello! Is that Turner, Turner, Turner and Turner? It is? Then good morning, good morning, good morning and good morning.' This first programme was in the last July of peace. Some of the very old comedians were still performing in the late Thirties: George Robey of pantomime dame fame, Harry Lauder and

Will Fyffe, both 'professional' Scotsmen.

Single acts usually had a particular trademark by which they were immediately recognisable and which contributes now to their dated *naïveté*: Claude Dampier as the consummate silly ass, Harry Helmsley with his child impersonations, diseuse Jeanne de Casalis, Gillie Potter from mythical Hogsnorton, Issy Bon with his Jewish patter. I can't place Stainless Stephen now, but he did make us laugh. Less highly regarded in our house was Max Millar – a decidedly vulgar Cockney.

There was usually a singing act; the orthodox sweetness of Anne Zeigler and Webster Booth contrasted with the earthiness of the lassie from Lancashire, our Gracie, Gracie Fields, just a few years younger than my parents. She took the eighteenth-century ballad of 'Sally' –

> Of all the girls that are so smart,
> There's none like pretty Sally.
> She is the darling of my heart,
> And she lives in our alley

– and made it into her very own song. She introduced the comic element into other sentimental ballads as she warbled, shrieked or belted out with consummate timing, 'The biggest [pause] Aspidistra in the world.' On stage or screen, she would scratch her back at a theoretically poignant moment or indicate that her feet were killing her. My parents approved of the poor girl from Rochdale who made good and became a Dame.

For Mother, the Bing Boys of the Great War were the thing. She was horrified by her daughter's burgeoning love of crooners and feared the worst. I've not lost my delight in the inimitable Bing Crosby, in the big sound of Adelaide Hall, the zest of Alexander's Ragtime Band. She could tolerate the so-English Jessie Matthews but was much less sure of Maurice Chevalier, projecting the image of the archetypal Frenchman in love.

There were orthodox bands still: Victor Sylvester, who actually gave instructions for ballroom dancing, Henry Hall and the BBC Dance Orchestra ('Here's to the *next* time') and Jack Payne. More modern bands and groups were taking over from Albert Sandler and the Palm Court Orchestra and were more to the taste of youngsters like myself with leanings to jazz rhythm – in fact, too many to mention all. Carroll Gibbons and his Savoy Hotel Orpheans, Harry Roy, Geraldo, Joe Loss, Ambrose – my parents could not accept all these, their limit being Troise and his Mandoliers. For me, Nat Gonella and the tango, Charlie Kunz and syncopation on the piano, and the blacked-up Kentucky Minstrels all ring a bell or cause a frisson of adventure even now. The Ink Spots were one of the first black singing groups to have hits over here.

I am indulging myself in this letter and shall continue to do so. Have you ever heard of these men and women? In other words, has the reputation of any of them survived? I wonder too, who were the heroes and heroines of your childhood and adolescence and how many of them still live with you and will survive?

Entertainment outside the Home

Cinemas were excitingly new. The lights dimmed gradually and you watched in the dark with other people – cinemas were often full – a massive programme by today's standards. A short film preceded the news – Pathé Gazette, Gaumont British or British Movietone, dependent on which chain ran the place – then advertisements, a cartoon (Mickey Mouse, Donald Duck), a trailer for the following week, maybe a 'short', and finally the main film. In the larger city cinemas, an organ would rise from the pit, with the organist playing his signature tune loudly to be greeted with applause. The best known of this kind was Reginald Dixon in the Tower Ballroom, Blackpool.

The lucky ones enjoyed the thrill of sitting in the back row, holding hands with a boy. This didn't come my way then, although I do recall the excitement of 'when these people leave, we'll pinch their seats'. You could sometimes manage to stay on and see everything twice round, all for 6d or 9d at most.

At the end of the programme, there was a rush to get as near as possible to the exit before 'God Save the King' – if you didn't make it, this stopped you dead in your tracks in the same way as in the game of musical statues.

Liverpool was well supplied with picture palaces, an accurate description as far as we were concerned: a brightly lit large foyer, marble pillars (we didn't suspect that they were false), deep carpets and brass rails in the auditorium: Forum, Futurist, Scala, Palais de Luxe and the (new) Trocadero. The Tatler, with commissionaires and midweek change of programme, was essentially a provider of news and cartoons, these last being a novelty.

Nearer the suburbs were the Rialto (frowned upon) and the Grand (it wasn't) in Smithdown Road. Woolton was allowed for *Mr Deeds Goes to Town* ('passed three boys and talked. That's all.') and remained a fleapit as did Garston Empire – whether justifiably, I can't judge. When we left Hunts Cross, our local was the much-liked and much-patronised Plaza. When we returned to Liverpool for the last time, it was being knocked down; some of our youth went with it.

Some of the pictures (they weren't called films then) which we enjoyed would be unwatchable now; don't forget, their makers and actors were technical pioneers and the viewers were pioneers too. You have only to watch again some of the early television programmes to realise the same phenomenon. In general terms, the pictures I was allowed to see divide into several groups.

The first was dependent on the star or stars; the titles are often a giveaway. On that basis, Mother determined what should not be seen and often forbade me to go with Mary. One, untraced, had a ventriloquial act, which gave me nightmares and for a time put paid to all cinema entertainment.

Such were the capers of ukulele-playing George Formby – 'I'm leaning on a lamppost at the corner of the street in case a certain little lady passes by. O me! O my!' (Oh well!) – in *Keep Fit*, Mickey Rooney in *Out West with the Hardys*, Will Hay in *Where There's a Will*, the *Three Maxims* with the ageing W. C. Fields, and, of course, Charlie Chaplin in *City Lights* and *Modern Times*. His screen persona was obviously innocent, so that was fine; we knew nothing of his private life.

Another unsophisticated group appealed to family viewing: the innocence of *A Hundred Men and a Girl* with Deanna Durbin and another Frenchman, Adolphe Menjou, Jessie Matthews in *You Shall Have Music*, the young Shirley Temple in *Heidi* and singing 'The Good Ship Lollipop', the operatic Grace Moore ('v. marvellous') in *Wings of Song*, the sweetness of *Marie Antoinette* with Norma Shearer and Tyrone Power, the saccharine *Snow White* and *Goodbye Mr Chips*, when the tears flowed. I don't think that I could sit through any of them now. We all fell in love with *Showboat* and the magical voice of Paul Robeson, his wholesome religious approach captivating my parents.

Others were full of *Boy's Own* derring-do, with titles such as *The General Died at Dawn*, and were mainly imports from Hollywood; Gary Cooper was our heart-throb. *Dawn Patrol* starred Errol Flynn and Basil Rathbone, *Spies in the Air* Barry K. Barnes.

We learned such shocking Americanisms as 'swell'. Immortal lines included the voluptuous Mae West's suggestive 'Come up and see me sometime' and Garbo's expressed desire to be alone.

Some were dramatic, with favourite stars or were good transfers of books to the silver screen: *Victoria the Great*, with majestic Anna Neagle and Anton Walbrook (probably more attractive than Albert ever was) and Shaw's *Pygmalion*.

What I enjoyed most at that stage, apart from the occasional weepie, was the comic, whether inherent in the plot as in *Climbing High* with Michael Redgrave (much loved from Liverpool Repertory days) and the inimitably long-faced Alastair Sim, *A Yank at Oxford* with Robert Taylor, the beautiful Vivien Leigh and Lionel Barrymore of the great family, or as prolonged comic turns translated from the stage. *Then*, the pinnacle was reached by the Marx Brothers, the wily Chico, the dumb, blonde-chasing Harpo and the quick-fire Groucho in, for example, *Duck Soup* and *A Night at the Opera*. I still loved them after the War but I don't know how I'd react to them now, when they are enjoying a cult success.

Theatre

As you may have gathered from what I've told you of Liverpool homes, and, indeed, ours, we were not 'into' Art. One visit took place on the Friday afternoon of a half-term holiday to the Walker Art Gallery (now the northern outpost of the London Tate) to see an exhibition by Liverpool amateur photographers; as we took in the Wirral that same afternoon, this could not have absorbed us for long. Equally briefly viewed was a display by part-time Art students at Wavertree Tech. Art appreciation lessons at school would surely have been more beneficial than drawing unstable cups and saucers.

Whilst musical comedy was in vogue, there was little real, non-sacred music either, although I recall many song titles, some tunes and a few words, mainly from films and wireless: 'Love in Bloom', 'Indian Love Lyrics', 'Some day my Prince will come', 'Did you ever see a dream walking?', 'Dancing cheek to cheek', 'If I had a talking picture of you (hoo)'.

> Some day I'll find you,
> Moonlight behind you…

Or:

> Darling, je vous aime beaucoup,
> Je ne sais pas what to do,
> Vous avez completely stolen my 'eart.
> Matin, midi et le soir,
> Toujours wondering 'ow you are...

They are mostly indistinguishable in attitude, namely the assumption that 'Love is the sweetest thing', completely an affair of sentiment or emotion and quite non-sexual. At least the words made some sort of sense.

At church concerts, young men warbled 'Where'er you walk', 'Who is Sylvia, what is she?', 'It was a Lover and his Lass' or Ben Jonson's

> Drink to me only with thine eyes
> And I will pledge with mine...

and:

> I think that I shall never see
> A poem lovely as a tree.
> Poems are made by fools like me,
> But only God can make a tree...

even:

> Come into the garden, Maud,
> For the black bat, Night, has flown.

Budding pianists struggled with Handel's *Largo* (6d), 'Londonderry Air' ('may be performed without fee or licence') or Ketelby's 'In a Monastery Garden'; the more accomplished, or daring, performed Chopin's *Preludes, Polonaises, Marche Funèbre* or the *Moonlight Sonata* or Mozart's Sonata in G ('suitable for general practice and for use at Local Examination Centre Examinations').

The sole exception was for Gilbert and Sullivan, staged by the official D'Oyly Carte Company, which often did a Liverpool season. We all enjoyed *The Gondoliers*, *The Mikado*, *HMS Pinafore* and, my own favourite at that time, *Patience*. The comedy in words and acting helped. Mother hated the slightest deviation from the 'business' laid down by Sir Henry Lytton, Bertha Lewis (whose autographs she had) and Darrell Fancourt (such a splendid name); the younger Martyn Green carried on the tradition. Not one of us made the transition to opera which I, regrettably, still find funny.

Other touring companies were less elevated – variety, ballet, the odd West End production and, of course, pantomimes of the spectacular kind which have rarely appealed, although one year, eleven of us from school unexpectedly enjoyed *Snow White*, probably more because we were out without grown-ups than due to appreciation of the subject matter.

Advertising as 'The Theatre with the Social Air', the Royal Court considered itself, in comparison with the Empire, 'upmarket', although the term was not yet in use. Had not Sir Henry Irving and Ellen Terry trodden its boards? It too presented a Christmas pantomime. In 1938, Emile Littler's All-Star *Humpty Dumpty* included sixteen Tiller Girls, of which Betty Boothroyd, the recent successful Speaker of the House of Commons, was once a shining example. More characteristic, perhaps, was *Victoria Regina* (designer Rex Whistler) with Pamela Stanley and Paul von Henreid. I judged it OK, which meant mediocre. I realise as I write that Mother must have been well aware of the old lady, for she was twelve when the Queen died. Both parents were eventually proud of having lived in six reigns. I can manage only four and they include the months of the uncrowned Edward VIII.

The Shakespeare Theatre staged only variety and was therefore bound to be vulgar, so we didn't go there, nor to the

Everyman, for its plays had a cutting edge, with political views – and you shouldn't mix pleasure and politics! The Unity was even worse. Amateur dramatics – you don't often hear the phrase now – flourished; the best appeared at the David Lewis Theatre. There was the unique occasion when we trailed to the Winter Gardens – I've no idea now where that was – for *The Arcadians* ('V. Good').

I remain eternally grateful for my parents' regular patronage of The Playhouse, for it was The Playhouse with the Liverpool Repertory Company, evenings 7.45 p.m., Saturday matinees 2.30 p.m., which was The Theatre.

The Playhouse, it was nationally accepted, was unique, being the oldest and probably the most successful unsubsidised repertory in the country. It started in 1910 with a trial season of six weeks at Kelly's Theatre in downtown Paradise Street. The Star Theatre in Williamson Square, the home of melodrama and seating about 1,000, was bought for £28,000, and completely altered and redecorated in some three and a half months; it opened on 11 November 1911, with *Strife*, its author, Galsworthy, in the stalls, Lord Derby in one box, Miss Horniman (founder of Dublin's Abbey Theatre) in the other. It was started with no hope of public subsidy, a board of directors who knew nothing about theatre management, an inexperienced producer in Basil Dean, and a debt.

It even managed to survive the Great War, with actors and staff taking over everything as a commonwealth, before it returned to repertory by 1916. A year later, it was christened The Playhouse. Gradually, it put on plays for a fortnight or three weeks according to their success. It had its troubles – bricks stolen by strikers, a fire – but by the time my parents were patrons, it had become a source of civic pride. At its Silver Jubilee, J. B. Priestley suggested swapping half a dozen commercial theatres full of imbecility for it. His own *Time and the Conways* was performed here. St John Irvine wished it long life and 'down with the damned "pictures" '. For its seventieth birthday, the then poet laureate, John Masefield, wrote an ode.

The theatre was small enough to feel intimate, not so large that a short-sighted child might feel lost. We took a small box of chocolates for the intervals. Opera glasses were fixed to the back of the seat in front. Like a railway or supermarket trolley nowadays, they could be liberated by a coin – was it 1/- then? I'm sure, however, that you couldn't get your money back!

Mother wore a cloche hat, occasionally secured with hat-pins, so that it did not obstruct the view of other patrons.

At one time, we had season or subscription tickets for the Circle, or, more often, the Upper Circle (1/6 or, in the front rows, 1/9); surely that was preferable to the expensive stalls or one of the two even more extravagant boxes! The licensee, Maud Carpenter, was one of the most famous women managers in the country; devoted to the theatre, she saw to everything – the annual repainting of the outside, contracts, taxes, carpets, stocking the tea, chocolates, etc.

In the Sixth form, I enjoyed occasionally the ritual of queuing with school friends prior to sitting in the gods (Gallery) for 6d, a thrill which neither parent could under-stand. 'Why queue when you can come with us and have a more expensive seat into the bargain?' Three of us queued for an hour for Clifford Bax's *The Venetian*. I remember nothing of the play; I do remember queuing!

The pianist, Joseph Smith, played before and after the per-formance as well as during the intervals; the lights dimmed, the hush was instantaneous. A curtain raiser gave an opportunity to less experienced actors and ensured that the faithful many could enjoy an adequately long entertainment. For us, it was simply two for the price of one. It wasn't a permanent feature. George Harris designed the programmes and many of the sets.

Writers not only allowed their work to be performed, but often gave Liverpool the first production, so that many transferred successfully to London. I judged one of these, *Mrs Lipscombe's Birthday*, to be pathetic.

I recall only one Shakespeare play, *Twelfth Night*, with Michael Redgrave and Rachel Kempson, partly because we enjoyed their romance, never dreaming of the theatrical dynasty which would result. Maybe we didn't go to such productions – too highbrow for my parents and because I had enough of him at school? The reason remains obscure.

The fare was often good and solid: no cheese-paring, no triviality. A list would be tedious for you to read. Although evocative for me, sadly many ring no bells after more than sixty years. Let me think now: almost all of G. B. Shaw, Ibsen, Granville Barker, Oscar Wilde, Sheridan, Lascelles Abercrombie, Barrie (*The Boy David*), Elmer Rice (a modern, serious drama, *Judgment Day*), West End thrillers such as *I Killed the Count* or the ripping adventure of *The Circus Boy*, *The Barretts of Wimpole Street*, *Reunion in Vienna*, James Bridie's *The Anatomist*, *The Brontës* (written by company member Alfred Sangster who played the Rev. Patrick), and *Jane Eyre*. For this last, I queued outside then had to stand throughout at the back of the gallery; I still thought the play quite good. The comedies were tremendous: *George and Margaret*, *You Can't Take It With You*, *The Late Christopher Bean* ('marvellous').

Sad to think that most have sunk without trace, killed off by the War, television and more sophisticated tastes. Have you heard of any of them? I was not as choosy then as I am now; I thought at the time that most of them were 'v.g.', a few were marvellous, several merely good, and a couple only OK. Apart from that première, not one was considered a flop by me. It was a wonderful initiation. I glued newspaper cuttings and reviews in an unwieldy album; all first nights were extensively reviewed in the *LDP*.

I kept the programmes, 6d each, until the other day. Their adverts and superfluous pages had already gone for wartime salvage; the centrefold of cast, acts, scenery, photos of the company, notes on the authors and successes of past members remained. The theatre opened at the beginning of September and closed in mid-June, the highlight being 'the enormous fun' of the last night with speeches, bouquets, etc. At Christmas in 1938, The Playhouse put on a single show of songs, playlets and a piano recital with all proceeds going to the charitable Goodfellow Fund. 'Whatever you pay for coffee or tea (in the interval) is a direct contribution to the proceeds of this concert.'

There was always a Christmas play for children. The first that I remember was in 1929, *Toad of Toad Hall*. Others were *Alice and Thomas and Jane*, *The Toymaker of Nuremburg*, *The Wind in the Willows* and a James Laver première, *The House That Went To Sea*.

Despite not always good or even regular pay, actors clamoured to come. Noel Coward and Gertrude Lawrence (albeit as an understudy) made their first professional appearances here.

Backed up by a nucleus of reliable old faithfuls such as Marjorie Fielding ('never in her life did she hope to be happier than she was at Liverpool'), Louise Frodsham, Lloyd Pearson, Deidre Doyle, Eleanor Elder and others stayed for several seasons. Many found greater fame on the box and in films, stardom in London and America: Liverpudlian Deryck Guyler (amongst other characters, Frisby Dyke in wartime ITMA), A. E. Matthews, Felix Aylmer, Megs Jenkins, Herbert Lomas, Cecil Parker, Robert Donat, Diana Wynyard, Catherine Lacey, Harry Andrews. There were occasional star returners: Judy Campbell and Wyndham Goldie who took the lead in *Parnell*. The boys adored Ruth Lodge, especially as St Joan; we girls swooned over the handsome Denis Webb, Alan's younger brother. We never sought any autographs as we had done in Stratford; that would have been an invasion of the privacy of admired and respected 'friends'.

Forgive me – I've enjoyed reliving one of the best parts of my pre-War life. Partly escapism, but more the appreciation of excellence.

Maintaining such a high standard must have been hard

going: choosing plays which fitted the strengths and limitations of the company and satisfied audiences with widely different tastes, having good actors leaving for London and being replaced by energetic but inexperienced newcomers, producing more than a dozen full-length plays and perhaps ten playlets with the strain on director and one-time actor William Armstrong and on performers' memories and stamina, to be venturesome yet keep the public – but I have realised this only with hindsight. We simply took the high standard for granted.

FIFTEEN

Adolescence

Growing up

Growing up is a trial even in the most understanding of families. It has many pains, physical, mental and emotional, with, at the time, few rewards. For me it was, perhaps, more difficult than the average, not simply as an only child in a family where the rules were strict because God-given, but also as a much younger and clumsy swot in my form at school.

How maddening were the remarks of grown-ups. I disapproved of adults who greeted me with, 'My, how you've grown!' and disliked intensely those who greeted me then said to Mother, 'My, how she's grown!' I felt that it would have been odder had I remained stunted. Those who did not refer to this normal course of nature got high marks. Now, I know how difficult it is not to refer to this phenomenon as I bite back the same comments. 'When you go out into the world…' was nearly as bad. What did they mean when they said, alarmingly, 'She's outgrowing her strength'?

Clothes

Non-school clothes caused distress. Your generation seems more tolerant, more willing to experiment and to throw away disliked or out-of-fashion garments. That would not have been permitted; the War reinforced this need for prudence, and it's hard to combat such training. My generation still has anxious moments: What to wear? Will it be suitable for the occasion?

Does this go with that? The greater worry then was whether it was on a level with the outfits of others, for clothes were the means of social, even moral differentiations.

Not that I was offered any choice! When I was fourteen, a new outfit was bought for me: blue hat and coat, blue costume (now called suit – jacket and, of course, skirt), blue blouse, blue shoes, gloves (brown kid) and a mac. This last must have been navy or brown, for I don't recall any other colours for macs. Question: What is your favourite colour? Answer: sky-blue pink with a finny addy (from haddock?) border.

For teenagers (the word was not known, or at least, never used; we were adolescents), ankle socks were still worn on holidays and for tennis, but otherwise, woollen stockings. Tights and synthetic fibres had not been invented. There was the thrill of graduating, outside school, from wool to lisle. Getting the back seams straight was far from easy. Silk, for Sundays, was not for the likes of us – fortunately, as in addition to a spud or potato (hole) in the toe or heel, they laddered all too easily.

Shoes, quite simply, *never* fitted; when they were new, they caused agony. This is marginally less so nowadays because of wider fittings. Sadly, my feet have got wider too. Young people can now affect the market in a way inconceivable to my age group, and so many have big, wide feet.

Auntie Florrie and her daughter Kathie made several of my outer garments. Ready-made clothes bore almost a stigma in the family. For well-to-do ladies, there was usually a tame dressmaker, someone good with her needle. Trouble loomed if a dress rucked up or got creased. I preferred my red check gingham, 2d a yard, so a dress cost 6d – 2½p, or, to put it another way, a week's pocket money. Mildly disliked were pinafore dresses, but most hated were puff sleeves for best or party dresses.

A jersey too could be knitted for 6d. A penny hank of one ounce had first to be wound into a ball (already wound, it cost

2d); one person held the skein taut over both wrists, moving hands from side to side, or if there were no one amenable to hand, it was draped round a chair back. Mother was willing to buy the wool as long as I was able and willing to knit it. Steel needles, numbered from fourteen, hopelessly fine, to one, thick as a walking stick, were needed. Polo necks were frowned on as they might conceal a goitre on the old, or, more relevantly, a tidemark on the young.

Shapeless dresses and blouses, boleros, bum-freezer jackets, skirts over the knees, clodhopper shoes – these were the clothes of the Thirties in my sphere. My first grown-up grey wool coat (I think I was seventeen) with a tie belt cost the enormous sum of £6. It lasted years and I loved it.

Most underclothes remained the same: itchy com(b)s, which did at least keep you warm, although the short sleeves showed as a bulge under a long-sleeved blouse or dress; vests with built-up shoulders – it proved quite an excitement to graduate to straps!

Physical matters

How I hated my enlarging figure and struggled to push in the burgeoning protuberances! The misery of buying my first 'bust bodice' (bra to you) is with me still. As Libby Purves wisely lamented some years ago, 'The history of the bra is a history of discomfort.' Other girls longed for this symbol of adulthood.

Paramount in one's early teens were 'growing pains'. I don't know how much your mother and elder sister told you. When, years later, I reproached my mother for not warning me of what would happen, what it meant and what it involved, she maintained that she had told me about growing up and 'woman's lot', but that I had blotted it out. She had probably said that it was the cross that all women had to bear. Anyway, forewarned or not, the curse (periods, a baffling idea just as 'change of life' is) came as a devastating shock, especially as it was usually very heavy and often accompanied by nosebleeds. This distressing and demeaning feature every seventeen to twenty-one days remained hell throughout my reproductive days. Mother claimed that I would be sorry when it stopped – well, I haven't been so far!

The subject was never mentioned in front of my father, indeed not in front of anyone. A recent serious article in *The Times* on the subject, a television programme – such could not have even been contemplated. We didn't discuss it or any bodily function at school, possibly because mine obviously came later than for everyone else in my form, and these older girls shielded me. I was never bullied as I had been on the train from Fairlie. It was a great pity that medication was not available as it is now.

Mother had, years before, made heavy flannel/towelling squares for this eventuality. They were folded like a nappy and secured with safety pins and had to be brought home, or saved on holidays or sent on. They were boiled each day. A bath was forbidden for the duration. Even your best friend wouldn't tell you – I have, as you know, no sense of smell. Apparently Mother inflicted gynaecological details on my best friend; I discovered this only twelve or thirteen years ago when Mary told me how much she disliked her. I didn't know if other girls bought towels and, if they did, where from, because they were invisible in the shops. I did not buy disposable ones until I left home.

This long ruined self-esteem and made participation in many activities tiring and, all too often, shaming. I even feel a bit embarrassed telling you about it now.

It was all part and parcel of the parental attitude to sex. I can see it now as understandable, especially for my father, who had seen the results of the selfish sexual appetite of his father. The spoof injunction to 'lie back and think of England' was not wildly off the mark. For me, with minimal and unscientific information, the word sex was a naughty word, but a sentimental longing for the unattainable was alive. Grown-ups mocked one's blushes in respect of boys. The whole business seemed dubious especially as one didn't have any of the adults' privileges.

Cosmetics were and remained a sign of moral depravity – illogical when 'perms' were permitted.

> Little grains of powder,
> Little dabs of paint,
> Make a girl's complexion
> Look like what it ain't.

Even Pond's vanishing cream was accounted daring. I found a Tangee lipstick in a loo once and guarded it carefully, not daring to try it, for anyone wearing lipstick was certainly no better than she ought to be. The height of excitement was my first compact some years later. A present, but not from my parents! Eau de cologne was permissible, scent was not. When Mother died, I inherited no fewer than eight unopened tins of talcum powder and a large bottle of 4711.

Adolescence was made still more unhappy because of the lack of mutual trust between Mother and myself. I was rebuked for actions or thoughts ('Don't care was made to care') which could have been known only from my diary. I could leave nothing personal like that lying about, because she read it. Her world was so narrow in comparison with what I was beginning to envisage.

An occasional escape next door, once until 10.45 p.m., when both parents were out at a church function and home-work had to be done, was 'gear'. The neighbours too enjoyed 'cheap' music; Gershwin symbolised freedom. I wasn't trusted even at sixteen to be in the house alone at night.

Relations with Mother grew more and more strained. The atmosphere must have been uncomfortable for me to describe myself in that diary as 'edgy and short-tempered. Mother got out of bed the wrong side this morning. All rows and nothing else… Awful row re the Mothers' Bright Hour party, a bit of a bust-up… another row re lacrosse match.' I broke a vase, there were rows about returning to school, outside activities, the lot. She called me 'mardy' (miserable) or like a bull in a china shop.

That she had periods of being unwell is now clear; she gave up the Sewing Meeting and walked very little but she never expressed or explained her martyrdom. As I was struggling to come to terms with my own increasingly difficult body, I did not know that she was probably menopausal – not a word I had ever heard of then. She believed in, or derived pleasure from, suffering silently – which was very noticeable, but one did not ask questions.

Dad was a buffer, although I'm not sure how much he knew of the tension or if he made a conscious decision to hold his peace. Mother never attacked me in his presence and I wouldn't have dared to say anything derogatory. I even helped him a great deal in the garden, although that made her jealous – 'You never help me in the kitchen.' When she spent a few days away, probably in Shrewsbury, Dad and I played pelmonism ('I won easily') and together we cleaned the house; the windows (my bit) were not to her liking. I cooked the fish for supper and topped and tailed the gooseberries. We went for a walk together once; Miss Amy (Smith) picked us up and took us for a ride in the car; the enjoyment was totally destroyed on our return.

When Dad was on overtime or, worse, when he spent two weekends in Shrewsbury to see his sister who was dying of TB and a third for her funeral when I was thirteen, life was truly wretched. Perhaps you can appreciate this more readily when I tell you that Mother could still reduce me to tears when I was much older than you are now.

Dad had also to go over to Belfast for two nights on the death of his father after several strokes; he was now head of the family. 'I got up, made tea, laid table – terrible day.' Some compensation came in the 'lots of funny stories' that he brought back about Granddad and how his determined second wife, little Sarah, got her own way – alas, all forgotten now.

The worst was probably when Mother was unwell and Dad had a bilious attack! He was tough, partly due to a good constitution and partly through his mental approach. He did suffer from fibrositis; embrocation was rubbed on. When he did get flu, however, it caused chestiness – there were no injections then. Once, he had to sleep in my room, so I was horrified to have to spend four nights in the front room's double bed with Mother. The spare bed in the winter/summer room was not to be made up out of season.

Then there was Sex – although I didn't recognise it, nor was the dirty word ever uttered. I was longing for a boy friend, the two words being milder, more factual and more accurate than boyfriend, now used to denote a steady partner. Yet at the same time I was bored and disgusted, longing for a boy to make a move, yet petrified if one did. Liberation was, by modern standards, incredibly slow in coming. We giggled at Menlove Avenue – that men love 'aving you – but at the words, not understanding the notion.

A kiss was desperately important; on the other hand, could a kiss bring a baby? This was a common enough notion in the Thirties and apparently has some currency even now. My knowledge of anatomy was still limited to:

Slugs and snails and puppy dogs' tails,
That's what little boys are made of.

Kissing on the cheek was unknown in the family circle, so that relations, family friends, honorary aunts and uncles all kissed one on the lips, as did my father – his one rather sloppy failure for me at that time. Presumably none of them counted in baby-making.

Adults had funny expressions: sweet seventeen and never been kissed, to be sweet on someone. Walking out with or, more common still, courting, was good; this meant going steady, and the female could with propriety refer to 'her young man'. In due time, there was an engagement, then marriage and babies were the inevitable end.

But spooning, such as holding hands, making goo-goo or sheep's eyes at a male, sealing a letter with SWA(L)K (sealed with a (loving) kiss) were all held by grown-ups in the highest contempt. My diary suggests a most unhealthy preoccupation with it all. I'd forgotten the intensity, but thinking of it now brings it all back. There was one small mercy for me: no adolescent spots.

The sad thing is that I now have no idea to whom the diary entries refer! For example, in January, when I was fourteen: 'Didn't see my boy today, although I looked for him.' Then worse: 'Saw him but he never spoke to me. I cried. I feel so on my own all the time.' This last reveals the crux of the matter – lonely and wanting to be self-indulgent without any reason for self-indulgence. It was safe too! 'Thank goodness, Ma and Pa don't know who it is,' but it was clearly someone from church, probably someone in the Boys' Brigade who was clearly older than I was as he had a car. Some of the entries remain too embarrassing to repeat.

After sixteen days without seeing him, I felt that a vision was urgently needed but, having seen him again, the desire tailed off. Absence did not make the heart grow fonder. Indeed, 'I've forsaken him now for another.' This one also proved elusive, so there followed another crush which lasted several months. He with a friend was invited to Sunday tea. He then made the fatal mistake of writing me a note: the poor lad's presumptuousness signified the end of that emotion. These yearnings seem to have absorbed about eighteen months.

Holidays

Holidays began to widen horizons. One of the most delightful was a very special one just for Dad and me in London when I was nearly fourteen. Mother stayed at home unwell, coming on later when we all headed for the Isle of Wight. Dad was delighted that, forty years on, we both remembered it with pleasure; it seemed like an out-of-school adventure for just the two of us.

We caught the 10.10 train from Mossley Hill to Euston. It seemed odd to say proudly that we were going *up* to London when clearly it was *down* on the map.

Dad had booked a bed and breakfast in Pimlico. Mrs Lewis, the landlady, shook me by coming unannounced into my spartan room when I was in my new bra and knickers (the term 'pants' hadn't been invented). Ill at ease in them at the best of times, embarrassed and shy, I didn't know how to cope so, for no reason, I bent down and remained thus. We queued up for the landing lavatory like the other customers. The best hotels, I learned, had 20 to 300 rooms; a single, with bath and breakfast, cost all of 11/6, whilst a double was 21/- or 23/-.

Tea was in an ABC (a non-alcoholic café), a meal at the Strand Corner House, our night drink in a milk bar or Lyons. Waitresses were called Nippies, presumably because they were nippy on their feet. The last of the 250 or so closed in the Seventies.

There was very little that we didn't see. I listed everything in the diary; just to read it more than sixty years later is exhausting.

Day 1: Cenotaph, Number 10 (you could go right along Downing Street in those relatively carefree days), Westminster Bridge, the Houses of Parliament and the Law Courts ('both looked like churches'), flats, Big Ben, Scotland Yard, the Dismissal of the Guards, Lambeth Palace (admittedly in the distance), Whitehall, Trafalgar Square, Boadicea, the Zoo (photographed showing the guidebook), Somerset House,

Ministry of Health, two war memorials, amusement and picture palaces.

Day 2 brought not only a 'marvellous' big breakfast, a 'marvellous' dinner and a 'marvellous' visit to Madame Tussaud's, but also St Paul's (up and down 369 stairs, 'marvellous'), the Tower (more steps) and the Tube to Pinner to see the Misses Bridgwater and Hopkins who had retired there from Hunts Cross. We didn't get back to our digs, by Tube and bus, until 12.30 a.m.! We were both equally excited.

Day 3 saw us at Buckingham and St James' Palaces, with the Changing of the Guard. Although I now cringe to admit it, I even thought Westminster Cathedral 'marvellous', whereas the Abbey was merely 'very nice, but too many monuments'. We walked to Marble Arch for Oxford Street, 'quite good'. At some point, we called on a missionary in Jamaica Road and at the East End Mission in Billingsgate. *Captain January* (Shirley Temple?) at the cinema was, you've guessed it, 'marvellous'.

Day 4 morning only, meant the House of Lords and the Commons and inspecting stamps and manuscripts in the British Museum.

The school magazine did not accept my remarks on London, which I had deemed an education in itself. What impressed a *naïve* Scouser? The awesome loftiness of the buildings which made any small construction look odd; the 'morbid propensity for elaborate monuments and tombstones'; buses, red and plenty of them, horribly shaky and with outside staircases; cabs built for service not for comfort; roads and cars which seemed new, yet with chaos and confusion in the streets; the gentleness of the river; the lovely tone of Big Ben; the very few 'To Let' notices, which probably indicated what is now called the North–South divide; 'Cockneys', very obliging and jocular; cleanliness despite seeming disorder, for it was the first time that I was aware of how dirty my home town was: 'Liverpool ought to be ashamed.'

In the mid-Thirties, Dad discovered the CEHH, or Christian Endeavour Holiday Homes. Each housed 80 to 100, mainly young people and were run by a hostess, usually a pleasant, comfortable, outgoing widow, often of a minister, with two or three energetic and extrovert excursion leaders, often ministerial trainees. Christianity of the nonconformist sort (that is, non C of E), evangelical but not tub-thumping, was clearly the basis of the movement. They catered primarily for the 'working classes'. Wakes Weeks in the Lancashire cotton towns meant that factories closed for an August week; more precisely, the whole town closed.

Tables were for ten to twelve; self-help was the order of the day as all the helpers were scarcely paid volunteers. There was, of course, no 'strong drink'. The young slept in dormitories, lights out normally at 11 p.m. Small prizes were awarded at the end of the week for the best kept, for the most helpful table and the like. For the few venerable couples such as my parents, there were several private bedrooms, but all lavatories and washbasins were in corridors.

Such holidays transformed the lives of the whole family, enabling each one to get away from the others for a little while. Mother stayed put with middle-aged, sedentary women of her own kind, which left Dad free to join in youthful activities. He and I went on many long walks together; six miles or so meant a nice trot, thirteen or fourteen were about my maximum.

I obviously enjoyed meeting, listening and talking to and laughing with so many people, an experience sadly lacking out of school. These young, cheerful, uncomplaining factory workers encouraged a new concept of social conditions different from those in Liverpool. I especially relished the company of overseas guests: Hugh, a negro from Barbados studying Law in London, an Indian from Bombay at Manchester College of Technology, a Danish girl from Copenhagen, a German girl from the town where Dad had been a Prisoner of War; this interested him greatly, but in no way upset him or his creed of tolerance.

'We found it very interesting to mix with these people, who, we found, were just the same as we are in many ways.' This patronising comment indicates just how sheltered and restricted was our circle.

Activities? A get-to-know-each-other walk ('a spit and a draw' meant not too far), tennis and croquet tournaments, clock golf, beetle drives, charades, clumps, musical knees, murder, hangman, I spy (with my little eye), the inevitable treasure hunts, general knowledge competitions, in which Clever Clogs was sure to shine, and concerts. Walks, longer hikes encumbered with rucksacks alternated with thrice-weekly, well-organised excursions in 'charras' – we certainly got around. It was very good value for money.

As well as such verbal infelicities as 'Jersey, Guernsey, Underwear and Socks' (for the uninitiated, Alderney and Sark) and 'Jamaica? No, she came of her own accord', we also learned some silly rhymes.

> My face I don't mind it,
> For I am behind it,
> The people in front get the jar...

Unhelpful to one's fragile confidence about one's appearance.
At 'good old sing-songs', we sang the tuneful

> So be kind to your four-footed friend,
> For he may have been somebody's brother.

I have forgotten the rest. Then there was the most naughty of all:

> The moon shines bright on Mrs Porter,
> And on her daughter,
> A reg'lar snorter,
> And she washed her dirty hands in dirty water,
> She didn't oughter,
> The dirty cat...

not to mention such cheerful ditties as:

> There's a hole in my bucket, dear Lisa, dear Lisa,
> There's a hole in my bucket, dear Lisa, a hole.
> Then mend it, dear Lisa, dear Lisa, etc.
> With what shall I mend it, dear Lisa...

This is extendible according to the verbal inventiveness of the group. The words of Ashby de la Zouche, Castle Bromwich have completely disappeared from my mind.

One often met friends from previous holidays at these Homes and occasionally a mammoth reunion took place in St George's Hall.

A daily informal breakfast service was taken by guests at their tables, an official one on Sundays, nightly family prayers, a sacred concert, a CE meeting for which I often played the piano as even I could manage hymn tunes and which was sometimes addressed by a local worthy or, once, by the president of the CE Union, Dr Maldwyn Edwards, son of one of the hostesses. We all attended the local church of whatever nonconformist denomination.

So where did we stay?

On the Isle of Man, advertised as an ideal holiday resort, all the young element set out, making a terrific din, round the Castletown streets to the jetty on the very end of which was a small tower with a Red Knob. 'We all dance round and sing and have great fun and then retire to bed.' And now we dare to criticise the young! But it was all so innocent, so non-destructive and such a release from inhibitions.

You will remember that the famous London trip preceded the Isle of Wight. Travel was complicated even in those days when public transport was the norm: train to Portsmouth, boat to Ryde, train to Ventnor, bus to St Rhadagunds. There were walks along the cliffs, table tennis, visits to various villages and castles and beaches such as Alum Bay with the different coloured sands (I kept a fat test tube full for years) or to Blackgang Chine, a deep narrow ravine that had sadly been closed to the public when I tried to revisit it a few years ago. There is now a children's park at the top. We even saw the *Queen Mary*, an aircraft carrier and a destroyer, but didn't associate them with preparations for war. The return journey was somewhat fraught: 10.10 to Ryde, a packed boat to Portsmouth (no Hovercraft then), 11.43 crowded train to Waterloo arriving an hour late (not a modern phenomenon, but no refunds then), Euston connection missed but compensated for by having tea on the 3.50 p.m., arrival Lime Street 7.50, walk to Central Station reaching Hunts Cross at 8.50. The trunk arrived three days later.

At Saltburn in Yorkshire I was allowed to ride a horse; Kents Bank was convenient for Lake District excursions; from Penmaenmawr we used to visit the village of Dwygyflychi. Although we knew the right pronunciation, we childishly enjoyed calling it Dwigh-ghee-fligh-kigh.

In 1937, another tortuous journey involved a long cold wait at Llandudno Junction on the way to Plas-y-Nant; I fell off a borrowed bicycle on the rough track at the foot of 3,359'-high Snowdon, getting concussion and a permanently scarred knee. 'They' say that this might have contributed to my frontal lobe epilepsy, or *petit mal*, nearly fifty years later. In those days, men had to wear cycle clips on their trousers – not that my father could have been allowed near a bicycle. On one of the occasional visits to the cinema in Caernarvon, we saw *Dancing on the Ceiling*. Mother was ill and couldn't go; she was cross because I had enjoyed it. I have never learned the necessary tact; sadly, I have inherited her stubbornness.

We spent at least four pre-War Christmases in North Wales and one in the Lake District, where Mother gave Dad *In the Steps of St Paul* for his present. Such a holiday gave her some relief, but she still made all the celebratory fare for our return. We reached Kents Bank by mixed transport: bus from Hunts

Cross ('a crowd of drunkards' – just pre-Christmas merry, I suspect), tram to town, train from Exchange Station, a change for Grange-over-Sands. On one of our long walks, probably taken to reduce the effects of vast meals, I drank milk, untreated, straight from the cow – a procedure which would surely be condemned now.

Whereas I now shy away from group activities, it was then a 'marvellous' way to begin to learn how to get on with people; but even with all this excitement, moments of boredom and of frustration that I could not explain crept in.

SIXTEEN
Public Life

Public figures

Life in the world outside began to impinge. We were all Royalists in those pre-War days. The monarch was the father of the nation; it was *lèse-majesté*, a personal affront to the King, almost high treason, for which you might land in gaol, to put stamps upside down on an envelope. I still feel mildly uncomfortable doing this, although more because it is like hanging a picture upside down. In my 1935 diary are listed eleven kings, two princes (Monaco and Lichtenstein), one grand duchess (Luxembourg), one regent (Hungary) and seventeen presidents.

My parents had been aware of Queen Victoria's Jubilee in 1897; Mother was eight years old and Dad nearly six; they knew that grown-ups wore black when the old lady died and that the coronation of Edward VII had to be postponed because the royal appendix had to be removed. Mother had thrilled at the Relief of Mafeking and the consequent rejoicings. This battle in faraway South Africa occurred on 15 October 1899, so that she would have been nearly eleven; her memory would not be surprising until one asks the question: How did she hear about it? The family had no money for newspapers and showed no political awareness. As far as I know, none of its members was involved. There was no wireless, no television. Did the Town Crier make an announcement? How did *he* know? I never thought to ask her.

She had her likes and dislikes of public figures; there

seemed little reason involved. Ramsey MacDonald was misguidedly admired, more perhaps because he came from a poor family than for any political acumen. Dad's approval was reluctant; he preferred 'honest' Stanley Baldwin, as did Miss Macrae. George Lansbury appealed to the pacifist element in him; he expressed amazement at the daring of the 'little Welsh wizard', Lloyd George.

He kept up to date with his newspaper, never questioning its impartiality or accuracy. *The Children's Newspaper* avoided all controversy, so there was little news in it. In 1937, Tom Harrison had begun Mass Observation, but its publications had not reached our house. The broadsheets passed on by the Smiths, right wing in religion and politics, served to cater for and satisfy orthodox opinions already held.

Both parents always voted in local and national elections, for that was their duty. Neither would be drawn on which way they cast their votes, for the ballot was secret, wasn't it? – and anyway, not suitable for children. My guess is that it would be for the Liberals; I cannot see Mother supporting Labour, for that would have reminded her of her origins, nor Conservative, for that would have been above her station. Dad was a Gladstonian Liberal; not for him such as *John Bull*. Such were his scruples that he would not be taken by car to the polling station if he were not voting for that particular party.

For a Parliamentary contest, we had a day's holiday, which was 'wasted' one year by buying a new skirt and jersey in town. Photos and names of candidates appeared in the church hall in Hunts Cross. In 1934, Randolph Churchill stood as an Independent Conservative for the Wavertree division of Liverpool. I learned that he had thus split the Tory vote and so let Labour in.

Contemporary Royalty

I am looking at a cheap circular medallion on a safety pin, presented to all children. On the front, through a tunnel, a car is going one way and a lorry the other. Round the circumference, the words 'Presented by the Mersey Tunnel Joint Committee' encircle a representation of traffic under an arch. On the back, with Liverpool at the top and Birkenhead at the bottom, with the respective coat of arms to left and right, is the legend:

OPENED

BY

HIS MAJESTY

KING GEORGE V

ACCOMPANIED BY

HER MAJESTY

THE QUEEN

18 JULY 1934

Its construction had taken nine years.

Merzy Dotes and Dozy Dotes (originally 'Mares eat oats' and 'does eat oats') was replaced by the Scouse version – Mersey Docks and Harbour Board. As the second line was 'And little lambs eat ivy', the whole thing remains somewhat baffling.

Earlier, for four days only, everyone was allowed to walk through the £3,000,000 miracle before it was given over to vehicles; 66,500 of us on Good Friday made the trip of just over two miles and by Monday night the number had risen to 266,578. A collection for hospitals for this privilege raised nearly £7,000.

Interest in the monarchy was stimulated on 6 May 1935, with the Silver Jubilee of King George V. School presented a medal on this occasion. I received also a commemorative mug featuring the King and his Consort. It joined an attractive small one of Victoria's Golden or Diamond Jubilee and larger ones for the coronations of Edward VII and George V.

The sole survivor of my cigarette card collection is one of a supplementary series of twelve Jubilee pictures, which were issued by Senior Service (ten for 6d), Junior Member (twenty for 1/4) and Illingworth's Number 10 (twenty-five for 1/-). On the back is printed, somewhat ungrammatically: 'To the delight of tens of thousands, their Majesties, with members of their family, assembled on the balcony of the Palace. In the evening the climax to this never-to-be-forgotten Jubilee night, the Palace being floodlit, the cheering crowd still remaining.'

On the front, and apparently separated by about a yard, an unsmiling George V and Queen Mary (the Garter ribbon across her ample bosom) stood on the balcony in their finery. It was impossible to feel any warmth in or to the Queen, especially when we learned that she had been engaged to George's elder brother, known as Prince Eddy. When he died, she was, so to speak, passed on to the next brother.

That same year, Princess Marina married George, Duke of Kent; attractively vivacious, she remained a favourite minor member of the royal family. Pre-War, those last two words would have begun with capital letters.

The King reviewed his Navy. Souvenirs proliferated.

Apart from the wireless announcement that we were at war with Germany, the bulletin best remembered by my generation is, I guess, that on George V: 'The King's life is drawing peacefully to its close.'

1936: the year of the three kings, as we irrationally boasted. George V died at 11.55 p.m. on 28 January. The *Daily Post* ran a supplement of pictures. There were no radio programmes on the day of the funeral. How different from the television coverage of Princess Diana's obsequies!

For me, his death came as a shock. Kings were not like other men; he should have gone on and on, as his grandmother Victoria had done.

He was succeeded by the bachelor Prince of Wales. Another shock: kings, by definition, had beards. The popular Edward VIII was clean-shaven and younger, more modern. I don't know who it was who aptly described him as 'a symbol of continuity to the elderly and a lively promise to those of his own generation'.

Royal broadcasts were always listened to in total silence; his broadcast of dedication was impressive.

Mother, like all her generation, felt that he should be married. The problem of succession was involved. You will know much more about him now than we did then. There was no prurient media interest in his personal life – at least not on the BBC or in the *LDP* – and we believed what we heard on the one and read in the other. There was a conspiracy of silence.

In my diary for 10 December, I have written 'KING ABDICATED'; his famous broadcast indicated that he could no longer reign without the support of the woman he loved.

How romantic, we swooned! Everyone in my form was on his side. A new word then cropped up – morganatic; that is, he could marry Mrs Simpson, but she would not be queen. The change in attitude to divorce was just beginning, but kings are not as other men. Prince Charles has faced a not dissimilar problem over sixty years later.

Our ignorance of Edward's personal behaviour and political views multiplied the force of the explosion. Known today but still somewhat controversial, they make crystal clear his unsuitability as monarch, particularly so at that sensitive time.

As it was near Christmas, we sang: 'Hark the herald angels sing! Mrs Simpson's pinched our King.'

His shy, stammering, unglamorous brother, the Duke of York, became the third King that year; his wife, later the centenarian Queen Mother, became Queen. His brother's coronation had been scheduled for 12 May 1937; presumably, arrangements were too far advanced to be cancelled or changed.

The mug prepared as Edward's souvenir became a collector's item; even his stamps had greater sale value! This mug, together with the previous three and the one of the new king,

were war casualties; they had disappeared when I wanted to
take them to my new home after the War. There were economies; the paper medallion on the ribbon was converted from
Edward VIII by a sticker to George VI; as time went by, the
sticker loosened. There were, of course, more new stamps.

The Coronation

The institution of monarchy had been damaged by the goings-
on, but George VI and Queen Elizabeth won sympathy for
their unexpected elevation to a life in public and more than
made up lost ground by their steadfast behaviour during the
War.

We went down to Pitt Street, then the heart of Chinatown
where we would not normally venture, to see their decorations, even more exotic than they had been for the Silver
Jubilee. Three Sixth formers represented CHS at the great
Empire Rally of Youth at the Royal Albert Hall. At school, each
girl received a large certificate. The crown was in the centre at
the top; along the sides were pink, white, blue and green
drawings to symbolise different races of the Empire. Red
Indians were at the centre below. It read thus:

THE

CORONATION

OF

THEIR MAJESTIES

KING GEORGE VI

AND

QUEEN ELIZABETH

12TH MAY 1937

PRESENTED BY THE CORPORATION OF LIVERPOOL

TO…

Miss Macrae then had to write the name of each girl and of the
school. At the Garden Party, we seniors wore white shifts with

tricolour hair ribbons for our display. On the wireless, we heard 'The fleet's all lit up'; the commentator was too!

Relations with the Corporation were close. School had been open in 1935 to visitors in connection with the local government centenary celebrations. Now we each received a reprint of the City's Coronation programme in the form of a copy of King John's Letters Patent making Liverpool a Borough and a Port, 28 August 1207 (on sale for 2d). The original Latin was translated freely by one Robert Gladstone.

Northern Ireland

We did not spend the Coronation holiday at home, but in Northern Ireland. Overwhelmed by my father's family, I loved every minute of our stay. The ferry from Liverpool ran overnight and on arrival at 7.25 a.m. we were met by two uncles: Martin, the youngest whom I knew; and George, whom I never got to know and, despite enquiries, have never heard of since. I felt a weird pride in having so many more relations than anyone in my form. We travelled to Gortgrib, Gilnahirk, to stay with my grandfather and his second wife Sarah.

The actual lovely hot dry day was spent in Belfast. We listened to the service, were again overwhelmed by yet another uncle, aunt and cousin (Alfred, Irene and Phyllis), visited Dundonald cemetery (presumably Granny was buried there) and, more interestingly, enjoyed huge ice creams. Uncle Harry arrived to listen with us to the Empire Homage and the Coronation Party on the wireless. Unsurprisingly, I was 'very tired'.

The following day, even more strenuous, began by pumping water as Granddad Hinchliffe had done. I showed off in Granddad Cherry's garden; my party piece was putting my foot in my mouth – literally this time! A photo was taken of the three generations: Granddad in bowler hat and suit, Dad in a Harris tweed suit which lasted for many a day and me in my school blazer. We collected newspapers from the village shop, and after midday dinner took the bus into Belfast. A guide showed us round parts of the City Hall 'where only 1 in 10,000 go' (?). The Post Office was selling the new Coronation stamp. After foot-slogging round the city and having tea in the Carlton, we took a tram to see yet another uncle, Eric this time. 'I played with Gillian [identity undiscovered], Eric and the whole tribe'.

Next day, Sarah took us to Knock to see her sons. Tea was with Martin and his wife Lily at their house. At the cinema, we saw the Coronation and a Variety Parade before returning to Granddad's. Obviously, all this gave us the strength to walk six miles to Harry's house and enjoy a little walk with his daughter Norah. Tea, piano, 'laughed and laughed', hen, ducklings, wild flowers, finch, cuckoo and corncrakes.

On our last full day, we went to the Presbyterian Church of Ireland. Auntie Mabel came; church again, then a gathering of the clan with Fred, his wife Annie and her sister Violet, Fric, his wife and their children.

Shopping in Belfast, dinner at Gilnahirk, a walk over ploughed fields and we were seen off by Harry, George, Fred and Annie. We arrived at the Pier Head at 6 a.m. and caught the train home.

This wasn't my first visit but it was my last. Apart from Martin, who joined the RAF, I have never seen any of the family again. I did have a breathless letter from Sarah before Denys and I got married.

My dear Joan

I hear you have decided to Love, Honour and <u>Obey</u> another woman's son and I am glad for there is nothing to compare with happy married life and that happiness depends on you both try to see the best in each other and forget the little differences that may arise we all have our faults you know no one is perfect in this life so Joan and — (I forget the name), we wish you every success in your new home.

Love from Sarah and Dad

I should have said Gran and Granddad

P.S. (Gran) (Dad) thanks you for remembering his birthday in all your excitement over the happy event. Eighty-five years old.

My first visit had been at the age of ten. We had gone in the MV Ulster Green, a ship of the Ulster Imperial Line. Mother and I travelled First Class in a cabin for two, Dad in steerage where all dossed down together, presumably to save money. Ships were taken out from the Landing Stage beyond the Liver Buildings by the Mersey Pilot boat as far as the Bar. I've mentioned that 'Crossing the Bar' was a religious metaphor for death so you'll understand that I found the beginning of the journey not merely confusing but frightening.

All that remains in my mind now is seeing Auntie Agnes and her husband George at Ballymena and another relative (which one?) at Ballnahinch (such lovely names), the magical Giant's Causeway and apparent hordes of relations all talking at once with strong accents already after some twenty years in Ireland. I enjoyed seeing them all; it was exciting to an only child to feel that all these people were my family. Mother grumbled about them behind their backs, but never to their faces. She simply froze. I rediscovered Auntie Agnes when she was ninety-eight. She died this summer, aged 103.

I was most impressed by my stocky grandfather, who was kindness and patience personified to me, even to saving, flattening and sending hundreds of Oxo cube wrappings to be exchanged for a cricket bat. I am glad that no one disturbed my illusions until I was grown-up and able to take in how differently and cruelly he had behaved to his own children. Granny Cherry terrified me: small, head bent right over, she didn't seem real. All adults seem old to children; grandparents, by definition, looked and were very old. She looked like a witch.

Not yet writing a diary, I made some notes under three headings:

1. Irish folk a) happy-go-lucky ways b) serving things on plates c) popping in at any time d) expressions

2. Ireland a) more concentrated towns b) no piers c) soon out into the country d) difference in fields e) gorse and wild flowers

3. Irish houses/cottages a) little conveniences – go to pump, no baths, ranges b) text cards over houses c) plenty of wirelesses

4. One post a day when only 1" out of boundary; postman often not bothered to do that much

Talk of jumping to conclusions on the pathetically unreliable evidence of the migrant, non-Irish Cherry family observed over one short week!

SEVENTEEN

The Outside World

Growing awareness

Our knowledge of public affairs was superficial. So much has been revealed subsequently in books and on television that you possibly know more of what went on then than we did at the time. Nothing was open. Children were especially protected. This led to a selective interest or, more frequently, to a lack of interest. I've tried not to let hindsight creep in.

Broadcasting had actually begun in the year of my birth; not that we were pioneer beneficiaries. The wireless gave a gentlemanly view of what was to me then the unchanging world. The earliest news that I remember was the first Royal Christmas message when I was ten. As I've mentioned, each cinema programme showed a newsreel; were they not all passed by a censor?

The *Daily Post* printed an annual review in January of the previous year's events, and in George V's Silver Jubilee year of 1935, those of his reign. It then recorded, for example, the assassination of the King of Greece (1913), of the Archduke Franz Ferdinand at Sarajevo (1914), of the Czar of Russia and his family after the Great War and of President Doumer of France. At home, pit disasters (1,109 men killed altogether) were brought home to us by the distressing loss of 200 lives at Gresford Colliery. In ships sunk, 3,851 had drowned, including those on the *Titanic*. More parochial was the opening of Gladstone Dock (and its subsequent extension) by the King himself. Amongst novelties which would shortly revolutionise the world was Lindberg's solo flight over the Atlantic in 1927.

At school, we sported boat race favours, but that was hardly an informed choice or relevant to the state of the nation. In 1934, we were excited by Belisha Beacons for safe pedestrian crossings, by the discovery of Nessie the Loch Ness Monster, the birth of the Dionne quintuplets in Ontario and the Trunk Murders in Brighton.

I kept a newspaper summary of that same year, an indication of a love of collecting and hoarding rather than of political sensitivity.

It commented, in true British fashion, on the weather; New Year's Day greeted by the worst fog in living memory, with 8,000 square miles of England blotted out, the hottest April day, 76 °F, for forty-one years, the worst August gale for fourteen; on Jean Batten in eight and a half days beating Amy Johnson's flight record to Australia; on natural disasters such as an Indian earthquake, a Japanese typhoon and Australian floods; on sporting triumphs such as Manchester winning the FA Cup, Windsor the Derby, Henry Cotton, the Open Golf championship; on miscellanea such as 6d off income tax, the launching and naming of the *Queen Mary* and car hooting being made illegal after 11.30 p.m.

The signs of political unrest were there for older people to ponder: Paris riots in January and February, the mountaineering Albert, King of the Belgians, killed, civil strife in Austria, the first Hitler purge with seventeen executions, eighty Spanish dead in an October revolt with the King of Spain threatening abdication if his powers were curtailed, the assassination of the King of Yugoslavia and the French foreign minister.

My own first interest in the big wide world came with the invasion of Abyssinia by Mussolini's Italians, which the League of Nations had failed to prevent. When his country was annexed, Emperor Haile Selassie, the Lion of Judah, became a dignified exile. The pronunciation of the country's capital

proved worrying: first it was Addis Abába, then it settled as
Addis Ábaba. The country is now Ethiopia.

In 1936, the strutting Mussolini ordered all workers in
munitions factories to do twenty hours of overtime each week,
whilst naval and air power was greatly increased. Every so
often, he was sneered at as a figure of little real substance. I
quote Sagittarius although this particular verse dates from
1939:

> For the Duce's inflated ideas
> We can offer but two panaceas –
> Either give him Gibraltar,
> Suez, Cyprus and Malta,
> Or a kick in the Pantellerias

– volcanic islands off Sicily which were taken by the Allies in
1943.

An article by J. C. Trewin two years later reminds me of
what I knew, or thought, to be interesting or significant then.
The death of King Fuad of Egypt meant attractive new stamps.
More important was the Spanish Civil War which began in
1936 and the rise to power of General Franco. At first, he was
acceptable because he had begun a revolution and therefore
was exciting; but despite Germany's signature to the Non-
Intervention Pact, 5,000 Germans joined him and the bombing
(a new facet of war) of the Basque town of Guernica in 1937
soon disabused most of us. 'We will remember Guernica when
black birds [namely bombers] descending our cities set on
fire.' The brutal war dragged on for three more years with
mass killings on both sides and with forced labour camps
usually run by the invaders. More than half a million died.
There is now a monument to the 2,400 British volunteers who
fought against Franco. The idealistic International Brigade and
Arthur Koestler's *Spanish Testament* and *Dialogue with Death*
showed the folly of approval. Perhaps you've seen Picasso's
painting and wondered what it represented: revulsion at over

1,600 civilian casualties, fear for the future. At home, it meant knitting for Basque refugees. ETA, the Basque separatist movement, fights on to this day.

Until then, and despite his call for colonies, Hitler too had been generally regarded as a nasty man, rather a silly fellow with a moustache, a comic salute and the outlandish emblem of a swastika. The name comes from Sanskrit, indicating well-being, but its form was a crooked cross, and offensive to many. A photo of the holiday party on the Isle of Man showed them all giving a derisive Hitler salute. And as for fatty Goering!

School's efforts

Miss Macrae did her best to bring the world outside into school. Armistice Day, 11 November, was always celebrated in the Hall at 11 a.m., the date and time of the end of the Great War. We stood in our form lines. Those two minutes seemed eternal. I could feel no relationship with, no involvement in, an event which had happened four years before I was even born. The only excitement was in seeing which Mistresses wore engagement rings in memory of their dead fiancés. We thought this odd, if not macabre, as we could have no conception of the horrifying slaughter of young men. I was moved to sobs when, a few years ago, we visited Arras with its rows of unnamed graves, and Vimy Ridge with its endless inscribed names, our filthy trenches so close to those of the enemy.

Even as a youngster, I felt it was horrid to have two different kinds of poppy according to the size of the donation, the silky one costing more than the papery version.

Refusing to participate in thinking during the Silence, I received a detention one year for fiddling with my wool stockings as we stood there; they seemed to itch more then than at any other time. For Mother, it was a sacred day; although none of her family was killed or wounded, she made no attempt to comprehend my lack of understanding or to explain why it meant so much to her generation. Dad had lost a brother-in-law.

My insensitive and childish petulance at the proceedings has hardened to distaste at the hypocrisy of thinking about my parents' war and remembering mine, in which several friends died, for two stipulated minutes each year. I remember in my own time and in my own unregimented way.

The Head gave a patriotic address on Empire Day, urging the duty of each individual to do her bit for far-flung bits of the world. We were bidden to wave flags when the King and Queen visited Liverpool in May 1938; we assembled in school groups on Wavertree playground – a tedious and pointless exercise.

When I was in the Fifths, CHS was host to a group of German girls. Most of us were a bit wary, as was my father, who was not at ease as England was becoming more aware of German aspirations, for Hitler had already begun his purges. They attended some lessons; we went with them to places of civic interest such as the Liver Buildings, the Town Hall and the Walker Art Gallery, where we all had tea. As far as I know, there was no follow-up in exchanges of letters or pupils.

It was decided that the Sixth form should be better informed; a Civics lesson was timetabled, presided over by either the Head or Miss MacCregor (History). Few Mistresses were capable of spurring us on and, in any case, they were and still are hindered from putting forward any party line. This was too often interpreted to mean the withholding of all facts which might actually prove something.

Luckily for me, I joined the Lower, or first year, Sixth when I was just fourteen, so began earlier than many to take a more informed interest. This was part of growing up, for this outside world did not function according to the teaching and philosophy of Wesleyan Methodists. An insidious doubt crept in very, very slowly: could it be that we were not the only ones who were always right?

The Spanish Consul for Ecuador addressed us incomprehensibly, but, apart from a few lectures, we were expected to prepare the odd paper and to question the views of others. One of my papers was on 'Prisons' and the second on 'The Doings of Russia'.

From 1936 to 1938, other than a discussion on alcohol ('very good too' – we were not even aware of drugs in those days), the only topics seem to have been political. We thought about local government, the budget, trade unions, the law courts and trial by jury, parliament, cabinet and king, the Great War. We debated the League of Nations of which Germany was a member; there was even a short-lived League of Nations Society.

European problems dominated: German colonies and our own with consequent troubles in Africa; Yugoslavia, where a twelve-year-old boy had been proclaimed King; Egypt; India; Hitler's re-occupation of the Rhineland.

This isn't a history lesson; indeed, events may be out of chronological sequence. I'm simply telling you how one girl remembers it all.

With examination pressure delayed, there was time to look around, to learn, to read. Penguin Specials steered towards a more belligerent frame of mind, as did Philip Gibbs' *European Journey*, Stefan Lorant's *I was Hitler's Prisoner* and a reprint of Edmund Blunden's *Undertones of War*.

In the public sphere, the last years of the decade were spent in first avoiding then preparing for war. One of the first shots had occurred as far back as 1934 when the Austrian Chancellor, Dollfuss, had been murdered by Austrian Nazis, but, such was our insularity, our separation from the continent, that there was for me, and I suspect the majority, still no idea that this might concern us, still no suspicion of the future.

There was a strong clamour for 'appeasement' – that is, wagging an admonishing finger at Germany but acceding to Hitler's demands in the hope that our kindly understanding would make him a better boy. Just writing the word appease-ment brings the tense atmosphere back. The 1935 pact between the English Hoare and the French Laval encouraged the feeling 'Don't let's be beastly to the Germans', and, more especially, the Italians ('Down with the panic-mongers'); it took the stuffing out of the League of Nations. Our Prime Minister, Neville Chamberlain, even felt able to toast the King of Italy as Emperor of Abyssinia. France had enough to cope with in her own country and gave no approval for risk-taking. Blackshirted Oswald Mosley and his party (the British Union of Fascists) stirred up riots especially in London with anti-Jewish and pro-Nazi sentiments. In the midst of these growing public and personal concerns, we moved house.

EIGHTEEN

Moving

48 Chalfont Road

I still don't know why we moved, but we did in 1938. There was clearly some unpleasantness at church which never surfaced. I suspected, without any real grounds, that there had been problems with Mr C. – which was doubly awkward as his daughter went to my school. I noted in my diary that Dad defended me in some matter saying that it was not my fault. It is now buried in the mist of time. When I later taxed him with this secrecy, he was astounded. All he would say was, 'I didn't think you would be interested.' He still did not divulge anything.

This time, I was informed about six weeks before the move, but was kept in ignorance of all financial matters and specifically of the technical trials of buying, selling and moving. I did wonder why an apparently straightforward matter – I sell, you buy – should need an agent. Mr Gill, from the next road, was not a family favourite, yet my parents saw much of him and seemed preoccupied for weeks.

The new property was not finished when I made the first of four visits to it. I was impressed, perhaps most by the builder, a big, burly man of Persian extraction.

For a question in English, I later wrote this verse:

Opportunity

A new house, plus large 'garden' is now ours.
The wasteland or estate

Has been the dumping ground of the neighbours
For sticks, sad to relate,
Bricks and concrete against which we seem so frail.
Soon you'll see 'New Modern Houses, now for Sale'.

Two days before Removal Day, I spent time removing stones and wood from the garden, and the next day I cleaned cupboards.

The actual day was sheer joy; it was sunny Easter time and was the last day of term. I shuttled to and fro on my bicycle, transporting I don't know what, even making meals, feeling that a new life was beginning. In this, I was not mistaken. Subsequently, I 'worked hard' in the appalling mess of the garden.

48 Chalfont Road was bigger than the Roskell Road house. Sykes Waterhouse and Co., estate agents with a local branch in Allerton Road, advertised it on my father's death in 1979 as a 'superior and well-planned semi-detached house conveniently situated in a quiet cul-de-sac off Mather Avenue and close to Allerton Road and the Allerton golf course. The property enjoys a delightful open outlook over school playing fields at the rear. The accommodation is bright, well-planned and labour-saving but the house is in need of some modernisation.' The asking price was then £24,500, Liverpool prices being much lower than for an equivalent property in the South. Visitors were to be accompanied.

The playing fields are still there; the groundsman used to pass over quantities of wood for the fire.

On the gate was the old name plate of Trelystan. There was a pull-out bell as well as a door knocker. The telephone was installed on a hook in the hall; Mother was never at ease with it.

The cold lounge (note the change of word) and dining room were similar, if a trifle bigger and lighter, to those in Hunts Cross; at the back a French window led to the rear garden. In theory, we could thus step out on to the narrow path which encircled a flower bed, mainly of roses. It was, very occasionally, opened; if we did go out, we had to return via the back door to avoid 'treading in' dirt.

Memory now fails me. 'A morning room with modern tiled fireplace with slow-burning fitment heating the water' – in 1938, a range – and a kitchen 'with Enamel Sink Unit with double drawers, half-tiled walls and tiled floor. Point for cooker' was advertised. I simply cannot visualise these two spaces. It may be that unhappy times have blotted them out, it may have been my strong sense that this could never really be my home.

> Ever let the fancy roam!
> Pleasure never is at home.

I had only two consecutive years, 1938–1940, there, although it was my home address for three more. It may be that the estate agent's jargon flatters the rooms. I visualise a small, badly organised kitchenette (a new word) leading to a pantry/larder/cooking-cum-laundry space.

There were three 'good' bedrooms. In the back one was my new bureau, a present for HSC that summer. I now write daily at it in our little study. Best of all, it had a key, so that I could have a few private things.

This was when I began to be aware of my parents as distinct persons, separate from their relationship to me, and also able to question the whole church set-up, which increasingly seemed restrictive. Questioning dogma and faith came later during the War when I was out of their orbit. Mother disapproved of this investigative approach: 'As sharp as a knife, so sharp you'll cut yourself.' It did not 'do' to be a smart alec.

I also had a new bed; a spring mattress this time, instead of the comfortable, floppy old feather bed. This took some getting used to. I hoovered my room.

Apart from the parental front bedroom, there was the usual

smaller third room. The airing cupboard with its hot water cylinder was in the bathroom; the WC remained separate. When we came to sell the house, we found in the attic old hats and hatpins; this time, the newspapers lagging the pipes belonged to 1938.

The 'ample garage space' is now a garage. We again had a large coal shed as well as a garden shed. The rear garden was described as exceptionally large, the result of the oddly shaped playing fields. I am amused by the small print: 'None of the statements contained in these particulars as to this property are to be relied on as statements or representations of facts.' What are they for, then?

In the other half of the semi lived the McCasseys. I pitied her, without any justification, for her misguided obligation to go to pre-breakfast Mass. Sadly later stricken by Parkinson's, she provided sanctuary on several occasions when relations with Mother became too strained. Their house name was Lisieux; they had probably made the pilgrimage to the shrine of Sainte Thérèse.

The Taylors were younger. Helen had been to my school. Because of her father's job, she often had free passes for Trade Shows in the cinema, usually the Paramount in town. Her husband Dick joined the Territorials during the War; he must have been in a reserved occupation. They were excellent neighbours who also comforted me on occasion. Whereas at Hunts Cross there had been a little boy as a companion, here there was a perky little off-brown puppy called Puck, an enjoyed companion on many walks.

Mother continued to shop at the Co-op, with its useful 'divi' stamps. I was more interested in the shops along Allerton Road, several of which advertised in the school magazine. Most were privately owned, village-like establishments: Allday's, the newsagent; A. E. Briggs, the chemist; Mr Parry, the family butcher; Wm. Griffiths, Repair Service; The Craft Shop. Alas, they too have gone.

Consequences

Strangely, I often cycled over to St James' at Woolton, but my parents returned to Trinity, Grove Street, after a twelve-year gap. I kept in touch with people in Hunts Cross, but only for a year or so. It was now much nearer to go to school along the residential part of Allerton Road – upmarket houses on one side, still unspoiled on the other because of playing fields and the golf course beyond its old stone wall. Next came Calderstones Park. From Allerton Road, I turned right and puffed my way up the steep Harthill Road and past Quarry Bank. The comparative nearness meant the enlarging of my circle of school friends.

Back at Trinity for a few months before the War, I found little to record. Sunday morning saw fewer visits, presumably because of the distance – twenty-five minutes or so by bus; too far to walk, expensive to ride. I was also left at home quite often on Sunday evenings to do my homework.

There were special occasions: Recognition Service for new members, John Wesley Bicentenary Celebrations, Bible and Temperance Sundays. This last was a misnomer: not Temperance but Total Abstinence; war against the Demon Drink. At a Cricket Evening, I played the piano and Dad took the chair. It sounds odd. I wonder what happened.

Generally speaking, a little more friendliness was forth-coming as both parents were happier there; this brought a few more visitors, including at least one of the earlier hockey 'girls' and the faithful Auntie Bea.

Much later, a frightening lady, Mrs Ethel Wear, then widow of Mr William Wear (called Billy behind his back, to take him, at least in our minds, down a peg), wrote in Mother's autograph book.

Faith

Lord, give me faith! to love from day to day,
With tranquil heart to do my simple part,

And with my hand in Thine, just go Thy way.
Lord, give me faith! to trust, if not to know;
With quiet mind in all things Thee to find,
And, child-like, go where Thou would'st have me go.
Lord, give me faith! to leave it all to Thee,
The future is Thy gift, I would not lift the veil
Thy love has hung twixt it and me.

(John Oxenham, a much quoted religious versifier)

Elsie Gamblin was a great stalwart; here is her contribution, untitled and unattributed:

Said the robin to the sparrow:
'I should really like to know
Why these pious human beings
Rush about and worry so.'
Said the sparrow to the robin,
'Friend, I think that it must be
That they have no Heavenly Father
Such as cares for you and me.'

Life was certainly simpler half a century ago for those who could believe without soul-searching.

A parson and his wife who had once been at Woolton now came to Trinity. Like us, he played tennis at the Smiths. The Reverend John T. Gray's offering was written 'In Sincerity':

The Celestial Surgeon

If I have faltered more or less
In my great task of happiness;
If I have moved among my race
And shown no glorious morning face;
If beams from happy human eyes
Have moved me not; if morning skies,
Books, and my food, and summer rain

Knock on my sullen heart in vain:
Lord, thy most pointed pleasure take
And stab my spirit broad awake.

R. L. S. (Robert Louis Stevenson)

Awake and Christ shall give thee light.

The parson's wife, Catherine May, wrote more briefly:

No man ever went to Heaven alone; he must either
find friends or make them.

John Wesley

O blessed life, the mind that sees
Whatever change the years may bring,
A mercy still in everything,
And shining through all mysteries.

You are probably reeling under this barrage of quotations. I have deliberately included them as they, like hymns, illustrate so clearly the atmosphere by which I was surrounded.

NINETEEN

Return to the Outside World

Crises

Meanwhile, the outside world was impinging more and more on normal, ordinary lives. Alarms proliferated. Sagittarius, already in 1936, had summed up the attitude of the British government:

> We weigh the pro against the con,
> count consequence on consequence,
> perched imperturbably upon
> the fence.

In 1937, for an English essay, I wrote *An Answer to a Warmonger*. Deplorable as it seems now in both style and content, it does show how sharply my views subsequently clarified.

> 'War! War! War!' is all they cry,
> The Hitlers and the Mussolinis,
> 'Kill anything for glory!'
> Oh why? Oh why?
> For when they are gone, still, still,
> Will nature in her beauty linger,
> She can't be killed for glory,
> Why try? Why try?

1938 brought the first of the major crises. In March, Hitler wanted to absorb Austria immediately after her plebiscite on the pretext that his own Nazis in Sudetenland had the right of self-determination, that is, to become part of the Fatherland. Germany was given an ultimatum – 'Stop this, or…' – a threat which was postponed. The Austrian leader committed suicide. Yugoslavia, Romania and Czechoslovakia banded together in the Little Entente. Would we support these countries also under Germany's threat?

In September, Neville Chamberlain flew to Munich – some called it a gallant gesture – to see the dictator, to whom he always gave the prefix Herr, by whom he felt that he was treated with marked respect and courtesy. I was in France at the time; everyone shook me by the hand, stating, as they had done many times previously, that the issue depended on England. A quarter of the Paris taxis had been mobilised, Parisians rushed for their valuables and retired to the country-side which caused a rush on the property market, sandbags were distributed and reservists recalled.

Chamberlain, wearing his trademark old-fashioned stiff pointed collar, returned waving a piece of paper and hailed his 'victory'. This featured in all the cinema newsreels. You may have seen and heard him in television anniversary documentaries, usually holding his long black umbrella. Peace with Honour, it was not. Peace in our time, it was not. Appeasement, it certainly was.

It was greeted with both horror (was Britain's word to prove the same as Hitler's?) and relief; I wrote 'PAIX' in my diary with a sense of betrayal, although I remember thinking thank goodness for the necessary breathing space. For too many as they flocked to churches to give thanks, it meant no war. I am not being wise after the event when I tell you that to me it simply meant no war *yet*. For my generation, the name Munich still brings a chill of recognition, of shame.

Gas masks in individual cardboard boxes were distributed to London and the provinces; air raid precaution (ARP) notes were issued to householders. Unknown to us at the time, plans for evacuating schoolchildren were formulated and eight Tube stations in London were closed, whilst parks and squares were trenched ready for air raid shelters.

Emancipation?

In that summer, I was marking time in the Sixth and no one knew what to do with me. What with the strikes and scandals in France – so that someone could comment that if the French could form a government that lasted one week, that would be something in French public life – together with the problem of a Catholic country, it was only after much heart-searching that my parents agreed to the pressure from Miss Macrae; I was to go to France.

Dad took me to London. We were tourists again – Hampton Court, Kew, the Changing of the Guard; we enjoyed *French Without Tears* at the Criterion (which would be taken over during the War by the BBC) with great contemporary stars such as Rex Harrison, Trevor Howard, Roland Culver; less well-known, but brilliant to me, were Guy Middleton, Hubert Gregg, Lueen MacGrath and Avice Landon. We enjoyed Avice's company years later when she was on holiday with her wonderfully named husband, Bruno Barnabe (pronounced Barnaby). One reviewer felt that no one could come to London without seeing the plays – 'It completes your education.' It seemed a most suitable choice in the circumstances and we laughed and laughed.

The highlight for us both was being taken into the House of Commons by the great Eleanor Rathbone, MP, much admired by my father. She had been the first woman member of Liverpool City Council, the first woman MP for Lancashire and was currently the Independent MP for the Combined Universities, Oxford and Cambridge then enjoying this extra privileged representation.

With first-hand knowledge of Liverpool slums, she sought to relieve the dreary life of local women, but it wasn't until after the War, in fact in the year before she died, that a measly family allowance was paid for the second child and any subsequent offspring.

I sat in the Ladies' Gallery, Dad opposite in the General Gallery. The visit was 'interesting more for picking out the men than for listening to what they said, for the majority talked piffling, trifling nonsense'. *Plus ça change…* The Speaker's remarks were inaudible. Chamberlain was very poor in contrast with Winnie (Winston Churchill), little Herbert Morrison and Mr Attlee. Both of these Labour men, horror of horrors, put their feet on the table.

We saw *The Thirty-Nine Steps* (Madeleine Carroll and heart-throb Robert Donat) and *Boys Will be Boys* (Will Hay). I still didn't appreciate how much Dad relished these special breaks – just the two of us.

Aged fifteen, I was despatched to Newhaven, all by myself for the very first time, to live with a non-English-speaking family in the depths of Normandy for three whole months. There was confusion over passports and a *Carte de Voyage Touristique* which gave 40% reduction on French railways (SNCF, anglicised as Snifka and standing for Société Nation-ale de Chemins de Fer Français) as long as one had a return ticket. It was stamped by a customs officer at Dieppe. In 1938, it cost 30F, the following year 40F, so there was inflation even then.

Domi (Dominique, the daughter of the household, proba-bly twenty or so then), scheduled to look after me, met me at the port. Brimming with self-confidence, she lived either in her own little house in the extensive grounds or in an annexe.

Everything thrilled: porters in their smocks, *le train omnibus* (stopping local train) with Second and Third Class carriages (the latter with wooden seats) and a very high step up. It wound its way through the main street. Like so many English travellers, I was struck by the hedgeless fields, the trees in straight lines, the boringly immaculate gardens and learned that an untidy one was known as *un jardin anglais*.

I was initiated into family life of a certain social status not matched by financial standing. Mme Jacques Bayle must have been in her late fifties or early sixties. As a widow, probably from the Great War, she wore the customary black and ruled not only her immediate household, but her family, however distant, and several other unrelated families who had second homes nearby. She seemed most venerable, more like a grandmother. She enjoyed her mid-afternoon *tisane de verveine*.

The black-framed notification of her death in 1960, naming over fifty relations carefully listed in order of consanguinity – sons, daughter, nephew, nieces, cousins, grandchildren and their families – indicates that she was at the centre of a great web. I can identify only a few now because of changes of name on marriage.

Monsieur et Madame Pierre BAYLE [the elder son was recalled in 1938 to the navy at Brest], le Capitaine de Frégate de réserve et Madame Luc-Marie BAYLE [Luc was in the Admiralty in Paris and appeared from time to time];

Madame Michel GOMART [Domi?];

Le Quartier-Maître Claude BAYLE [brother-in-law?], Messieurs Pascal et Laurent BAYLE, Mesdemoiselles Martine et Adeline BAYLE;

Messieurs Emanuel, Jacques-Martin, Jean-René et José GOMART,

Mesdemoiselles Catherine et Anne GOMART;

Monsieur et Madame Jean CARON;

Madame Henri CLEMENT et ses fils;

Monsieur et Madame Claude CHARPENTIER;

Mademoiselle Claude CARON;

Monsieur et Madame Louis LEPETIT, leurs enfants et petits-enfants, Monsieur Jean LEPETIT, son fils et ses petits-enfants [General Lepetit and his daughter Guiguite were most hospitable];

Madame VIGUÈS, Madame Louis Lestelle, ses enfants et
petits-enfants;
Monsieur et Madame Charles VILLEMANT et leurs enfants;
Mademoiselle Antoinette VILLEMANT;
Mademoiselle Thérèse LEGAY

Ont la douleur de vous faire part de la perte qu'ils viennent
d'éprouver en la personne de

MADAME JACQUES BAYLE,
Née Marie-Louise CARON.

How different from my one-child household, with relatives
discouraged! While similar notifications occur to this day in
France, they tend to be shorter. This one also suggests the
longevity of women, whether as widows or old maids.

Mme Bayle died at her home, Le Frêne, in the village of
Houlbec-Cocherel in the *département* of Eure. The house itself
struck me as 'terribly old-fashioned, with stone floors, rush
matting, iron banisters and old wooden beds and cupboards'.
She supplemented her income by boarding people like me for
£2 or two guineas per week, payable in English money. She
was able to make a handsome profit in three months.

I was dependent on others for excursions and the like,
whilst neighbours such as the almost equally venerable Mlle
Clarice supplemented Domi's desultory dictations. Armorel
from CHS got Paris and the Loire *châteaux* thrown in during
her one month's stay. What I did not appreciate at the time was
how excellent was this total immersion in the French language
and in French social life of a now bygone age. I had never
before known this socialising – a post-War word. There was a
constant coming and going of friends, neighbours, acquaintances, close and distant relatives, so that eighteen eating dinner,
outside whenever possible, was not unusual. Social habits have
changed: no one ever used the familiar *tu* to me. There was
one overworked and not over-bright *bonne à tout faire*, a put-

upon girl who seemed to be permanently on the go.

During my stay, Madame celebrated both her *fête*, *le quinze août*, *la fête de l'Assomption*, as her name was Marie, and her birth-day.

How did I spend my days, apart from reading? Country walks, visits to M. le Curé, knitting, searching for Crabbe (the dog, who made a habit of going missing), tea with various unattached ladies, bridge most evenings (on the learners' table), playing word games and the piano, blackberrying, bathing in the river, enjoying pancakes, writing letters. Dad wrote regularly as he continued to do throughout his life; I have never received a single note from Mother.

I once attended High Mass, fearful of the wrath of my Protestant God, especially as I went eleven weeks without a 'proper' church service.

On rickety hired bikes, the tyres of which punctured with monotonous regularity, with back pedal brakes, we cycled round the local villages. I marvelled over glow-worms, which I had never seen before. We took picnics to the river bank, enjoyed village fêtes or *Kermesses*; we played ping-pong, deck quoits and tennis against wealthy neighbours on their private courts (great celebrations when I won the ladies' singles) and once in the regional tournament. I had no idea what I was letting myself in for, especially as these courts were shale, not grass. I lost in the final to a woman then ranked number fifteen in France!

We younger ones often spent the evening at the local Hôtel de la Paix, talking over lemonades.

On my sixteenth birthday, Auntie Edie sent a six-word greetings telegram, handed in at the Shropshire hamlet of Marshbrouck [sic] at 9.29 a.m., which arrived at the Norman hamlet of Houlbec that same day about 2 p.m.! She always sent us a carefully packed box of dampened snowdrops in midwinter and, a rarer treat, a subsequent present of cowslips; both flowers always bring Church Stretton to mind. The two

Pavy girls gave me the equivalent of a gift voucher, *Bons Vœux! Bon pour une 'discrétion' de la part de Colette et Jacqueline*. I wonder what I bought with it? I do remember the three of us happily spending ages in Galeries Lafayette.

Neighbours took me to the nearest market town of Vernon and on a trip round Vironvay (panorama) and Louviers (beautiful church). I was teased and soon learned enough French – and confidence – to tease back. A cousin, René Pila, used to avoid Mass by volunteering to look after his two children; he subsequently sent me a card: 'You can't any more pull my legs, and, of course, I'm having a good rest.' His wife, Monique, joined in everything.

French breakfasts were unsatisfactory for me. How I love them now! Forks and bread served as knives at dinnertime, each serviette was sensibly kept in its own linen envelope, and the oldest married woman was served first.

I owed most to the Pavy family; Madame, a younger cousin of Mme Bayle, Monsieur Jean and their two daughters, Colette (Coco) then seventeen and Jacqueline (Kiki), three years younger. Kiki married and emigrated to South America. I kept in touch until her death a few years ago with the not over-strong Coco who never went out to work.

One trip which the three of us made with Domi stands out. We went to Rouen, all finding the outing more expensive than we had budgeted for, the journey itself costing 6F too much! Besides admiring all the churches and houses of the lovely old town, we seem to have indulged in éclairs at the *pâtisserie* in the rue de la Grosse Horloge, several ice creams (one with a packet of chips!), also apple and pineapple tarts. I tried to change a 10/- note (technically replaced now by 50p), but it was too late after we had climbed the 793 steps to the top of the cathedral spire. I still have the 2F ticket to prove that feat.

Their house in the village was nearly finished, but Monsieur Jean did his utmost to make me welcome by taking me with them to their spacious apartment (flat is too small a word), 29 Villa Molitor, Auteuil, on the outskirts of Paris. The family showed me Paris. I noted the remains of the World Fair at the Trocadero, l'Etoile, the Senate buildings, le Palais de Justice, the *quais* and bookstalls, the fashionable streets and shops.

At the bus stop, you pulled a lever to secure a numbered ticket, so that when the bus arrived, you called out your number – a cumbersome process, but it reduced queue-jumping. Seats were reserved on both bus and Metro for the Great War wounded. I dined with the family's friends, and had tea at a pavement café. I was thrilled beyond measure; this was living, *le high life*, pronounced 'hig' to rhyme with 'fig', whilst 'life' rhymed with 'leaf'.

My visit paled into insignificance beside the Royal Visit, delayed, fortunately from my point of view, by the death of the Queen's mother. An *Entente Cordiale* badge was produced, French on one side, English on the other. In retrospect, it seems like the last gleaming of sumptuous hospitality and elegance. This, 'the most perfect day in my life – so far', was enlivened by the wonderful illuminations, fountain displays and fireworks, by the Arab Spahis, the Garde Républicaine, regular soldiers and police at the Arc de Triomphe. I basked in reflected glory as the band of the busby-wearing Grenadier Guards played. We all enjoyed 'the most perfect ices at the Hungaria Restaurant on the Champs Elysées about 11.40 p.m., while a Hungarian gypsy orchestra played'.

On a second stay a few weeks later, Versailles, the Louvre, la Sainte Chapelle and les Invalides (2F to visit the tomb of Napoleon) proved highlights. We visited shops: 'Toute femme élégante est cliente du Printemps.' The film *l'Impossible Monsieur Bébé* was too long; we had to wake Monsieur Jean when it was over.

The family sent cards to 'Mademoiselle Joan' from their summer travels in the Loire Valley and in Champagne.

Jean was a laughable and laughing scatterbrain. I have no

idea what he did (if anything much) to enable the family to live a life of such luxury; questions of this kind were, of course, never asked. On my return, Dad wrote to thank him for what he had done for me. He managed to reply on 23 December. The letter brings him back to life.

Dear Sir, [this sounds more stilted in English than does Cher Monsieur]

I am very, very sorry to have left your kind letter of September without any answer. I wonder if you will ever forgive me such impoliteness.

We were very pleased when receiving your so kind letter and my idea was to answer you immediately and tell you all the satisfaction my girls found in Joan's company. Then came some awful alarming days [Munich] and what is not done in time you can never do afterwards. What will you think of French people? We had really no merit in procuring Joan drives and sports for she was for everybody of us a charming friend, especially for my two girls who were really delighted by her gay and equal character very lively and kind too. She is very clever too and has for her age a great knowledge; this was a very good example for our girls. Thanks to her and to her professor we could win the little championship at our friend's Dupont.

I hope you and your family had a good winter till now, here everybody is all right, at Mme Bayle's too. We have had frost and snow as I never saw in Paris. Anyhow we go to the country for Christmas and take with us skates having no skis yet.

The months to come will bring us, I fear, still very anxious days but we must hope, thanks to a stout English–French agreement, we will go through all right. Inside, France looks better.

I thank Joan very much for the photograph, it is quite nice.

We, all four, wish you, Mrs Cherry and Joan a very merry
and happy Christmas and too a good and agreeable New Year.
Many friendships to Joan.

I apologise again for my inexcusable behaviour.

Very sincerely yours,

J Pavy

Dear Jean – he claimed that the reason he never went to
confession was that he had forgotten his sins by the time he
reached the church. It wouldn't surprise me if this excuse were
really justified. I never saw him again.

I found this letter over forty years later in my father's files.
If only I had seen it at the time, what confidence it could have
given me in my fight for greater freedom to know how
someone outside the family could think of me. It was not
addressed to me; I expect my parents thought, as usual, that
praise would make me big-headed.

The end of this bliss came on 24 September. Monsieur Le
Clair took me to Vernon at 9.20; I changed trains for Rouen at
10.15, having to stand in the corridor to get some fresh air. I
registered my luggage and had my passport checked at Dieppe.
On the overfull boat, according to my diary, 'a young English-
man gave me his seat', but, sadly, this chivalry has gone from
my mind. English customs were 'gruelling'.

Dad met me in London, we ate 'lunch' at half-past seven in
the evening at an ABC café, for I had had nothing since my
continental breakfast at half-past eight that morning, walked in
the pouring rain to theatreland where 'University folk were
yelling Arms for Spain or Help for Czechoslavakia', saw a film
and caught the 1.30 a.m. train, securing two comfortable seats
each for the long journey, arriving in Allerton at 6.30 a.m.

I noted 'CRISIS APPROACHING. ULTIMATUM until Saturday', but you know already how that worked out. I wrote my
diary in French for several days, for I had truly been thinking
in that language.

I wrote to Mme Bayle as soon as it became possible. She

replied on a Carte de Correspondence aux Armées. Printed instructions read: '*Pour assurer la transmission n'indiquer aucune opération militaire passée, présente ou futur, ni lieu autre que le secteur Postal.*' It bore the stamp of Gouvernement Provisoire de la République Française, and the time 23h45, nov, 44, Eure.

She had written in her old-fashioned and difficult to read handwriting:

> *Chère Joan. Quel plaisir de pouvoir enfin échanger des nouvelles. Nous allons tous bien. Domi est mariée depuis quatre ans et Luc depuis deux ans. Domi vient d'avoir deux jumeaux au mois d'Août. Nous avons passé par des moments bien pénibles mais nous n'avons que des dégâts matériels à déplorer. Le calme est revenu et j'espère que nous verrons bientôt la fin de toutes nos misères. Donnez-moi de vos nouvelles plus longuement. Domi va vous écrire.* [She didn't.] *Tous nos bien affectueux souvenirs.*

M L Bayle

We never met again.

The last days of non-war

In 1938's magazine, an Old Girl wrote enthusiastically, if in vague terms, on BYPA – the British Youth Peace Assembly – and its attempts to achieve justice and peace.

Things had got, and were getting, worse. Germany occupied Czechoslovakia in defiance of the Munich agreement, Hitler entered its capital, Prague. Danzig, then a free port under the League of Nations, was 'visited' by Nazi storm troupers disguised as tourists. The Spanish problem continued, Madrid being taken by Franco's forces. China and Japan were at war. Italy invaded Albania. Sagittarius had written back in February about our government's attitude to Mussolini:

> Resolved to stick at no expense
> To set aggression on its feet,

> We bribe with simple confidence
> This bankrupt and unquestioned cheat
> Who, once assisted to the top,
> Will scheme to make as shut up shop.

School, however, carried on normally, apart from lectures, practices and examinations in First Aid. Liverpool folk were 'upset by the sinking of the submarine *Thetis* off Liverpool Bay in June with the loss of 99 sailors'; it wasn't simply the disaster, but what were submarines doing so close to home?

I was allowed to see in the New Year for the first time in 1939. I was surprised to find an ornate document in nineteen different languages indicating that, in the junior section, Juan Hinchliffe Cherry, Gr. [sic] Britain, had won a medal in a contest (essay competition) on Christ and World Friendship organised by the Ecumenical Youth Commission, based in Geneva. A forlorn cause. Twelve seniors from twelve different countries won prizes; forty-one received medals (Gt. Britain heading the list with three) and sixty-four had Honourable Mentions, Gt. Britain being the only one of twenty-four countries to reach double figures. Perhaps the most noteworthy in the circumstances were two Germans. Juniors won fewer awards overall: eleven prize-winners from ten countries (no British this time), forty-three medallists (we tied with Hungary, seven each) and only nineteen Honourable Mentions from twelve countries, including Siam (one).

Of all the essays received in twenty languages from thirty-nine different countries in the five continents, we topped the award list with thirty-five, Hungary came second with twenty-four, then Switzerland eighteen, Denmark fifteen and Bulgaria ten. The fourteen countries with one achiever each represented many different religions between them – from China and Ceylon to New Zealand and the Philippines, Syria, Lebanon and Madagascar to Peru and the Union of South Africa. An incredible encouragement of hope – which failed.

The domestic atmosphere was not softened by the fact that Dad's sister Edith spent four nights early in July with us before Yvonne came to spend a month from mid-July.

An exchange had been decreed a good idea and my parents pushed the boat out. Yvonne was no linguist, so I had more practice in French than she did in English. We still keep in annual touch, although we have little in common now as she became a Protestant nun with the title of Soeur Béatrice.

We took her to Liverpool to see the cathedral, over the water into the Wirral, to Oglet for a picnic, to school, to see a film of Mickey Rooney. The Smiths invited us twice for tennis. We apparently struggled with a jigsaw of the Prince of Wales; this must have been a few years old as there had been no such person since 1936.

More importantly, she came on holiday with us for a fortnight to the CE guest house at Penmaenmawr, the journey involving a bus ride through the Mersey Tunnel. We enjoyed all the usual activities, indoors and in the countryside. She was the young sister of Gustave from Neuilly, a 'good' suburb of Paris. Then a trainee Protestant pastor, he had spent some time as a leader there the previous year. We had been notified of his wedding a week before Yvonne came over.

Madame Adolphe Handisyde, Monsieur et Madame André Lagny ont l'honneur de vous faire part du marriage du pasteur Gustave Lagny, leur petit-fils et fils, avec Mademoiselle Hélène Trocmé. La Bénédiction Nuptiale leur sera donnée le mercredi 12 juillet, 1939, à 11 heures, au Temple de l'Église Réformée de Saint Quentin.

A similar note came from Hélène's grandfathers (one a pasteur) and parents.

Dad took us both up to London by the 2.15 train which arrived in Euston at 6.20. We stayed at the Drury's boarding house and showed Yvonne Westminster Abbey, Hyde Park

Corner and Knightsbridge one day, the Docks and the real East End of Cable Street on another, and again ate at milk bars and the Strand Corner House.

I went back with her, again via Newhaven and Dieppe; her father collected us in a taxi at Gare St Lazare in Paris. In four exciting and exhausting days, we saw everything: all the famous sights of 1938 plus the Panthéon, the Sorbonne, three churches (St Etienne du Mont, 'very old and you can see the staircase to separate the monks from the congregation', St Séverin, with five naves, and St Julien-le-Pauvre) and the Luxembourg Gardens. I noted a blistered foot and that there were crowds and crowds of English in Paris. But after four days it seemed likely that war was imminent. Yvonne's family did not feel able to take any further responsibility for me. I was impotently furious – but they were right, of course. They took me to see *Rose Marie* and sent me home the next morning.

I came across the letter which Monsieur Lagny sent on, I think, 25 August. It is stilted in the old French tradition (I wonder how Dad understood it), but indicates clearly both his own sense of responsibility and the general atmosphere.

Apparently, he had already written, but felt that he dared not wait for a reply as events had overtaken him. After '*mûre réflexion*', he had recalled his own son. He sought my father's approval as in the day's newspapers, all who had no immediate reason to be in Paris were urged to leave while trains were still running. Once transport was handed over for military needs, civilians would find it difficult to get away. He was upset for '*la pauvre petite*' facing the prospect of '*un bien vilain voyage*' with considerable crowds and no one to meet her in London. No mobile phones then. He sent a telegram giving the train time, having assured himself that I could get on it. He felt that I could manage by myself. I didn't know this until long after. Had I been aware of it, I'd have been more proud than tearful. He expressed sadness because all had enjoyed my company. Should the situation calm down, they would love to have me in 1940! I never saw him or his wife again. The letter ends '*Votre tout dévoué*', which polite and now dated phrase must have puzzled the recipients.

I caught the 9.15 train from Paris. In fact, there were four trains packed with returners, but I did get a seat. The fifteenth boat left Dieppe at 1.25 p.m. and arrived at Newhaven at 4.15. I was pushed on to First Class and had not only to stand but to pay excess. It took twenty minutes to disembark. After customs, a kind porter took my luggage and me to another train, on which I secured 'a bit of a seat' and reached London in the rain at 6.30.

The eight o'clock train to Crewe ran late. Crewe, the unloveliest of stations at the best of times, caused Howard Spring to ask: 'At Crewe, what can the impressionable traveller do but abandon himself to the worst forebodings?' The next connection at half-past eleven also ran late so that I arrived in Liverpool at ten past two in the morning. My parents met me – I wonder now how long and anxiously they had been waiting – and we took a taxi home and I fell into bed.

The tiniest details of those few days are indelibly fixed; others had better, more had worse, journeys. Mine was simply the worst I had had to date: fear of the unknown, fear that my parents would in some way blame me for a premature return, panic that I'd do something silly like miss a train or get on the wrong one, terror that war might break out at any time.

The unknown was the trouble. What was war like? We, young and wise, knew that it could not be the same as last time. I, an English girl, was impatient with the French who seemed to want to turn tail and flee once more to a negotiated 'peace'. I, then, had no notion of their suffering 1914–1918. Would *Rose Marie*, that charming but dated musical, be the last show I would ever see in my life? Would we be in a state of siege in our own houses, venturing out, with our gas masks on, only to be decontaminated?

This was certainly *it*, whatever *it* might be.

Yet again, Sagittarius' verse, dated 2 September, gives the feeling of jitters:

Nerves

I think I'll get a paper,
I think I'd better wait.
I'll hear the news at 6 o'clock,
That's much more up to date.

It's just like last September,
Absurd how time stands still;
They're bound to make a statement,
I don't suppose they will.

I think I'd better stroll around.
Perhaps it's best to stay.
I think I'll have a whiskey neat
I can't this time of day.

I think I'll have another smoke.
I don't know what to do.
I promised to ring someone;
I can't remember who.

They say it's been averted.
They say we're on the brink.
I'll wait for the *New Statesman*.
I wonder what they think.

They're shouting. It's a special.
It's not. It's just street cries.
I think the heat is frightful.
God damn these bloody flies.

I see the nation's keeping cool,
The public calm is fine.

This crisis can't shake England's nerves.
It's playing hell with mine.

Life was irritatingly normal for a few days, which increased my resentment – tennis at school, church on Sunday, but on 28 August, there was an evacuation rehearsal. The following day, we collected our examination results and on the 31st, each took to school a blanket which would be brought to our evacuation town – wherever that might be.

Germany finally went too far for the Western Allies and invaded Poland on 1 September. Chamberlain had announced in March that Britain and France were committed to helping Poland if it were invaded. We now had no choice whatsoever.

Schoolchildren were evacuated between 1 and 4 September (but that is another and a different story); compulsory military service for men aged eighteen to forty-one, although opposed by Labour MPs, was announced. On 3 September, the British Ambassador in Berlin handed over an ultimatum stating that a reply must be received by 11 a.m. to the demand that Germany should immediately withdraw. This time, there could be no fudging even by our Prime Minister, Chamberlain: 'I have to tell you that no such undertaking has been received and that consequently this country is at war with Germany.'

For me, as for many, this declaration was welcome. H. G. Wells summed up the feeling: 'People had been so long oppressed by the threat of and preparation for war that its arrival came with an effect of positive relief.' I certainly remember gasping with relief.

Battle lines were joined, to use the jargon of previous war/wars, although this was not to be a war like any other. We were all sure, rightly, that it would mean the end of life as we had hitherto known it, but that was all anyone knew.

TWENTY

Looking Back

Rereading these letters, I feel a stranger. I find that I don't like this girl overmuch: she took too many pleasant things for granted, she sulked, she was often ungrateful, unkind and spiteful, and made too little effort to understand and feel with others.

Yet I feel sorry for her. She was lonely and struggling to find both friends and her own personality and approach to life. Little could be spontaneous. She spent too much of her adolescent years in fear: fear of lack of money, fear of people, fear that she would not get on with them, fear of what they would think of her, fear of growing up, fear of the independence which she craved, fear of not being able to live up to the expectations of others, fear of boys especially, all made worse by a lack of social grace and physical coordination.

The stirrings of a social and political conscience are there, for she was eager and wanted to be outgoing, but she was stifled by the dominance of religion of the limited, orthodox, unthinking kind; it could not stand up to an awakening mind. Take away that mainstay, however, and what was left? Fear of a vindictive God. She questioned, not yet constructively and sometimes woundingly, in her efforts to make sense of the adult world.

The other main restriction was the solidity of the class structure, its grip on everyday life, indeed its simplicity. Not for that girl the freedom to do her own thing, yet she was brighter and luckier than so many who had the same limited financial and social status.

Her home life was confusing. You may think that she was too vindictive towards her mother. True in part at this stage of her life, but her later, even more, hurtful experiences hardened her feelings. She felt less culpable when she heard from family how much they disliked and feared her mother too. She has never found anyone who genuinely liked her. She was totally in her mother's charge from 8.30 in the morning until 5.50 in the evening each working day.

> Crabbed Age and Youth
> Cannot live together.

She had her books and she had her father, especially on non-working days. She had not fully taken in before how deep was the pleasure they took in each other's company and how much she gained from him. She is increasingly grateful for his love which continued to grow, thankful for his determination to give her the best education available at the time, and recognises his deep sincerity and concern for her welfare – spiritual, material and literary. She did not realise how fearful he was of emotion. It is sad that it is now too late to thank him.

She would soon grow up fast and in another world when everyone had to take hold of life too quickly, as it had a greater value. I'll try to tell you about this another time.

Much love,

Joan

Index

A

advertisements, 45, 70, 71, 73, 78, 84, 91, 98, 105, 123, 191–93, 208, 226, 237, 263, 304

alcohol, 32, 98, 125, 138, 166, 252, 279, 299, 305

animals, 46, 66, 92, 304, 314

autographs, 31, 94, 155, 163, 207, 248, 263, 305–6

B

Bayle family, 311–15, 317, 318–19

Bible, 53, 73, 110, 146, 151, 175, 177, 240, 305

bicycle, 99, 106–7, 213, 215, 216–18, 282, 302, 305, 314

birthdays
  Dad, 64
  family/friends, 88, 99, 104, 201, 292, 314
  mine, 28, 118, 231, 254, 314
  Mother, 66, 79, 89

books, 192, 202, 212, 229, 299
  Dad, 32, 282

mine, 72, 80, 116–19, 134, 156, 173–77, 187, 206, 208–9, 222, 239–44, 327

C

charity, 30, 35, 139, 156–59

Cherry family, 290–93
  grandparents, 275, 290–91, 292
  uncles/aunts, 28, 65, 87, 188, 251, 253, 274, 290–93, 298

Christmas
  celebrations/entertainment, 21, 154, 203, 263, 267, 282, 294
  parties, 148, 151–53
  presents, 28, 32, 101, 104, 115, 117, 118, 254, 282
  traditions, 35, 63–66, 89, 128

church
  activities, 27, 28, 35, 49, 141, 146–49, 152, 156, 157, 262, 273, 305
  churches
    St James's, Woolton, 128, 133–48, 157, 301, 305

D

background, 16, 18, 20–21, 26, 38, 52–53, 107, 263, 284, 285, 297
birthday, 66, 79, 89
church/religion/beliefs, 26, 74, 92, 136, 147, 148, 158
health/constitution, 38, 41, 43, 170, 223, 274, 275, 277, 282
leisure/enjoyments, 119, 132, 147–48, 257, 263
likes/dislikes/attitudes, 20, 73, 87, 98, 101, 125, 162, 222, 239, 254
personality, 28, 38, 48, 52, 58, 59, 60, 64, 98, 101, 103, 201, 212, 248, 302
relations
with both families, 15, 24, 25, 27, 48, 65, 87, 144, 185, 186, 252, 253–54, 292
with others, 17, 28, 31, 32, 33, 97, 125, 144, 161, 288
Mussolini, 295–96, 319
Myers family, 21, 29, 218

N

neighbours, 33, 97–103, 137, 161–62, 273, 304
New Year, 64, 66, 143, 295
newspapers, 90, 92, 129, 203, 252, 291, 322
Liverpool Daily Post (*LDP*), 21, 35, 165,

189, 199, 209, 266, 287, 288, 294
others, 21, 119, 165, 203, 254, 285
use of, 20, 61, 63, 71, 76

P

parents
in general, 75, 101, 191, 198, 229, 232, 244, 246, 250
mine, 21–22, 29, 41, 50, 53, 59, 64, 71, 89, 101, 103, 127, 135, 141, 144, 162, 166, 260, 263, 264, 273, 279, 284, 285, 303, 305, 310, 318, 321, 323
parties, 99, 290
church, 147, 148, 151, 153, 156, 274
private, 99, 216, 218
photographs, 15, 62, 123, 133, 290, 297, 317
piano, 57, 58, 100–101, 152, 281, 291, 305, 314
politics, 31, 285, 294, 295–98

R

racism, 18, 22, 34, 108, 112, 116

S

sayings, 36–38, 53, 78–81, 86, 87, 93–95, 102, 130, 145–46, 185, *See* Scouse

Printed in the United Kingdom
by Lightning Source UK Ltd.
127405UK00001B/1-9/A